THE WEALTHY KIDS' GUIDE

EQUIPPING CHILDREN FOR LIFELONG FINANCIAL SUCCESS

Soumya Alexander
Jaison Mathew

To all the parents, caregivers, and educators who believe in the power of financial education and its ability to shape the lives of our children,

This book is dedicated to you.

You have recognized the importance of equipping our young ones with the knowledge and skills they need to thrive in a world where money plays a central role. You understand that financial literacy is not just a luxury but a necessity for their future success and well-being.

To the parents who teach their children the value of a dollar, the joy of saving, and the significance of giving back—we honor your dedication.

We salute your commitment to the caregivers who go above and beyond to provide a stable foundation, teach the basics of money management, and help children develop healthy financial habits.

To the educators who inspire and empower young minds, making financial literacy an integral part of their education —we commend your efforts.

May this book serve as a resource to support your tireless efforts in nurturing financially responsible and empowered children. May it be a guiding light, igniting curiosity and fostering a love for learning about money.

Our children are our greatest assets, and we are investing in a brighter future by equipping them with the tools for financial success. Together, let us raise a generation of financially savvy individuals equipped to make wise decisions, embrace opportunities, and overcome financial challenges.

Thank you for joining us on this journey to empower the next generation and for your commitment to ensuring a lifetime of financial success for our kids.

With heartfelt appreciation,
Soumya Alexander
Jaison Mathew

To all the parents, caregivers, and educators who believe in the power of financial education and its ability to shape the lives of our children,

This book is dedicated to you.

You have recognized the importance of equipping our young ones with the knowledge and skills they need to thrive in a world where money plays a central role. You understand that financial literacy is not just a luxury but a necessity for their future success and well-being.

To the parents who teach their children the value of a dollar, the joy of saving, and the significance of giving back—we honor your dedication.

We salute your commitment to the caregivers who go above and beyond to provide a stable foundation, teach the basics of money management, and help children develop healthy financial habits.

To the educators who inspire and empower young minds, making financial literacy an integral part of their education —we commend your efforts.

May this book serve as a resource to support your tireless efforts in nurturing financially responsible and empowered children. May it be a guiding light, igniting curiosity and fostering a love for learning about money.

Our children are our greatest assets, and we are investing in a brighter future by equipping them with the tools for financial success. Together, let us raise a generation of financially savvy individuals equipped to make wise decisions, embrace opportunities, and overcome financial challenges.

Thank you for joining us on this journey to empower the next generation and for your commitment to ensuring a lifetime of financial success for our kids.

With heartfelt appreciation,

Soumya Alexander

Jaison Mathew

CONTENTS

Title Page

Dedication

Introduction

Preface

Prologue

Understanding the Value of Money   1

Building a Strong Financial Foundation   27

Money Management for Kids   43

Teaching Kids about Debt   64

Investing for Kids   87

Giving Back   106

Practical Money Skills   123

Financial Literacy at School   157

Parental Responsibility   179

Preparing Kids for Adulthood   198

Empowering Future Financial Success   240

Beyond the Basics   309

Unlock Financial Success   354

Play Your Way to Financial Literacy   367

Unlocking the Language of Finance   394

Recommended Actions 417

Recommended reading 420

Epilogue 423

About The Author 425

About The Author 427

Books By This Author 429

Books By This Author 431

INTRODUCTION

"The Wealthy Kids' Guide: Equipping Children for Lifelong Financial Success" is a comprehensive and engaging book that serves as a roadmap for parents and children to navigate the world of personal finance. With a focus on building a solid foundation for financial literacy, this book offers practical strategies, essential knowledge, and valuable insights to help children develop the skills they need to achieve lifelong financial success.

Through its informative and accessible content, "The Wealthy Kids' Guide" covers various topics, including budgeting, saving, investing, entrepreneurship, and responsible spending. It provides age-appropriate explanations and interactive activities that make learning about money enjoyable and relatable for young readers.

This book empowers children to make informed financial decisions, instilling in them the importance of setting goals, making wise choices, and understanding the value of money. It encourages critical thinking, resourcefulness, and creativity as children explore financial concepts through engaging examples and real-life scenarios.

"The Wealthy Kids' Guide" also emphasizes the significance of cultivating healthy money habits early and teaches children how to manage their money wisely. It introduces them to financial independence and helps them develop a mindset focused on long-term wealth creation and financial security.

"The Wealthy Kids' Guide" sets children on a path toward financial freedom and empowers them to take control of their financial future by equipping them with the necessary tools, knowledge, and skills. This book is a trusted resource for parents, educators, and children, ensuring that the next generation is well-prepared to navigate the complex world of personal finance with confidence and success.

"The Wealthy Kids' Guide: Equipping Children for Lifelong Financial Success" is a comprehensive and empowering resource that lays the foundation for children to achieve prosperity and financial independence. This engaging book focuses on essential financial concepts and provides practical strategies to equip children with the knowledge and skills they need to navigate the complex world of personal finance.

Through this guide, children will learn valuable money management skills, including budgeting, saving, and making wise spending choices. They will develop a strong understanding of financial literacy, grasping concepts such as income, expenses, credit, and investments. With a practical and age-appropriate approach, this book encourages children to take charge of their financial future, teaching them the importance of setting goals and working diligently to achieve them.

"The Wealthy Kids' Guide" also introduces children to the world of investing and entrepreneurship, showcasing the benefits of long-term thinking and the potential for wealth creation. It emphasizes the significance of financial planning and equips children with the tools to create budgets, track expenses, and make informed financial decisions aligned with their objectives.

Written in a clear and engaging style, this book nurtures a positive money mindset in children, instilling the values of responsibility, diligence, and financial independence. By equipping children with the knowledge and skills to make sound financial choices, "The Wealthy Kids' Guide" empowers them to build a solid financial future, laying the groundwork for lifelong financial success.

With its accessible language, practical activities, and inspiring examples, "The Wealthy Kids' Guide" is an invaluable resource for parents, educators, and children alike, making it an essential read for anyone seeking to provide children with the tools they need to thrive financially and unlock a lifetime of financial success.

PREFACE

In a world where financial literacy and money management skills are crucial for success, a significant gap exists in our children's education and preparation. Parents, caregivers, and educators often focus on imparting academic knowledge and essential life skills to our young ones. However, we tend to overlook one fundamental aspect that can profoundly shape their future— financial well-being.

Introducing "The Wealthy Kids' Guide - Equipping Children for Lifelong Financial Success." This book is a labor of love, born out of a deep desire to empower the next generation with the tools and knowledge they need to navigate the complex world of personal finance confidently.

The book addresses the critical need for financial education specifically tailored to children. It provides a comprehensive roadmap for parents and guardians to guide their kids toward financial literacy and independence. It is a resource designed to empower children, teaching them how to make informed decisions, manage money responsibly, and build a solid foundation for a financially secure future.

"The Wealthy Kids' Guide" offers practical advice, real-life examples, and engaging activities to make learning about money enjoyable for young readers. From understanding the value of money and setting financial goals to budgeting, saving, investing, and even entrepreneurship, this book covers various topics, equipping children with essential skills that will serve them well throughout their lives.

Moreover, this guide emphasizes the importance of instilling positive money habits early on, emphasizing the significance of delayed gratification, responsible spending, and the value of giving back. It encourages children to develop a healthy relationship with money, nurturing attitudes of gratitude, discipline, and generosity.

We sincerely hope that "The Wealthy Kids' Guide" will spark conversations and create opportunities for families to explore the world of finance together. By empowering children with knowledge, skills, and confidence, we can foster a financially astute, resilient generation capable of making sound financial decisions.

Remember, financial success is not about acquiring vast wealth but understanding money, respecting it, and using it wisely. Equipping our children with the right tools sets them on a path toward a lifetime of financial security and freedom.

Let us embark on this journey together, opening doors to a brighter financial future for our children. With "The Wealthy Kids' Guide - Equipping Children for Lifelong Financial Success" in hand, let's empower our kids to become the masters of their financial destinies.

We wish you and your children a prosperous journey ahead!

Sincerely,

Soumya Alexander

Jaison Mathew

PROLOGUE

In the hustle and bustle of our daily lives, it's easy to overlook one of the most critical aspects of preparing our children for the future—their financial well-being. As parents and caregivers, we strive to give our kids the best education, a nurturing environment, and a solid foundation for their dreams. Yet, often, the subject of money is left unexplored, untouched, and underestimated.

But what if we could change that? What if we could equip our children with the knowledge and skills to navigate the complex world of personal finance confidently? What if we could teach them the principles of earning, saving, investing, and giving back from an early age? The potential impact on their lives would be immeasurable.

"The Wealthy Kids' Guide - Equipping Children for Lifelong Financial Success" is here to bridge that gap. It is a roadmap designed to empower parents, caregivers, and educators in nurturing financially astute and independent children. This guide aims to instill a solid financial foundation, arming our young ones with the tools to make wise decisions, set goals, and manage money effectively.

Within these pages, you will find a wealth of knowledge, actionable advice, and engaging activities that make learning about money enjoyable for children. We will explore the value of money, budgeting, saving, the power of compounding, the basics of investing, and even the concepts of entrepreneurship and giving back.

"The Wealthy Kids' Guide" is about accumulating wealth and

fostering a healthy relationship with money—a relationship built on knowledge, discipline, and responsible decision-making. It encourages children to think critically, question, and develop financial habits that will serve them well into adulthood.

As we embark on this journey together, let us remember that financial literacy is not just about numbers and transactions; it's about empowering our children to create a future of abundance, security, and freedom. It's about teaching them to be masters of their financial destinies, to embrace opportunities, and to overcome challenges.

Now is the time to make a difference in our children's lives. With "The Wealthy Kids' Guide" in hand, let us empower the next generation with the knowledge and skills they need to flourish in an ever-changing financial landscape.

Are you ready? Let's embark on this transformative journey together and equip our children for lifelong financial success.

Chapter 1: Understanding the Value of Money. Turn the page and let the adventure begin.

UNDERSTANDING THE VALUE OF MONEY

Teaching Children About Money

The value of money is not in its possession, but in its purpose.

Thomas Jefferson

Money is essential to our daily lives, and understanding its value is crucial for every child's financial literacy. In This, we will explore different ways to teach kids about money, from basic concepts to practical applications.

The importance of financial literacy: In today's world, financial literacy is more important than ever. As children grow up, they need to know how to manage their money, create budgets, save for their goals, and avoid debt. Unfortunately, many young adults lack these essential skills, leading to financial struggles later in life.

As parents or caregivers, it's our responsibility to ensure that children learn about money management from a young age. By teaching them good financial habits early on, we can help them avoid common financial pitfalls and set them on a path to financial success.

Basic Money Concepts: The first step in teaching kids about money is introducing them to basic money concepts. Children need to understand the value of money, how it's earned, and how we can use it to purchase goods and services.

Parents can start by explaining the difference between needs and want and how we can use the money to satisfy both. They can also teach kids about the different currencies and coins and how to count money.

Saving and Spending: Once children understand the basics of money, parents can introduce them to the concepts of saving and spending. They can teach kids how to set financial goals, create budgets, and save money for the future.

Parents can also teach kids the importance of spending wisely, distinguishing between essential and non-essential expenses, and making smart purchasing decisions. In addition, they can use real-life examples and activities to make these concepts more tangible and relatable for children.

Earning Money: Earning money is an essential part of the financial equation, and parents can encourage children to earn money through various means, such as allowance, chores, or part-time jobs. In addition, they can teach children the value of hard work, responsibility, and financial independence.

Giving Back: Teaching children about the value of money also involves teaching them the importance of giving back. For example, parents can encourage children to donate to charity or volunteer in their communities, instilling a sense of empathy and social responsibility.

In this chapter, we discussed the importance of financial literacy for children and explored different ways to teach kids about money, from basic concepts to practical applications. Parents can set their children on a path to financial success and security by starting early and providing age-appropriate financial education.

THE IMPORTANCE OF FINANCIAL LITERACY

Financial literacy is essential because it helps us manage our money wisely. It's like a map that helps us navigate our financial journey; just as we learn to read and write, learning how to manage money is essential.

If we don't learn how to manage our money, we spend it all on things we don't need or use credit cards without understanding how to repay them. This can lead to debt and financial troubles in the future.

Financial literacy can help us make intelligent decisions with our money. It can teach us how to create a budget, save money, and invest wisely. By learning these skills early on, we can develop good habits that will help us throughout our lives.

So, it's essential to start learning about money management as early as possible. By understanding the value of money and how to use it wisely, we can make better financial decisions and achieve our financial goals.

Here are some ways to explain the importance of financial literacy to a kid:

Start by explaining what money is and where it comes from: Teach kids that money is earned through hard work and that it's essential to use it wisely.

Use real-life examples: Use examples from their everyday life to help them understand the importance of financial literacy. For instance, explain how saving up for a new toy can help them avoid spending all their money on candy and toys in one go.

Teach them about budgeting: Help kids understand how budgeting works by creating a budget for their allowance or any money they earn. This can teach them to prioritize spending, save money, and avoid impulse buying.

Talk about the value of money: Explain to kids that money has value and that it's essential to be mindful of how they spend it. Please encourage them to think about what they need versus what they want.

Teach them about the consequences of poor financial decisions: Help kids understand that poor financial decisions can lead to debt and financial problems in the future. Teach them that they can avoid these negative consequences by learning about financial literacy and making intelligent financial decisions.

By teaching kids about financial literacy, you can help them develop good money management habits that will serve them well throughout their lives.

CONVERSATIONS BETWEEN PARENTS AND CHILDREN: (THE IMPORTANCE OF FINANCIAL LITERACY)

EXAMPLE-1:
Child: Mom/Dad, what is financial literacy?
Parent: Financial literacy means knowing how to manage your money and make sound financial decisions. It's essential to learn about money to make wise choices with your money as

you grow up.

Child: Why is it important to learn about money?

Parent: Learning about money can help ensure you have enough for your needs and wants. It can also help you avoid debt and save money for the future.

Child: How can I learn more about money?

Parent: There are lots of ways to learn about money. We can talk about it together, read books about money, and play games that teach us about money. You can also learn by earning, saving, and spending wisely.

Child: Why do I need to learn about earning money?

Parent: Earning money can help you become more independent and allow you to buy things you want or need. Learning how to earn money to care for yourself and achieve your goals is essential.

Child: Can you give me an example of earning money?

Parent: Sure, you can earn money by doing chores around the house, babysitting, or selling items you don't need anymore.

Child: That sounds cool! What about giving back related money?

Parent: Giving back related to money means sharing some of your money with people or organizations that need it more than we do. It's important to help others who may be less fortunate than us is crucial, and giving back to our community is essential.

Child: I understand. Learning about money is essential, and I want to be good with my money when I grow up.

Parent: That's great to hear! We'll work together to learn more about money and ensure you have the tools to make intelligent financial decisions.

EXAMPLE-2:

Parent: Hey, do you have a minute to chat? I wanted to talk to you about something important.

Child: Sure, what's up?

Parent: I wanted to talk to you about financial literacy. Do you know what that means?

Child: Not really, no.

Parent: Financial literacy means understanding how to manage your money, save, and invest for the future. It's important because it helps you make better decisions with your money, which can set you up for success in the long run.

Child: Oh, okay. But why is it so important? Can't I spend my money however I want?

Parent: You can, but there might not be better ideas. Financial literacy can help you avoid making mistakes with your money that could hurt you. For example, if you don't know how to budget, you might spend more than you make and get into debt. But if you have good financial literacy skills, you can create a budget and ensure you only spend what you can afford.

Child: I see. So what can I do to learn more about financial literacy?

Parent: There are lots of things you can do! You can start by reading books or articles about personal finance, watching videos, attending workshops, or even playing financial literacy games or simulations. And, of course, you can always come to another trusted adult or me for advice.

Child: Okay, I'll try to learn more about it. Thanks for explaining it to me, Mom/Dad!

Parent: Of course! It's essential to start thinking about these things to prepare for the future. And remember, I'm always here to help you if needed.

EXAMPLE-3:

Parent: I wanted to discuss something vital with you. It's about money management.

Child: Okay, what's that?

Parent: Money management is about learning to save, spend, and invest your money wisely. It's important because it can help you make sound financial decisions and avoid financial problems in the future.

Child: Okay, I understand. But why is it important to start learning about money management now?

Parent: Well, the sooner you start learning about money management, the better off you'll be in the future. By learning good money habits now, you'll be able to set yourself up for success in the long run. You'll also be better prepared for unexpected expenses or emergencies that may come up.

Child: I see. So, how can I start learning about money management?

Parent: There are many ways to start learning about money management. One way is to start keeping track of your spending. You can do this by keeping a log of everything you spend your money on. This will help you see where your money is going and where you can cut back.

Child: That's a good idea. What else can I do?

Parent: You can also start thinking about ways to earn some extra money. You can do chores around the house or help with a family business. By earning your own money, you'll be able to start learning how to manage it.

Child: Okay, I'll try to do that. Thanks for talking to me about this, Dad/Mom.

Parent: Of course! Learning about money management is an integral part of growing up, and I'm always here to help you if you have any questions or need any advice.

BASIC MONEY CONCEPTS

When explaining basic money concepts to a kid, it's essential to keep it simple and use relevant examples.

Here are some basic money concepts everyone should understand:

Income: Income refers to the money you earn from your jobs or other sources, such as investments or rental properties.

Expenses: Expenses are the costs of the goods and services you buy, such as rent, groceries, transportation, entertainment, and utilities.

Budgeting: Budgeting is creating a plan for your income and expenses. This helps you track your spending and ensure you have enough money to cover your needs and wants.

Saving: Saving refers to setting aside money for future needs or goals, such as emergencies, retirement, or a down payment on a house.

Investing: Investing is putting money into assets to earn a return on that investment over time.

Credit: Credit refers to the ability to borrow money, typically through a credit card or loan. This can help make large purchases or build a credit history but can also lead to debt if not managed properly.

Interest is the cost of borrowing money or the return you earn on your investment. Therefore, it's essential to understand how interest rates work and how they can affect your finances.

Money is earned: Explain that money is earned by working and that people exchange money for goods and services. Use examples like parents going to work to earn money for groceries or a toy.

Money has value: Teach kids that money has value and that different coins and bills represent different amounts. Show them the different denominations of coins and bills and explain what can be used to buy.

Budgeting: Teach kids about budgeting by giving them an allowance or helping them save for something they want. Explain how they can prioritize their spending and save money for the things they want.

Saving: Teach kids about saving by explaining that they can save money for a rainy day or a big purchase they want to make. Please encourage them to set aside a portion of their weekly allowance or earnings.

Needs vs. wants: Help kids understand the difference between needs and wants. Explain that needs are things we need to survive, like food, water, and shelter, while wants are things we would like to have but are unnecessary.

By teaching kids these basic money concepts, you can help them better understand money and how to manage it wisely. It's an excellent foundation for building good financial habits that can serve them well in the future.

Here are some ways to explain the importance of basic money concepts to a kid:

Money is a part of daily life: Explain to the kid that money is a part of our daily lives and that we use it to buy things we need and want. Help them understand that learning about money can help them make good choices with their spending.

Basic money concepts help us make good decisions: Teach the kid that basic money concepts like budgeting and saving can help them make good decisions with their money. They can learn to manage their money wisely by setting goals and prioritizing their spending.

Learning basic money concepts early can help build good habits: Help the kid understand that by learning about money at a young age, they can develop good habits that will serve them well in the future. By practicing sound money management skills now, they can avoid mistakes and make sound financial decisions later in life.

Money management skills are essential for achieving goals: Explain that basic money concepts like budgeting and saving can help them achieve their goals. Whether they want to save up for a new toy or a college education, good money management skills can help them get there.

Understanding money can give them independence: Help the kid understand that they can become more independent by learning about money. They can make their own financial decisions and manage their money without relying on others.

By teaching kids basic money concepts, you can help them develop good money management skills that will serve them well throughout their lives. It's an essential foundation for building financial independence and achieving their goals.

CONVERSATIONS BETWEEN PARENTS AND CHILDREN: (Basic Money Concepts)

EXAMPLE-1:
Child: Mom/Dad, what does it mean to save money?
Parent: Saving money means putting some of the money you earn or receive into a special place to use later.
Child: Why do we need to save money?
Parent: Saving money can help you buy things you want or need in the future, like toys, clothes, or even a car or house when you grow up.
Child: Can you show me how to save money?
Parent: Sure! We can start by setting up a savings account for you at the bank. You can put some of your allowance or any money into the account and watch it grow over time.
Child: What about spending money? What does that mean?
Parent: Spending money means using your money to buy things you want or need, like toys, clothes, or food.
Child: Can I spend all my money?
Parent: It's essential to spend your money wisely and not spend what you have. That's why we need to learn how to make a budget and a plan for using our money.
Child: What's a budget?
Parent: A budget is a plan for how you'll use your money. It includes how much you'll earn or receive, how much you plan to save, and how much you plan to spend on things like food, clothes, and toys.
Child: That sounds like a good idea. How can I make a budget?
Parent: We can work on making a budget together. We'll start by writing down how much money you have coming in, like your allowance or any money you earn. Then we'll list the things you need to spend money on, like food or clothes. We'll make sure to set aside some money for savings too.
Child: Okay, I think I understand. Saving money and making a budget can help me buy what I want and need and not spend

more than I have.

Parent: That's right! Learning about money can help you make intelligent decisions and be in control of your money. So we'll keep working on it together.

EXAMPLE-2:

Parent: Hey, Buddy/Princess, do you know what money is?

Child: Yeah, money is what we use to buy things, right?

Parent: That's right! Money is a medium of exchange to buy goods and services. Do you know what the different types of money are?

Child: Umm, no, I don't.

Parent: There are two main types of money: cash and digital. Cash is physical money, like coins and bills, you can hold. Digital money exists electronically, like using a debit card to buy something.

Child: Oh, okay. That makes sense. But why is it important to know about money?

Parent: Understanding basic money concepts is critical because it helps you make better decisions with your money. For example, if you understand the concept of saving, you'll be more likely to save your money for something you want rather than spend it on something you don't need.

Child: I see. So, how can I learn more about money?

Parent: One way to learn more about money is to start saving. You can ask for an allowance or do house chores to earn money. Then, you can put your money in a piggy bank or a savings account and watch it grow over time. You can also read books, watch videos about money, or talk to another trusted adult or me.

Child: That sounds like a good idea. I'll try to start saving my money and learn more about it. Thanks, Mom/Dad!

Parent: You're welcome! Learning about money is an integral part of growing up, and I'm always here to help you if you have any questions or need any advice.

EXAMPLE-3:

Parent: Hey, do you have a minute? I wanted to talk to you about some basic money concepts.

Child: Sure, what's up?

Parent: Do you know what a budget is?

Child: I've heard the word before but don't know what it means.

Parent: A budget is a plan for how you will spend your money. It lists everything you need to pay for, like rent or mortgage, utilities, food, transportation, and how much money you have for each.

Child: Oh, okay. So, why is it essential to have a budget?

Parent: A budget is essential because it helps ensure you have enough money to cover all your expenses. It also helps you avoid overspending and going into debt.

Child: That makes sense. How can I make a budget?

Parent: You can start by listing everything you must pay monthly and how much they cost. Then, you can add all those expenses and compare them to how much money you have each month. If your expenses exceed your income, you should find ways to reduce your spending.

Child: Okay, I think I understand. What are some other basic money concepts I should know about?

Parent: Another essential concept is saving. Saving means putting aside money for the future, like for emergencies or for something you want to buy. It's important to save because it helps you achieve your financial goals and can provide a safety net if something unexpected happens.

Child: I'll try to remember that. Thanks for explaining all this to me, Mom/Dad!

Parent: Of course! Learning about basic money concepts is an essential part of growing up, and I'm always here to help you if you have any questions or need any advice.

SAVING AND SPENDING

When explaining saving and spending to a kid, it's essential to keep it simple and use relevant examples. Here are some tips:

Explain the difference between saving and spending: Saving means putting money aside for a future purchase or goal, while spending means using money to buy something now.

Use examples: Use examples that are relevant to the kid's life. For example, explain how they can save money from their allowance to buy a new toy or game or save money for a future trip or activity.

Prioritize needs vs. wants: Teach the kid about the difference between needs and wants. Explain that needs are things we need to survive, like food and shelter, while wants are things we would like to have but are unnecessary. Please encourage them to prioritize their spending and save money for what they want.

Set goals: Help the kid set goals for saving and spending. For example, they might set a goal to save a certain amount of money for a specific purchase, or they might set a goal to limit their spending on non-essential items.

Teach the value of money: Explain to the kid that money is earned through hard work and that it's essential to spend it wisely. Please encourage them to think about the value of the items they want to buy and whether they're worth the money.

By teaching kids about saving and spending, you can help them develop good money management habits that will serve them well throughout their lives. It's a great way to help them understand the value of money and make informed decisions about their finances.

Here are some ways to help a kid understand the importance of money-saving:

Explain the concept of saving: Explain to the kid what saving means. You can use examples from their own life, such as putting aside money from their allowance or birthday gifts for a future purchase.

Show the benefits of saving: Help the kid understand the benefits of saving money. For example, explain that by saving, they can afford to buy bigger and better things in the future or have money for unexpected expenses or emergencies.

Encourage goal-setting: Help the kid set a savings goal, such as saving for a new toy or game they want. This will give them a concrete reason to save and help them develop good saving habits.

Teach delayed gratification: Explain to the kid that saving requires delayed gratification - waiting for some time before they can have what they want. This vital life skill will serve them well in many areas.

Make it fun: Saving doesn't have to be boring! Make it fun by creating a savings chart or jar where they can see their progress or by setting up a rewards system for reaching certain savings milestones.

By helping kids understand the importance of money saving, you can set them up for a lifetime of financial success. In addition, it's a great way to teach them about responsible money management and encourage good saving habits from an early age.

Here are some ways to help a kid understand the disadvantages of money spending:

Talk about opportunity cost: Explain to the kid that every time they spend money, they give up the opportunity to use it for something else. For example, if they spend their allowance on a new toy, they may need more money to save for something else they want.

Discuss the importance of needs vs. wants: Teach the kid about the difference between needs and wants, and encourage them to prioritize their spending on needs first. Explain that if they spend too much money on wants, they may need more money for things they need, like food and shelter.

Show the consequences of overspending: Help the kid understand the consequences of overspending. For example, if they spend all their money simultaneously, they may not have little left for unexpected expenses or emergencies. Or, if they use a credit card to buy something they can't afford, they may end up paying high-interest rates and getting into debt.

Teach the value of saving: Help the kid understand that saving money can have many benefits, such as being able to afford bigger and better things in the future or having a safety net for unexpected expenses.

Set limits: Encourage the kid to limit their spendings, such as only spending a certain amount of money each week or month. This will help them develop good spending habits and avoid overspending.

By helping kids understand the disadvantages of money spending, you can teach them to be more mindful and responsible with their money. It's a great way to encourage good financial habits early on and set them up for a lifetime of financial success.

CONVERSATIONS BETWEEN PARENTS AND
CHILDREN: (SAVING AND SPENDING)

EXAMPLE-1:
Child: Mom/Dad, can I buy this new toy I saw at the store?
Parent: Sure, you can buy it if you have enough money.
Child: I have some money saved, but not enough to buy it.
Parent: Well, you could wait and save up some more money before buying it.
Child: Why do I need to save money? I want to buy the toy now.
Parent: Saving money can help you buy things you want in the future. If you spend all your money now, you might need more for something else you want later.
Child: That makes sense. But how can I save more money?
Parent: We can help you make a budget, which is a plan for how to use your money. You can save money each week or month to save up for something you want.
Child: Okay, I'll try that. But can't I use my allowance to buy the toy now and save money later?

Parent: It's essential to balance your spending and saving. If you spend all your allowance now, you might need more left to save for something else you want later. We can work on making a budget together that includes saving some of your weekly allowances.

Child: That sounds like a good idea. I want to take advantage of something I want only after spending all my money.

Parent: It's essential to consider your long-term goals, and planning your spending and saving accordingly is essential. We'll work on it to help you be smart with your money.

EXAMPLE-2:

Parent: I wanted to talk to you about saving and spending money. Do you know what those words mean?

Child: Yeah, saving means putting money aside for later, and spending means using it to buy things we want or need.

Parent: That's right! Saving and spending are two essential parts of managing your money. Do you know why it's essential to save money?

Child: I'm not sure.

Parent: Saving money can help you achieve your financial goals, like buying a car or attending college. It can also help you be prepared for unexpected expenses, like if your phone breaks or you need to go to the doctor.

Child: Okay, I see. So how do I save money?

Parent: There are a few ways to save money. One way is to set a savings goal and then put a little bit of money aside each month to reach that goal. Another way is to avoid spending money on things you don't need, like buying snacks at school instead of bringing your own from home.

Child: That makes sense. But what about spending money?

Parent: Spending money is also essential, but it's essential to do it wisely. You should always try to spend money on important things that make you happy, but not waste it on things you don't need or that won't bring you long-term satisfaction.

Child: How do I know if something is good to spend money on?
Parent: That's a good question. One way to decide is to ask yourself if you want to buy something you need or if it's something you want because it's popular or because your friends have it. It's also a good idea to compare prices and shop around before making a big purchase.
Child: Okay, I'll try to remember all that. Thanks for talking to me about this, Mom/Dad!
Parent: You're welcome! Managing your money is an important life skill; I'm always here to help you learn more about it.

EXAMPLE-3:
Parent: I wanted to talk to you about saving and spending. Do you know what saving and spending mean?
Child: Yeah, saving means keeping money for later, and spending means using money to buy things we want or need.
Parent: That's right! Saving and spending are essential parts of managing your money. Do you know how to save money?
Child: Not really.
Parent: One way to save money is to set a savings goal, like saving for a new toy or a memorable trip, and then put aside a little bit of money each week or month to reach that goal. You can also save money by avoiding unnecessary spending, like buying snacks at school instead of bringing your own from home.
Child: Okay, I get it. But what about spending money?
Parent: Spending money is important too, but you have to be careful not to spend more than you can afford. One way to do this is to create a budget, which is a plan for how you will spend your money each month. That way, you can ensure you have enough money for everything you need and want without overspending.
Child: How do I create a budget?
Parent: You can start by listing everything you must pay for each month, like food, clothes, and school supplies. Then, you

can add up how much those things cost and compare it to how much money you have coming in each month. If your expenses exceed your income, you should find ways to reduce your spending.

Child: Okay, that sounds like a good plan. Thanks for explaining all this to me, Mom/Dad!

Parent: Of course! Learning about money saving and spending is essential to growing up, and I'm always here to help you learn more about it.

EARNING MONEY

Earning money is important because it teaches us the value of hard work and helps us to understand the concept of earning and spending. When we earn our own money, we learn to appreciate the value of money and the effort it takes to earn it. We also learn essential life skills such as budgeting, saving, and financial planning.

In addition, earning money can help us to achieve our goals and dreams. Whether buying a new toy, saving for college or starting our own business, earning money gives us the means to achieve our aspirations. It also gives us a sense of independence and self-sufficiency, which can help boost our self-confidence and self-esteem.

Furthermore, earning money can teach us important values such as responsibility, discipline, and perseverance. By working hard and earning money, we learn the importance of setting goals, staying focused, and overcoming obstacles. These valuable skills can help us succeed financially and in all aspects of our lives.

Overall, earning money is an integral pato growing up and learning to navigate the world. By teaching our children the value of hard work and the importance of earning their own money, we can help them develop essential life skills and set them on a path toward a successful future.

Here are some ways to make a kid aware of the importance of

earning money as a parent:

Give them opportunities to earn money: Offer your child ways to earn money around the house, such as doing extra chores or helping with a family business. This will help them understand the value of hard work and how earning money works.

Please encourage them to earn money and save a portion for future goals. This can help them understand the importance of saving for the future and the benefits of delayed gratification.

Teach them to set goals: Help your child set goals for what they want to achieve with their earnings, such as buying a new toy or saving for a special event. This can help them learn the importance of working towards goals and the sense of accomplishment that comes with achieving them.

Discuss the concept of earning: Talk to your child about how earning money works in the real world, such as through jobs or starting a business. This can help them understand the connection between effort and reward and how earning money can help them achieve their goals.

Be a positive role model: Show your child the importance of earning money by setting a good example. Talk to them about your experiences earning and saving money, and demonstrate the value of hard work and financial responsibility.

By taking these steps, you can help your child develop a strong understanding of the importance of earning money and the skills they need to succeed financially.

CONVERSATIONS BETWEEN PARENTS AND
CHILDREN: (EARNING MONEY)

EXAMPLE-1:

Parent: Hey, I wanted to talk to you about earning money. Do you know what that means?

Child: Yeah, earning money means doing something to get paid.

Parent: That's right! You can earn money in many ways, like

doing chores around the house, selling things you don't need anymore, or starting a small business. Do you have any ideas about how you might earn some money?

Child: I've been thinking about doing yard work for our neighbours or babysitting.

Parent: Those are both great ideas! It's important to remember that when you earn money, you also need to learn how to manage it wisely. Do you know what that means?

Child: Not really.

Parent: Managing your money means making sure you have enough to pay for the things you need, like food and clothes, and saving some for the things you want, like a new toy or a fun activity. Setting goals for how you want to spend and save your money is essential.

Child: Okay, I understand. But how do I manage my money?

Parent: One way to manage your money is to create a budget, which is a plan for how you will spend and save your money each month. You can also open a bank account and start saving your money there, which will help you earn interest and keep it safe.

Child: That sounds like a good idea. I want to save some of my money for a new video game I want.

Parent: That's a great goal! Remember, earning money is integral to being independent and learning to manage your finances. I'm proud of you for thinking about it.

Child: Thanks, Mom/Dad! I'll start thinking more about how to earn and manage money wisely.

EXAMPLE-2:

Child: Mom/Dad, can I have some money to buy a new video game?

Parent: Have you thought about ways to earn money yourself?

Child: What do you mean?

Parent: You could do extra chores around the house to earn money or offer to walk a neighbour's dog for a fee.

Child: Oh, I see. But why do I need to earn money? Can't you give it to me?

Parent: It is essential to learn the value of money and the hard work that goes into earning it. When you earn your own money, you can also learn how to manage it better and choose how to spend it.

Child: Okay, I could do some extra chores to earn money. How much do I need to earn to buy the video game?

Parent: First, let's determine how much the video game costs. Then we can talk about how much you need to earn and how you can reach that goal.

Child: That sounds like a plan. I'll get started on my chores right away!

Parent: Great, I'm proud of you for taking the initiative and working towards your goals. Remember, hard work pays off, and you'll appreciate what you buy with your money even more.

EXAMPLE-3:

Parent: Have you ever considered earning money?

Child: Yeah, but I don't know how to.

Parent: That's okay. There are many ways you can earn money. For example, you can ask your grandparents or other family members if they need help with anything around the house or yard work and offer to do it for a fee.

Child: That's a good idea. What else can I do?

Parent: You can also offer to walk dogs or pet-sit for people in your neighbourhood who might be busy or out of town. Or you can offer to run errands for people, like picking up groceries or walking to the post office.

Child: Okay, but how much money can I make?

Parent: That will depend on how much work you do and how much you charge. But remember, when you earn money, you must learn how to manage it wisely.

Child: How do I do that?

Parent: One way to manage your money is to create a budget, which is a plan for how you will spend and save your money each month. You can also open a savings account and start saving your money there, which will help you earn interest and keep it safe.

Child: Okay, I want to save money for a new bike.

Parent: That's a great goal! Remember, earning and managing money is an important life skill that will help you become more independent and responsible. And I'm here to help you along the way.

GIVING BACK

Giving back related to money means donating a portion of your income or savings to a charity, non-profit organization, or needy individual. It's a way of helping others and positively impacting your community using financial resources. Giving back can take many forms, such as making a one-time donation, setting up a regular giving plan, or giving gifts in kind.

There are many reasons why giving back related to money is essential. First and foremost, it helps support causes and organizations that positively impact the. For example, donating money can fund critical research, provide resources for needy individuals, or help support community programs and services.

Giving back related to money can also express gratitude for what we have in our lives and positively impact the world. For parents, teaching kids about giving back related to money can be a valuable lesson in empathy, kindness, and generosity. By encouraging kids to get involved in charitable giving, parents can help their kids develop a sense of social responsibility and a greater appreciation for the needs of others.

Giving back related to money is an important concept that can help us connect with others, make a positive difference in our communities, and foster a sense of compassion and gratitude.

Here's an explanation of the importance of giving back related to money in a language that a kid can understand:

When we have money, we can buy things we want or need, like toys or clothes. But did you know that money can also help other people who may not have as much as we do? Giving back related to money means sharing some of our money with people or organizations that need it more than we do.

When we give back related to money, we help others who may be less fortunate than us. For example, we can give money to a charity that helps people who are sick, or we can buy food for people who don't have enough to eat. Giving back related to money can make a difference in someone's life and help them feel better.

Giving back related to money can also make us feel good inside. When we help others, it can make us feel happy and proud of ourselves. We can also learn about the importance of sharing and caring for others.

You may have little money; even a tiny can make a big difference. For example, you can ask your parents if you can help you do some of them with your allowance or earnings from doing chores for charity or an organization you care about. It's a great way to help others and show kindness and generosity.

Overall, giving back related to money is an important concept that can help us positively impact the world and feel good about ourselves.

CONVERSATIONS BETWEEN PARENTS
AND CHILDREN: (GIVING BACK)

EXAMPLE-1:

Parent: Hey, Buddy/Princess! Do you remember when we talked about sharing and giving back to others?

Child: Yes, I remember! We shared our toys with our friends and donated some of our old clothes to charity.

Parent: That's right! And today, I want to talk about giving back on money. Do you know what that means?

Child: No, not really.

Parent: Giving back with money means helping less fortunate people by donating money to organizations that help them. When we donate, we can help others in need and make a difference in their lives.

Child: Why should we do that?

Parent: Many people worldwide struggle to get by and need our help. We can make a difference by sharing some of what we have with those who need it most. Essential to be grateful for what we have and to share it with others who are less fortunate.

Child: How can we do that?

Parent: We can donate money to organizations that help people in need, such as homeless shelters, food banks, or charities that support children who are sick. Even a small donation can make a big difference in someone's life.

Child: That sounds like a good idea! Can we donate some of my allowances to help others?

Parent: Of course! I'm proud of you for wanting to help others. Let's find a charity you're interested in and donate together.

EXAMPLE-2:

Parent: Hey, have you ever heard of donating money to a charity?

Child: I have heard of it but must learn what it means.

Parent: Well, donating money means giving some of our money to organizations that support causes we care about, like helping people who are sick, protecting the environment, or supporting education.

Child: That sounds like a good thing to do. But why do we do it?

Parent: We do it because many people need help, and sometimes the government or other organizations cannot provide more help. By donating our money, we can help make a difference and contribute to a better world.

Child: Okay, but how do we know which organizations to donate to?

Parent: That's a good question. We can start by researching organizations with good reputations and clear mission statements. We can also look for transparent organizations about their financials and how they use the donations they receive.

Child: That makes sense. But how much money should we donate?

Parent: That's up to you. We can start by setting aside a certain amount of our monthly income for donations or donate a percentage to charity.

Child: I want to donate some money to help children who don't have access to education.

Parent: That's a great cause! Remember, donating money to charity is crucial to give back to society and to help improve the world. And I'm proud of you for wanting to make a difference.

EXAMPLE-3:

Parent: Have you ever considered donating some of your money to a good cause?

Child: Donating my money? But I want to use it to buy toys and games.

Parent: I understand that, but donating some of your money to a good cause can also make you feel good and help others who may not have as much as we do.

Child: Okay, but how do I know which cause to donate to?

Parent: Well, we can research different organizations that help people or animals in need. For example, we can donate to a local food bank to help families who may not have enough to eat or donate to an animal shelter to help care for animals who may not have homes.

Child: That sounds like a good idea. But how much money should I donate?

Parent: That's up to you. We can start by setting aside a certain amount of your monthly allowance for donations, or you can donate a percentage of your allowance to charity.

Child: I want to donate some money to help kids who are sick. Parent: That's a great cause! Remember, donating money to charity is a crucial way to help improve the world. It can also teach us the value of generosity and empathy toward others. And I'm proud of you for wanting to impact the world positively.

BUILDING A STRONG FINANCIAL FOUNDATION

Starting Early with Kids

Financial freedom is not a privilege, but a right. It's the power to make your own choices and live life on your own terms.

Suze Orman

Teaching kids about finances from a young age can lay the foundation for a lifetime of financial stability and success. In this chapter, we will discuss the importance of starting early with financial education and provide tips on how to build a solid financial foundation for kids.

The Value of Starting Early:

Studies have shown that children as young as three can grasp basic financial concepts, such as the value of money and the importance of saving. Starting early with financial education can help children develop good financial habits and attitudes and establish a solid financial foundation to serve them well.

Teaching Kids About Money:

One of the first steps in building a solid financial foundation is to teach kids about money. This includes introducing them to basic financial concepts, such as earning, saving, spending, and giving. It is also important to involve kids in financial decisions and to model good financial behaviour.

Teaching kids about money can be done through various methods, such as games, stories, and hands-on activities. For example, parents can play games that teach kids about money management, read books that promote financial literacy, and involve kids in family budgeting and financial planning.

Establishing Good Habits:

Another essential aspect of building a solid financial foundation is establishing good habits. This includes teaching kids the importance of saving, setting financial goals, and avoiding debt.

Parents can help kids establish good financial habits by providing opportunities to earn and save money, such as through chores or allowances. Encouraging kids to set financial goals, such as saving for a specific item or experience, is also essential. Additionally, parents can teach kids about the dangers of debt and how to avoid it.

Building a solid financial foundation is essential in preparing kids for financial wisdom. By starting early and teaching kids about money, establishing good financial habits, and involving them in financial decisions, parents can help set their children on a path to financial success.

THE VALUE OF STARTING EARLY

The Value of Starting Early in finance refers to the benefits individuals can gain by saving and investing for their future financial goals as early as possible. By starting early, individuals have more time to let their investments grow, take advantage of the power of compound interest, and weather financial setbacks or market volatility. Additionally, starting early allows individuals to build good financial habits and establish a strong foundation for long-term financial security. Overall, starting early in finance can lead to significant benefits over the long run, including higher potential returns, lower risk, and more excellent financial stability.

Starting early in finance can significantly benefit individuals in the long run. Here are some reasons why:

Time is on your side: The earlier you start investing, the longer your money has to grow. Over time, even small contributions can add up to significant wealth due to the power of compound interest. Compound interest means earning interest on your initial investment and the interest that your investment generates. The longer your investment has to compound, the greater the potential returns.

Lower risk: Starting early allows you to take more risk with your investments. With a longer time horizon, you can invest in riskier assets, such as stocks, which have historically delivered higher returns than less risky assets, such as bonds. Over time, the stock market's volatility tends to even out, meaning the longer you stay invested, the less risky it becomes.

Ability to weather financial storms: Life is unpredictable, and unexpected expenses or emergencies can derail your financial plans. However, if you start saving and investing early, you can weather financial storms better. As a result, you have a longer time horizon to recover from setbacks and grow your wealth.

Building good habits: Starting early in finance can help you develop good financial habits. Saving and investing regularly can become a routine part of your life, and over time, you may need to pay attention to the money you're setting aside. By starting early, you can establish these habits and set yourself up for a lifetime of financial security.

Starting early in finance can be hugely beneficial for individuals. It allows you to take advantage of the power of compound interest, take more risks with your investments, weather financial storms, and build good financial habits.

CONVERSATIONS BETWEEN PARENTS AND CHILDREN: (THE VALUE OF STARTING EARLY)

EXAMPLE -1:

Parent: Have you heard the saying "the early bird catches the worm"?

Child: Yes, I have heard it, but what does it mean?

Parent: It means that you have a better chance of success if you start doing something early. This is true for many things, including money and saving.

Child: Saving money? I only have a little money to save.

Parent: That's okay, but it's essential to start saving early. Even if you can only save a bit, it can add up over time and help you reach your goals.

Child: What goals?

Parent: For example, you may want to save for something you want, like a new toy or game. Or you can save for something bigger, like a college education or a down payment on a house.

Child: But those things are so far away!

Parent: That's true, but starting early gives you more time to save and reach your goals. And it also teaches you the value of patience and discipline.

Child: That makes sense. But how do I save money?

Parent: We can start by setting a goal and then figuring out how much you need to save each week or month to reach that goal. We can also look for ways to save money, like avoiding impulse buys or shopping for sales.

Child: Okay, I want to save for a new game.

Parent: Great! Remember, starting early is a significant value, and it can help set you up for success in many areas of life, including money and finances. And I'm proud of you for wanting to learn and make intelligent choices with your money.

EXAMPLE -2:

Parent: Hey, Buddy/Princess! Do you chat about something important?

Child: Sure, what's up, Mom/Dad?

Parent: I wanted to talk to you about money and how important it is to start saving early.

Child: Why is that important, Mom/Dad?

Parent: Starting early means you have more time for your money to grow. Let's say you start saving $10 a week now and continue to do so until you're 25. If you invest that money wisely and earn a 7% annual return, by the time you're 65, you'll have over $270,000!

Child: Wow, that's a lot of money!

Parent: Yes, it is! But let's say you wait until 30 to save that same $10 a week. By age 65, you'll only have about $185,000.

Child: Oh, I see. So, starting early means, I'll have more money in the end?

Parent: Exactly! Starting early gives your money more time to grow and helps you establish good financial habits early on. Plus, life is unpredictable, and unexpected expenses can happen anytime. A savings cushion can help weather those storms without taking on debt.

Child: That makes sense, Mom/Dad. I'm going to start saving some of my allowances every week.

Parent: That's a great idea! And if you keep it up, you'll set yourself up for a financially secure future.

EXAMPLE -3:

Parent: Have you ever heard of the phrase "a penny saved is a penny earned"?

Child: Yes, I have heard that before. But I don't understand what it means.

Parent: Well, it means that when you save money, it's like earning money. For example, you have nothing left if you get $5 as an allowance and spend it all on candy. But if you save that $5 instead, you have $5 more than before.

Child: Oh, I get it. But what's the big deal about saving money?

Parent: Saving money is essential because it helps you prepare for unexpected expenses, like if your bike breaks down and needs to be fixed. It also helps you reach your goals, like buying a new toy or going on a trip with your family.

Child: How do I save money?

Parent: We can start by setting a savings goal, like $10 or $20 monthly. Then, we can look for ways to save money, like bringing lunch from home instead of buying it at school or asking for books from the library instead of buying them.

Child: Okay, I want to save for a new bike.

Parent: That's a great goal! Remember, every penny you save is like earning a penny, and it can help you prepare for unexpected expenses and reach your goals. And I'm proud of you for wanting to make wise choices with your money.

TEACHING KIDS ABOUT MONEY

Teaching kids about money refers to the process of educating children about financial concepts such as saving, budgeting, investing, and financial responsibility. The goal of teaching kids about money is to help them develop good financial habits and skills to set them up for long-term financial success. This includes teaching children about the value of money, how to set financial goals, how to save and budget effectively, and how to make informed financial decisions.

Parents and educators can help children establish good financial habits that will benefit them throughout their lives by teaching kids about money from an early age. It can also help children better understand money's role in their lives and the importance of responsible financial behaviour.

There are several ways to teach kids about money, including.

Leading by example: Kids learn extensively from watching their parents or caregivers. Parents can instil positive money habits in their children by modelling good financial habits like saving money, creating and sticking to a budget, and avoiding unnecessary debt.

Use real-life examples: Use real-life examples to help children understand financial concepts. For instance, when grocery shopping, explain to your child how you compare prices, use coupons, and stick to a budget.

Make it fun: Financial education doesn't have to be boring. You can make learning about money fun by playing games like Monopoly or creating a savings goal chart.

Give an allowance: Giving an allowance can be a great way to teach kids about money. It can help them learn to budget, save, and spend responsibly.

Start a savings account: Consider opening a savings account for your child. This can teach them about interest, saving, and the benefits of long-term investing.

Involve kids in family finances: Involve your children in family financial decisions, such as choosing a restaurant or planning a vacation. This can help them understand how money impacts everyday decisions.

Use online resources: Many online resources are available to help teach kids about money. For example, websites like

MoneyAsYouGrow.org and HandsOnBanking.org offer age-appropriate financial lessons and activities.

Overall, teaching kids about money is an ongoing process that requires patience and consistency. However, by using real-life examples, making it fun, and involving kids in family finances, parents can help set their children up for long-term financial success.

CONVERSATIONS BETWEEN PARENTS AND CHILDREN: (TEACHING KIDS ABOUT MONEY)

EXAMPLE -1:
Parent: Hey, Buddy/Princess! Let's talk about money for a bit.
Child: Sure, what's up, Mom/Dad?
Parent: Well, I wanted to talk to you about saving money. Do you know what saving money means?
Child: Kind of. It means spending only some of your money, right?
Parent: That's right! And when you save your money, you can use it to buy something you want or need in the future. So, let's say you have $10 and want to buy a toy that costs $20. How could you save up for that toy?
Child: I could save $1 daily for ten days.
Parent: Great idea! And when you save that money, you could put it in a piggy bank or a jar. Would you like to try that?
Child: Yes, that sounds like fun!
Parent: Awesome! And if you keep it up, you'll have enough money to buy that toy in no time. And remember, it's essential to save your money instead of spending it all at once.
Child: Okay, I will.
Parent: Also, it's essential to spend money wisely. Do you remember when we went grocery shopping last week?
Child: Yeah.
Parent: Do you remember how we compared prices and used coupons to save money?
Child: Yes.

Parent: Well, that's one way we save money. And it's essential to do that because then we have more money to save for things we want or need.

Child: Oh, I get it.

Parent: Great! And as you get older, we'll teach you more about money and how to use it wisely.

Child: Okay, I'm excited to learn more!

EXAMPLE -2:

Parent: Hey, sweetie! Do you know what a budget is?

Child: I'm still determining. Is it like a shopping list?

Parent: Well, it's like a shopping list for your money. A budget is a plan for how you spend your money. It helps ensure you have enough money for everything you need and want.

Child: Oh, okay. Can you give me an example?

Parent: Sure! Let's say you get $20 for your birthday and want to spend it on things you like. You can make a budget to decide how to spend that money. For example, you could write down that you want to spend $5 on a toy, $5 on some candy, $5 on a book, and $5 to save for later.

Child: Oh, I get it. So, you must decide how much money you want to spend on each thing.

Parent: Exactly! And it's essential to get, so you only spend all your money at a time and then have nothing left for other things you might want.

Child: That makes sense. Can I make a budget for my next birthday money?

Parent: Of course! That's a great idea. And if you stick to your budget, you'll have enough money for everything you want, and maybe even some left over to save for later.

Child: Okay, I'm excited to try it!

Parent: Great! And remember, making a budget is just one way to be smart with your money. As you age, we'll teach you more about money and how to use it wisely.

Child: Okay, I'm ready to learn!

EXAMPLE -3:

Parent: Hey, Buddy/Princess! I wanted to talk to you about the importance of earning money. Do you know what it means to earn money?

Child: Kind of. It means working for someone, and they give you money, right?

Parent: Yes, that's right! And when you earn money, you can use it to buy things you want or save it for something unique. So, let's say you want to earn some money. Do you have any ideas for what kind of work you could do?

Child: Hmm, I could help you clean the house, walk the dog, or mow the lawn.

Parent: Those are great ideas! And when you do those things, you can earn some money. How much would be fair for those jobs?

Child: Maybe $5 for walking the dog, $10 for mowing the lawn, and $2 for helping clean the house.

Parent: Those are fair prices! And when you earn that money, you can decide how to spend it or save it for something unique. Do you have any ideas for what you want to do with your money?

Child: I want to save up for a new bike!

Parent: That's a great goal! And if you keep working hard and earning money, you'll be able to buy that bike in no time.

Child: Yay! I can't wait!

Parent: Remember, working hard and earning money is essential, but spending it wisely and saving for the future is also essential.

Child: Okay, I will. Thank you, Mom/Dad!

GOOD HABITS IN MONEY MANAGEMENT

Establishing good financial habits means developing positive and responsible behaviours related to money management. It involves forming habits and routines that promote financial stability and well-being, such as budgeting, saving, investing, and avoiding excessive debt.

By establishing good financial habits, individuals can set themselves up for success in the long run and avoid common pitfalls like overspending, living pay check to pay check, or falling into debt. Good financial habits can also lead to increased financial freedom, allowing individuals to make choices and pursue opportunities they might not have been able to otherwise.

Some examples of good financial habits include creating a budget and sticking to it, saving regularly, avoiding unnecessary expenses, investing for the future, and paying bills on time. These habits can be learned and reinforced over time, increasing financial security and peace of mind.

Here are some ways to teach kids the importance of establishing good financial habits:

Set a good example: Children learn by observing their parents' behaviours. Therefore, it's essential for parents to model good financial habits and to talk openly with their kids about their own financial decisions.

Start young: Teaching kids about money and financial responsibility should start at a young age. Even simple activities, like giving kids an allowance and encouraging them to save a portion, can help establish good habits early on.

Use real-life scenarios: Kids may have difficulty understanding abstract concepts, so it's helpful to use real-life scenarios to help teach them about financial responsibility. For example, if you're at the grocery store, you can show them how to compare prices and make a budget for their shopping list.

Make it fun: Learning about finance doesn't have to be boring. You can make it fun by playing games that teach financial concepts, such as Monopoly or The Game of Life. This can make financial responsibility feel less daunting and more engaging.

Encourage goal setting: Setting financial goals can be an excellent motivator for kids. For example, you can encourage them to save for a specific item they want or to set a goal for how much they want to save over a certain period. This can help them establish good saving habits and build discipline.

Talk openly about money: Many parents avoid discussing it with their kids, and avoiding excessive debt is most important in financial matters. This can help kids understand the value of money and how to manage it responsibly.

Celebrate successes: When kids establish good financial habits, they imitate their successes. This can reinforce positive behaviours and encourage them to make intelligent financial decisions.

Here are some examples of good habits related to money:

Budgeting: Creating and sticking to a budget is one of the essential habits for managing money effectively. A budget helps you track your income and expenses and can help you avoid overspending and debt.

Saving: Saving money regularly is another vital habit for money-related habits. Aside from a portion of your income, savings can help you achieve your financial goals, build an emergency fund, and plan for the future.

Investing: Investing can be a great way to build wealth over time, but it's essential to do so wisely. Good investing habits include diversifying your portfolio, avoiding risky investments, and regularly reviewing and adjusting your investments.

Paying bills on time: Paying bills on time helps you avoid late fees and damage to your car. Setting up automatic payments or reminders can help establish this habit.

Avoiding debt: Debt can be a significant obstacle to financial stability, so avoiding excessive debt. Good habits related to debt include:

- Paying off credit card balances in full each month.
- Avoiding unnecessary loans.
- Living within your means.

Practicing frugality: Frugality is living simply and avoiding unnecessary expenses. Good habits related to frugality include shopping for bargains, using coupons, and avoiding impulse purchases.

Setting financial goals: Setting financial goals can help you stay motivated and focused on your financial objectives. Good habits related to goal-setting include breaking goals down into smaller, achievable steps, tracking progress regularly, and celebrating successes.

Establishing good money-related habits is crucial for achieving financial stability and well-being. Good habits such as budgeting, saving, investing, paying bills on time, avoiding debt, practicing frugality, and setting financial goals can help individuals make smart financial decisions and avoid common financial pitfalls. In addition, these habits can be learned and reinforced over time, leading to increased financial security, peace of mind, and the ability to choose and pursue opportunities that might not have been otherwise. By establishing good habits early on, individuals can set themselves up for success in the long run and enjoy the benefits of financial freedom and security.

CONVERSATIONS BETWEEN PARENTS AND CHILDREN:
(GOOD HABITS IN MONEY MANAGEMENT)

EXAMPLE -1:
Parent: Hi, have you ever thought about the importance of money management?
Child: Not really; what do you mean?
Parent: Well, managing money is an essential skill that can help you achieve financial stability and make intelligent decisions about your future. Establishing good habits related to money management can be the key to success.
Child: What kind of habits are you talking about?
Parent: There are several good habits related to money management, such as budgeting, saving, investing, paying bills on time, avoiding debt, practicing frugality, and setting

financial goals.

Child: That sounds like a lot to remember!

Parent: It may initially seem overwhelming, but establishing these habits is gradual. You can start by setting small goals, like saving a portion of your weekly allowance or creating a simple budget to track your spending.

Child: Why is it so essential to establish these habits?

Parent: Good money management habits can help avoid common financial pitfalls like overspending, debt, and stress. They can also help you achieve your financial goals, build an emergency fund, and plan for the future. By establishing these habits early on, you can set yourself up for success in the long run and enjoy the benefits of financial freedom and security.

Child: I see what you mean. These habits can help me make intelligent decisions about my money and avoid getting into trouble.

Parent: That's right. By practicing good habits related to money management, you can develop the skills and knowledge necessary to navigate the financial world and achieve your goals confidently. So, are you ready to start establishing these habits?

Child: Yes, I am! Thank you for explaining it to me.

EXAMPLE -2:

Parent: Hey, have you ever thought about what you want to do with your money?

Child: Not really; I spend it on things I like.

Parent: That's okay, but it's essential to establish good habits related to money management to make the most out of your money.

Child: What kind of habits are you talking about?

Parent: There are several habits that you can develop that can help you manage your money better. One crucial habit is budgeting. This means planning how much money you will spend and how much you will save.

Child: Why is budgeting important?

Parent: Budgeting is important because it helps you avoid overspending and getting into debt. It also helps you prioritize your spending to save money for things that are important to you.

Child: Okay, that makes sense. What are some other good habits?

Parent: Another good habit is saving. This means setting aside some of your money for things you want to buy in the future or for unexpected expenses. Saving can help you achieve your goals and feel more financially secure.

Child: I want to save money, but it's hard!

Parent: It can be challenging, but there are things you can do to make it easier. One way is to set a goal for yourself and work towards it. For example, you could set a goal to save up for a new toy or video game. Another way is to make saving a habit by setting aside a portion of your allowance or money from doing chores.

Child: What are some other habits?

Parent: Other good habits include investing, avoiding debt, and being frugal. Developing these habits allows you to set yourself up for a more secure financial future.

Child: I understand why these habits are essential now. Thanks for explaining it to me, Mom/Dad.

Parent: You're welcome! Remember, developing good money management habits is a gradual process, so take it one step at a time and be patient with yourself.

EXAMPLE -3:

Parent: Hey, have you ever thought about how to manage your money effectively?

Child: Not really; I spend it on whatever I want.

Parent: It's okay to spend money on things you want, but it's also essential to develop good habits related to money management. Doing this ensures you have enough money to do what you want and need.

Child: What are some good habits related to money

management?

Parent: One important habit is keeping track of your money. This means knowing how much money you have, how much you are spending, and where your money is going. Doing this can avoid overspending and ensure you always have enough money for your needs.

Child: How do I keep track of my money?

Parent: You can start by recording all the money you receive and spend. You can use a notebook or an app on your phone. At the end of each week and see where your money is going.

Child: What are some other good habits?

Parent: Another good habit is setting financial goals. This means deciding what to do with your money and working towards those goals. For example, you might set a goal to save up for a new toy or to donate money to a charity.

Child: That sounds like a good idea. What else can I do?

Parent: You can also develop good habits like saving money, avoiding debt, and being frugal. Doing these things ensures you always have enough money for your needs and wants.

Child: I understand why developing these habits is essential now. Thanks for explaining it to me, Mom/Dad.

Parent: You're welcome! Developing good money management habits takes time, so be patient and keep working.

MONEY MANAGEMENT FOR KIDS

Developing Good Saving and Spending Habits

Money is only a tool. It will take you wherever you wish, but it will not replace you as the driver.

Ayn Rand

Teaching children how to manage money is essential to their financial wisdom. Good money management habits can set the foundation for a successful financial future. This chapter will focus on developing good saving and spending habits in kids.

Understanding the Value of Money:

Before teaching kids how to manage their money, it's essential to help them understand the value of money. Kids need to know that money is earned through hard work and should be spent wisely. This section will cover different strategies parents can use to teach their kids the value of money, including setting a good example, using visual aids, and involving kids in decision-making.

Developing Good Saving Habits:

Saving money is an important habit that can help kids achieve their financial goals in the future. This section will focus on ways parents can encourage their kids to save money, including setting savings goals, creating a savings plan, and using incentives to motivate kids to save.

Developing Good Spending Habits:

Teaching kids how to spend money wisely is also important. Parents can teach their kids how to make wise spending decisions by involving them in family budgeting, setting spending limits, and teaching them the difference between needs and wants. This section will also cover strategies for avoiding impulse buying and teaching kids how to compare shops.

Teaching Kids About Debt:

As kids grow older, they may be exposed to debt. Therefore, parents must teach their kids about debt and how to manage it responsibly. This section will cover different types of debt, such as credit cards and loans, and provide tips for teaching kids how to use credit responsibly.

Teaching kids good money management habits is vital in preparing them for financial wisdom by helping them understand the value of money, developing good saving and spending habits, and teaching them about debt. As a result, parents can set their kids up for a successful financial future.

UNDERSTANDING THE VALUE OF MONEY

Refers to the ability to appreciate and comprehend money's worth in terms of its purchasing power, utility, and impact on personal financial well-being.
This involves having knowledge and awareness of financial concepts such as Budgeting, saving, investing, and managing debt, as well as making informed decisions about spending and prioritizing financial goals.
It also involves recognizing the economic and social factors that affect the value of money, such as inflation, interest rates, and market fluctuations. Overall, understanding the value of money is crucial for making sound financial decisions and achieving stability and security.

Teaching kids the importance of understanding the value of money is an essential aspect of their financial education. Here are some ways to do so:
Start with the basics: Begin by teaching your child about the different types of coins and bills, their denominations, and their values. This will help them understand the value of money and how it is used in everyday transactions.
Use real-life examples: Help your child understand the concept of money by giving them real-life examples, such as paying for groceries or buying a toy. This will help them see the practical applications of money and its value.
Encourage saving: Teach your child the importance of saving by setting up a savings account or piggy bank. Help them understand that saving money can help them achieve their

goals in the future.

Set a budget: Teach your child how to budget by creating a spending plan and allocating money for different expenses. This will help them understand the importance of making informed financial decisions and sticking to a budget.

Involve them in financial decisions: Involve your child in decisions such as choosing a family vacation or making a significant purchase. This will help them understand the financial decision-making process and the trade-offs involved.

Teach them about debt: Help your child understand the concept of debt and how it can impact their financial well-being. Teach them about interest rates and the importance of paying off debt promptly.

By teaching your child the importance of understanding the value of money, you can help them develop strong financial habits and skills that will benefit them throughout their lives.

Here are some specific examples of how you can teach the importance of understanding the value of money to kids:

Play money games: Many board games and online games teach kids about the value of money, Budgeting, and saving. For example, games like Monopoly, The Game of Life, and Financial Football can be fun and engaging ways to teach kids about financial concepts.

Set up a savings account: Help your child set up a savings account and encourage them to save a portion of their allowance or earnings. This will teach them the importance of saving and setting financial goals.

Discuss the cost of everyday items: When you're out shopping or paying bills, talk to your child about how they add up over time. For example, buying coffee daily can add up to a significant amount of money over a year.

Make a budget together: Work with your child to create a budget for a specific goal, such as saving for a vacation or a new toy. This will teach them how to allocate money and make informed financial decisions.

Encourage comparison shopping: Encourage your child to compare prices and look for deals when shopping for a specific item. This will teach them the value of researching options and making informed purchasing decisions.

Talk about the value of work: When your child earns money from doing chores or a part-time job, discuss the value of their work and how they can use their earnings to achieve their financial goals.

Incorporating these examples into your conversations and activities with your child can help them better understand money's value and financial literacy's importance.

CONVERSATIONS BETWEEN PARENTS AND CHILDREN:
(UNDERSTANDING THE VALUE OF MONEY)

EXAMPLE -1:

Parent: "Hey, Buddy/Princess! Do you remember the other day when we were shopping for groceries?"

Child: "Yeah, I remember. Why?"

Parent: "Well, do you remember how we had a list of items we needed to buy, and we were checking the prices of each item before putting them in our cart?"

Child: "Yeah, I remember that."

Parent: "Do you know why we were doing that?"

Child: "Uh, I don't know. To make sure we don't buy too much?"

Parent: "Yes, that's one reason. But another reason is that we want to ensure we're not spending too much money. By checking each item's prices, we can ensure we get the best deals by checking each item's prices without overspending. That's why it's important to understand the value of money."

EXAMPLE 2:

Parent: "Hey, sweetie! Do you want to help me create a budget for our next vacation?"

Child: "Sure, that sounds like fun! But what's a budget?"

Parent: "A budget is a plan that helps us allocate our money for different things we want or need. For example, if we're planning a vacation, we must have enough money for transportation, lodging, food, and activities. By creating a budget, we can ensure we're not overspending and enjoy our vacation without worrying about money."

Child: "Oh, I get it! So, we need to save money and plan how to spend it?"

Parent: "Exactly! And that's why it's important to understand the value of money. By making smart financial decisions and planning, we can achieve our goals and enjoy what we want without putting ourselves in financial trouble."

EXAMPLE -3:

Parent: "Hey, Buddy/Princess, do you know what it means to save money?"

Child: "I think it means not spending all of our money, right?"

Parent: "Yes, that's right! Saving money means putting some of our money aside for later. It's like having a little piggy bank for the future."

Child: "Why is saving money important?"

Parent: "Well, there are many reasons why saving money is important. For example, if we save money, we can use it to buy something special that we want, like a new toy or a video game. Or, if we save enough money, we can use it for a fun trip or vacation. Saving money can also help us be prepared for unexpected things that might happen in the future, like a surprise expense or an emergency."

Child: "Oh, I get it now! So, saving money is like putting away some of our money for later, and it can help us get the things we want and be ready for the future."

Parent: "Exactly! And that's why it's important to understand the value of money, so we can make smart financial decisions and use our money wisely."

EXAMPLE -4:

Parent: "Hey, Buddy/Princess, do you know what it means to budget our money?"
Child: "No, I don't. What does that mean?"
Parent: "Budgeting means planning how we will spend our money. It's like making a list of things we need and want and then deciding how much money we will spend on each. It helps us ensure we have enough money for everything we need and want without overspending."
Child: "Oh, I see. So, it's like making a plan so we don't run out of money?"
Parent: "Exactly! And it's also a way to help us save money and achieve our financial goals. For example, if we want to buy a new video game, we can budget our money and save up for it instead of spending all of our money right away. That way, we can get the game we want without putting ourselves in financial trouble."
Child: "That makes sense. So, Budgeting is important because it helps us plan for our money and ensure we don't overspend."
Parent: "Exactly! And by understanding the value of money and how to budget our money, we can make smart financial decisions and achieve our goals."

DEVELOPING GOOD SAVING HABITS

Developing good saving habits refers to regularly setting aside a portion of one's income or resources to build up savings. This involves consciously and consistently making choices about allocating money, prioritizing saving over spending on unnecessary items, and sticking to a savings plan.
Good saving habits can help individuals and families achieve financial goals, prepare for unexpected expenses or emergencies, and build long-term financial stability and security.

Here are some excellent saving habits for kids:
Setting aside a portion of their allowance or income: **Encourage** your child to save a portion of their allowance or

income, whether from doing chores or receiving money as gifts. This can help them develop the habit of saving regularly.

Saving for a specific goal: Encourage your child to set a savings goal, such as saving for a new toy or a special outing with friends. This will help them stay motivated and see the benefits of saving.

Saving windfall money: If your child receives unexpected money, such as a birthday gift or a bonus from a grandparent, encourage them to save at least part of it instead of spending it all right away.

Avoiding impulse buys: Teach your child to think before purchasing and consider whether they need the item or if it's just a fleeting desire. Encourage them to wait a day or two before purchasing to avoid impulse buys.

Comparing prices: Teach your child to shop and compare prices before purchasing. This will help them develop the habit of being a savvy consumer and getting the best value for their money.

Creating a savings plan: Help your child create a plan that outlines how much they want to save, what they are saving for, and how long it will take to reach their goal. This can help them stay focused and motivated.

By encouraging these good saving habits for kids, they can develop solid financial skills that will benefit them throughout their lives.

Here are some ways to teach kids the importance of developing good saving habits:

Start with a piggy bank: Introduce the concept of saving by giving your child a piggy bank or a jar where they can put their loose change or small amounts of money. Encourage them to save regularly and count their savings periodically.

Use visual aids: Create a visual representation of a savings goal, such as a chart or a graph, and encourage your child to track their progress. This will help them see the benefits of saving and staying motivated.

Set an example: Children learn by watching and imitating their parents' behaviour. For example, model good saving habits by regularly putting money aside for savings and discussing why it's essential.

Provide incentives: Consider offering a small reward or allowance for consistent saving behaviour. This can motivate your child to develop good saving habits and make it a fun and rewarding experience.

Talk about goals: Discuss with your child the reasons for saving money and how it can help them achieve their goals. Whether saving for a special toy or a family vacation, having a clear goal can help make saving more purposeful and rewarding.

Encourage delayed gratification: Teach your child that sometimes it's important to delay gratification and save up for something they want instead of buying something impulsively. This will help them develop the discipline to resist immediate impulses and make better financial decisions in the future.

Involve them in family financial decisions: Involve your child in discussions about family finances, such as Budgeting or planning for big purchases. This will help them understand the importance of saving and how it fits into the bigger picture of financial planning.

By teaching kids the importance of developing good saving habits at a young age, they can learn valuable financial skills that will serve them well throughout their lives.

CONVERSATIONS BETWEEN PARENTS AND CHILDREN:
(DEVELOPING GOOD SAVING HABITS)

EXAMPLE -1:
Parent: Hey, I noticed you got money for your birthday. What do you plan on doing with it?
Child: I was thinking about buying a new video game that just

came out.

Parent: That sounds fun, but have you considered saving money instead? You could save up for something even more significant than you want.

Child: Like what?

Parent: What about saving for a new bike or a special outing with your friends?

Child: Yeah, that sounds cool. How much should I save?

Parent: It's up to you, but you could start by putting half of your birthday money into your savings account. Then you can add to it with your allowance and any extra money you earn.

Child: Okay, I can do that. How long will it take to save enough for a new bike?

Parent: It depends on how much the bike costs and how much you save each week. We can make a plan together to help you reach your goal.

Child: That sounds like a good idea. I'm excited to save up for something I want!

This conversation illustrates how parents can encourage their children to develop good saving habits by helping them set a savings goal and plan to achieve it. By teaching children the value of saving and helping them develop good saving habits, parents can empower their children to make wise financial decisions and achieve their goals.

EXAMPLE -2:

Parent: Hey, I noticed you've been talking about wanting to buy a new toy. Have you considered saving up for it instead of buying it immediately?

Child: No, I want it now.

Parent: I understand, but saving up for it can be more rewarding. You'll appreciate it even more when you finally get it. Plus, it's a good habit to start saving money for things you want.

Child: How do I start?

Parent: Well, how much does the toy cost?

Child: It costs $20.

Parent: Great, let's set a goal to save $5 each week. That means you'll have enough money to buy the toy in four weeks!

Child: Okay, I can do that.

Parent: We can make it more fun by creating a savings chart to track your progress. We can put it on your wall and mark it off each week as you save.

Child: That sounds like fun! I can't wait to save up for my new toy.

This conversation shows how parents can encourage their children to develop good saving habits by helping them set a specific goal and providing support and motivation. In addition, by making saving fun and achievable, parents can help their children see the benefits of delayed gratification and develop good financial habits that will serve them well throughout their lives.

EXAMPLE -3:

Parent: I wanted to discuss your allowance. Do you know where your money is going each week?

Child: Not really. I spend it on whatever I want.

Parent: That's understandable, but learning to manage your money wisely is also important. What if we started setting aside some of your allowance for savings?

Child: What's that?

Parent: Savings is when you put money aside later, like for something you want in the future. It's a good habit to start doing now, so you can be prepared for more significant purchases or emergencies later on.

Child: Okay, how much should I save?

Parent: We could start with 10% of your allowance each week. That means if you get $10 for allowance, you could put $1 into savings.

Child: That's not much.

Parent: It may not seem like much, but it adds up over time. And if you get any extra money from doing chores or getting a gift, you could add that to your savings.
Child: Okay, that makes sense.
Parent: When you have enough money, you can decide what to spend it on. It could be something small or big, like a new bike or a memorable trip.
Child: That sounds cool! I want to start saving up now.

This conversation shows how parents can teach their children the importance of saving and budgeting money. By starting early and developing good financial habits, children can learn to manage their money responsibly and make intelligent decisions about their future financial goals.

DEVELOPING GOOD SPENDING HABITS

Developing good spending habits means learning to make responsible and wise choices about how to spend money. This includes understanding the difference between needs and wants, Budgeting, avoiding impulse purchases, and prioritizing long-term goals over short-term desires. Good spending habits also involve being aware of the value of money and using it wisely to achieve financial security and stability.

Here are some excellent saving habits for kids:
Understanding the difference between needs and wants: Teach your child the difference between things they need (such as food, clothing, and shelter) and things they want (such as toys or video games). Encourage them to prioritize their needs before spending money on wants.
Making a budget: Help your child create a simple budget with categories for saving, spending, and giving. Encourage them to set goals for each category and track their spending to stay on track.
Avoiding impulse purchases: Teach your child to think before making a purchase. First, encourage them to ask themselves

if they need the item and if it's worth the money. Then, teach them to wait a few days before avoiding impulse buying.

Prioritizing long-term goals: Help your child understand the importance of saving for the future, such as for college or a car. Encourage them to set aside some of their allowance or earnings towards these long-term goals rather than spending all their money on short-term wants.

Shopping wisely: Teach your child to compare prices and look for deals. Show them how to read labels, compare prices, and encourage them to shop at thrift stores or garage sales to save money.

Being responsible with credit: Teach your child the importance of paying bills on time and being responsible with credit. Explain how credit cards work and the importance of paying off the balance each month to avoid interest charges and debt.

By developing these good spending habits, kids can learn to make responsible and wise choices with their money, setting them up for financial success in the future.

Here are some tips for teaching kids the importance of developing good spending habits:

Lead by example: Children learn much from observing their parents and other adults. Model good spending habits, such as making a budget, saving money, and avoiding impulse purchases.

Involve kids in budgeting decisions: Talk to your kids about the family budget and involve them in decision-making when appropriate. For example, you could discuss the family's spending priorities or involve them in making a shopping list.

Encourage saving: Help your child develop a savings plan and encourage them to save for future goals. This can help them develop a sense of delayed gratification and prioritize long-term goals over short-term desires.

Teach the value of money: Help your child understand the value of money by talking about how it's earned and the effort that goes into earning it. Encourage them to think about the cost of items beyond just the price tag.

Set limits on your child's spending, such as a weekly allowance or budget for specific purchases. This can help them learn to prioritize and make responsible choices with their money.

Use real-life examples: Use real-life examples to teach your child about good spending habits. For example, you could discuss how a friend or family member made a wise financial decision or the consequences of making poor choices with money.

By teaching children the importance of developing good spending habits, you can help them develop financial literacy and set them on a path toward financial responsibility and success.

CONVERSATIONS BETWEEN PARENTS AND CHILDREN: (DEVELOPING GOOD SPENDING HABITS)

EXAMPLE -1:

Parent: Hey, Buddy/Princess! Can we talk about your spending habits?

Child: Sure, what's up?

Parent: I noticed you've been spending a lot on toys and video games lately. Do you make the best use of your money?

Child: I don't know, I just really wanted those things.

Parent: I understand, but it's essential to consider the long-term too. Remember how we discussed saving for a new bike or a memorable trip?

Child: Yeah, I remember.

Parent: If you keep spending all your money on toys and games, You have enough to save for those bigger goals. How about we make a budget together, with categories for saving, spending, and giving? That way, you can ensure you're putting your money toward what matters most.

Child: Okay, that sounds like a good idea.

Parent: Great! And let's also think about avoiding impulse purchases. Before buying something, ask yourself if it's something you really need or want right now. If it's not something you need, try waiting a few days to see if you still want it.

Child: Okay, I'll try that.

Parent: Remember, good spending habits aren't just about saving money. It's also about using your money wisely to achieve your goals and priorities. By making smart choices with your money now, you'll be setting yourself up for financial success in the future.

Child: Thanks, I understand now. I'll start being more careful with my spending.

EXAMPLE -2:

Parent: Hey, Buddy/Princess, have you thought about what you want to spend your birthday money on?

Child: I was thinking of getting a new video game and maybe some candy.

Parent: Those are some fun things to buy, but have you considered saving some of your birthday money for the future?

Child: What do you mean?

Parent: You could put some of your birthday money into your savings account. That way, you can save up for something more significant in the future, like a new bike or a memorable trip.

Child: Oh, that sounds like a good idea. But I want the video game and candy now.

Parent: I understand, but balancing your wants and needs is essential. Maybe You can use some of your birthday money for the video game and candy and set aside some for your savings account.

Child: Okay, I see what you mean.

Parent: And let's also think about being a savvy shopper. Before you buy something, do some research to find the best deal. You can compare prices online or look for coupons or sales.

Child: That's a good idea.

Parent: Remember to think about the actual cost of things. Sometimes, things seem cheap initially, but they cost a lot in the long run. For example, buying a cheap toy that breaks easily might seem like a good deal, but you'll have to buy another soon.

Child: Yeah, I get it. It's better to buy something that will last longer.

Parent: Exactly! By developing good spending habits now, you'll be setting yourself up for financial success in the future.

EXAMPLE -3:

Parent: Hey, sweetie, do you want to go to the store with me to buy groceries?

Child: Sure, can we get some ice cream too?

Parent: We can get some ice cream, but let's discuss our grocery list first. We need to ensure we're spending on things we don't need.

Child: Okay, what's on the list?

Parent: We need bread, milk, eggs, and some vegetables for dinner. And we can also get some fruit and snacks for you to bring to school.

Child: Can we get some chips and cookies too?

Parent: We can, but let's consider how much we want to spend on snacks. If we buy too many, they might go to waste, and that's not a good use of our money.

Child: Okay, I understand. How about we get one bag of chips and one box of cookies?

Parent: That sounds like a good plan. And let's also think about buying store brands instead of name brands. They usually cost less and are just as good.

Child: Can we still get the ice cream, though?

Parent: Of course! We can get some ice cream as a treat, but let's ensure we're not overspending on other things.

Child: Okay, I get it. It's essential to think about how we spend our money.

Parent: That's right! By making intelligent choices at the store, we can save money and ensure we're not wasting our resources. And that's a good habit to have for the future.

TEACHING KIDS ABOUT DEBT

Debt refers to the amount of money borrowed by one party from another with the agreement to repay the borrowed amount with interest over time. Debt can take many forms, including credit card debt, personal loans, student loans, mortgages, and business loans. The borrower typically incurs a debt when they receive money or services from the lender and agrees to pay it back over a certain period. Failure to repay the debt can result in penalties and negatively impact the borrower's credit score.

Here are some examples of debt:

Credit Card Debt: When a person makes purchases using a credit card and does not pay the entire balance on the due date, they incur credit card debt. The outstanding balance accumulates interest, and the borrower must make minimum monthly payments to avoid penalties.

Student Loans: These are loans that students take to finance their education. The loans accrue interest and must be paid back after graduation. Students can take out federal or private loans, and the repayment terms can vary depending on the type of loan.

Mortgage: A mortgage is a loan taken out to purchase a home. The borrower agrees to make regular payments over the loan term to pay off the principal plus interest. Failure to pay the mortgage can result in foreclosure.

Personal Loans: These are loans that individuals take out for personal expenses, such as medical bills or home renovations. The loans typically have a fixed repayment term and interest rate.

Business Loans: Businesses may take out loans to finance operations, purchase equipment, or expand. The terms and interest rates for business loans can vary depending on the lender's and borrower's creditworthiness.

Teaching kids about debt can be challenging, but it is an essential financial lesson that will benefit them in the long run. Here are some tips for teaching kids about debt:

Start with the basics: Before you teach kids about debt, they must understand what it is and how it works. Then, you can use straightforward language to explain that debt is borrowed money we must repay with interest over time.

Use real-life examples: Children learn best when they see how a concept applies to their lives. So you can use examples like buying a car or a house to help children understand how debt works in real-life situations.

Discuss the consequences of debt: It's essential to teach children that debt can have negative consequences if not appropriately managed. For example, you can explain how debt can lead to high-interest charges, late fees, and damage to credit scores.

Emphasize responsible borrowing: While debt can have negative consequences, it is also a necessary part of life. You can teach kids about responsible borrowings, such as only borrowing what you can afford to pay back and making payments on time.

Encourage saving: One way to avoid debt is to save money for big purchases instead of borrowing. Encourage your child to save money regularly and explain how saving can help them achieve their goals without going into debt.

Teaching kids about debt and managing it responsibly can help set them up for a more financially secure future.

CONVERSATIONS BETWEEN PARENTS AND
CHILDREN: (UNDERSTANDING ABOUT DEBT)

EXAMPLE -1:
Parent: Hey, Buddy/Princess, do you know what debt means?
Child: No, what is it?
Parent: Debt is when you borrow money from someone and then pay it back with interest. It's like a loan, but you must pay extra to borrow the money.
Child: Why would someone borrow money if they have to pay extra?
Parent: Sometimes, people need to borrow money to pay for things they can't afford, like buying a car or a house. But it's essential to be careful with debt because you must pay it back on time to avoid problems.
Child: What kind of problems?
Parent: If you don't pay back your debt, you can owe even more because of interest charges and late fees. Plus, getting loans or credit in the future can be tricky if you have too much debt.
Child: So, what can we do to avoid problems with debt?
Parent: One way to avoid problems with debt is only to borrow what you can afford to pay back and to make sure you pay it back on time. It's also good to save money for big purchases instead of borrowing. That way, you don't have to pay extra to borrow the money.
Child: That makes sense. Thanks for explaining it to me, Mom/ Dad.
Parent: You're welcome, sweetie. Understanding debt is essential so you can make intelligent decisions about your money.

EXAMPLE -2:
Parent: Hey, have you ever heard of debt?
Child: No, what is it?
Parent: Well, debt is when you borrow money from someone and have to pay it back later, usually with extra money called interest. For example, if you borrow $10 from your friend and promise to pay them $12 back the next week, that $2 extra is

the interest.

Child: Oh, I see. But why would someone want to borrow money?

Parent: Good question. People often borrow money to buy things they can't afford, like a house, a car, or a college. But it's important to understand that borrowing money also comes with risks.

Child: What kind of risks?

Parent: If you borrow too much money or don't pay it back on time, you can owe even more because of the interest and fees. This can make it harder for you to borrow money in the future, or it can hurt your credit score.

Child: What's a credit score?

Parent: A credit score is like a grade that shows how good you are at paying back borrowed money. It's essential to have a good credit score because it can affect your ability to get loans, buy a car or a house, and even get a job.

Child: Wow, I didn't know all of that. So, what can I do to avoid getting into debt?

Parent: One way to avoid debt is to save money for what you want to buy instead of borrowing. This means putting aside money weekly or monthly until you have enough to buy what you want. Of course, it takes longer, but it's safer than borrowing money you might not be able to pay back.

Child: That sounds like a good idea. Thanks, Mom/Dad.

Parent: You're welcome, honey. Remember, it's essential to be responsible with your money and avoid getting into too much debt.

EXAMPLE -3:

Parent: Do you know what credit cards are?

Child: They're like magic cards that let you buy whatever you want!

Parent: Credit cards are not magic and are not free money either. You borrow money from the company using a credit card to buy something. And just like any other borrowing, you must pay it back, usually with interest.

Child: What's your interest?

Parent: Interest is like a fee that you have to pay for borrowing money. So, for example, if you buy something for $50 with a credit card and the interest rate is 20%, you'll have to pay back $60 instead of $50.

Child: That's not fair! Why would anyone use a credit card, then?

Parent: Sometimes, using a credit card can be convenient, especially for emergencies or when you don't have cash. But using credit cards responsibly and paying back what you owe on time is essential. If you don't, you can have a lot of debt and hurt your credit score.

Child: What's a credit score?

Parent: A credit score is a number that shows how good you are at borrowing and paying back money. A good credit score means you're responsible with money and can help you get better loans or lower interest rates. But a bad credit score can make borrowing money harder or getting approved for apartments or jobs.

Child: Oh, I didn't know that. So, how can I use credit cards responsibly?

Parent: Well, one way is to only use your credit card for things you can afford to repay immediately and always pay off your balance in full each month. That way, you won't have to pay any interest, and you'll build good credit habits for the future.

Child: Okay, I'll remember that. Thanks, Mom/Dad!

Parent: You're welcome, sweetie. Credit cards can be helpful, but using them responsibly and always repaying what you owe on time is essential.

TEACHING KIDS ABOUT DEBT

Understanding Credit and Loans

Before you borrow money, make sure you know the true cost of debt. It's not just about the interest rate; it's about the impact on your financial freedom.

Suze Orman

In today's world, borrowing money is almost a way of life. Most people have some form of debt, whether a student loan, credit card, or mortgage. Therefore, kids need to learn about debt and how to manage it responsibly. This chapter aims to provide parents and educators with the tools and strategies to teach kids about credit and loans, including the benefits and pitfalls of borrowing money.

What is Debt?: In this section, we'll define debt and explain how it works. We'll discuss the different types of debt, such as secured and unsecured loans, and explain how interest rates work. We'll also explore the consequences of taking on too much debt, including the impact on credit scores and the potential for bankruptcy.

Good Debt vs. Bad Debt: Not all debt is created equal, and kids must understand the difference between good and bad debt. In this section, we'll discuss examples of each type of debt and explain why some types are considered beneficial while others can be harmful. We'll also discuss how to make informed decisions about borrowing money and avoid unnecessarily getting into debt.

Managing Debt Responsibly: Managing debt responsibly is crucial to avoid financial problems in the future. This section will provide tips and strategies for teaching kids how to manage debt effectively, including making timely payments, avoiding high-interest loans, and developing a budget. We'll also discuss the importance of building and maintaining a good credit score.

Teaching Kids about Loans: This section will discuss the different types of available loans and explain how they work. We'll discuss the pros and cons of most people have some form of debt, whether money and how to evaluate loan offers. We'll also explore the impact of interest rates on loan payments and how to calculate the cost of borrowing money.

Teaching kids about debt is an integral part of financial education. By providing them with the tools and strategies to manage debt responsibly, we can help them avoid financial problems in the future. There are many valuable lessons about credit and loans, whether understanding the difference between good and bad debt or learning how to manage loans effectively.

WHAT IS DEBT?

Debt is the amount of money or property one party (the borrower) owes to another (the lender). We can incur debt by borrowing money, purchasing goods or services on credit, or using a credit card. The borrower must repay the debt to the lender, usually with interest or fees, over a specified period.

Debt can be good or bad, depending on how it is used and managed. Good debt can help to build wealth and improve financial well-being, while lousy debt can lead to financial difficulties and negative consequences.

There are several different types of debts. Some examples include

Credit card debt: Credit card debt is when someone uses a credit card to purchase goods or services and doesn't pay the balance in full at the end of the billing cycle.

Student loan debt is when someone borrows money to pay for their education and must pay it back with interest.

Mortgage debt: Mortgage debt is when someone borrows money to buy a home and must pay it back with interest over the years.

Car loan debt: Car loan debt is when someone borrows money to buy a car and must pay it back over the years with interest.

Personal loan debt: This is when someone borrows money for personal expenses, such as home renovations, medical bills, or other large purchases, and must pay it back over the years with interest.

Payday loan debt: This short-term loan typically has very high-interest rates and fees and is intended to be paid back on the borrower's next payday.

SECURED AND UNSECURED LOANS:

Secured and unsecured loans are different types available to borrowers.

A secured loan is a loan that is backed by collateral. Collateral is an asset that the borrower puts up to guarantee the loan. If the borrower cannot repay the loan, the lender can seize the collateral and sell it to recover their losses. Some examples of secured loans include home, car, and secured personal loans.

An unsecured loan, on the other hand, does not require any collateral. Instead, the lender relies on the borrower's creditworthiness and income to determine if they can repay the loan. If the borrower defaults on the loan, the lender has no collateral to seize. Examples of unsecured loans include personal loans, credit card debt, and student loans.

Because secured loans offer more security for the lender, they often come with lower interest rates and longer repayment terms. On the other hand, unsecured loans usually come with higher interest rates and shorter repayment terms because they are riskier for the lender.

WHAT IS INTEREST?

Interest is the cost of borrowing money, typically expressed as a percentage of the borrowed amount over a set period. It is the amount a lender charges a borrower for using their money.

The interest rate can be fixed or variable, and the loan term length can also affect the interest paid over time. Interest is a way for lenders to make money from lending funds and for borrowers to pay for the privilege of using those funds.

Taking on too much debt can lead to several negative consequences, including

Financial stress: When you have too much debt, it can lead to financial stress and anxiety. You may need help to meet your monthly payments and worry about how you will pay off your debts.

Reduced credit score: Too much debt can negatively impact your credit score, making it harder to get credit approval. A lower credit score can also result in higher interest rates on loans and credit cards.

Limited financial flexibility: If you have too much debt, it can limit your ability to make critical financial decisions. For example, you may need help to take advantage of investment opportunities or make significant purchases.

Collection calls and legal action: If you cannot pay off your debts, you may start receiving collection calls from creditors. In some cases, creditors may also take legal action to recover the money owed to them.

Bankruptcy: If you cannot pay off your debts and your financial situation does not improve, you may need to file for bankruptcy. This can have long-term negative consequences on your credit score and financial future.

Teaching kids about secured and unsecured loans can be done in various ways:

Use simple language: Explain the concept of secured and unsecured loans in simple terms that are easy for kids to understand.

Give examples: Provide real-life examples of secured and unsecured loans, such as a mortgage or car loan, versus a credit card or personal loan.

Use visuals: Use visual aids such as pictures or diagrams to help illustrate the differences between secured and unsecured loans.

Role-play: Engage in role-play activities with your child to help them understand the difference between secured and unsecured loans. For example, you can pretend to be a banker and ask your child to apply for a loan.

Encourage your child to ask questions about secured and

unsecured loans. Answer their questions honestly and give them the information they need to understand the concept fully.

Provide resources: Utilize books, videos, and other educational resources that explain the concept of secured and unsecured loans in a way kids can understand.

Teaching kids about secured and unsecured loans requires patience, creativity, and a willingness to answer their questions honestly. By providing your child with the knowledge and understanding they need, you can help them make informed decisions about borrowing money in the future.

Teaching kids about the concept of interest can be done differently, depending on their age and level of understanding. Here are some suggestions:

Explain it simply: Interest is the money you must pay on top of the borrowed amount. So it's like a fee for borrowing money.

Use real-life examples: Show them how credit card interest works or explain the interest rate on a car loan. You could also show them how savings accounts earn interest.

Play games: There are plenty of games and activities with kids to help them understand the concept of interest. For example, you could have them pretend to be a bank and charge interest on loans to their stuffed animals.

Show them the math: Depending on their age, you could explain how interest is calculated using math equations. For younger kids, you could use visual aids like blocks or toys to demonstrate the concept.

Emphasize the importance of paying off debt: Talk to kids about how interest can add up over time and make it harder to pay off debt. Emphasize the importance of making timely payments and avoiding debt whenever possible.

CONVERSATIONS BETWEEN PARENTS AND CHILDREN: (SECURE AND UNSECURED LOANS)

Parent: Hey, Buddy/Princess, do you know what a loan is?

Child: Yeah, it's when you borrow money from someone and then pay it back later.

Parent: Great! Are there different types of loans, like secured and unsecured?

Child: No, what's the difference?

Parent: A secured loan is when you borrow money and use something valuable like your home, car, or savings account as collateral. If you can't repay the loan, the lender can take the collateral to get their money back.

An unsecured loan, on the other hand, doesn't require collateral.

Child: Oh, I see.

Parent: Let me give you an example. Suppose you want to buy a new bike and borrow money for it. If you take out a secured loan and use your old bike as collateral, the lender will have the right to take your old bike if you can't repay the loan. On the other hand, if you take out an unsecured loan, you won't need to provide any collateral, but the interest rate might be higher.

Child: Okay, I think I understand now.

Parent: Understanding the difference between secured and unsecured loans is essential because it impacts your ability to get approved for a loan and the loan terms, including the interest rate. It's always best to borrow only what you can afford to pay back and to read the loan terms carefully before signing anything.

CONVERSATIONS BETWEEN PARENTS
AND CHILDREN: (INTEREST)

Parent: Hi, have you ever heard of interest?

Child: No, what is it?

Parent: Interest is the additional money you must pay on top of your borrowed money. For example, if you borrow $100 from someone and agree to pay back $110, $10 is the interest.

Child: Oh, I get it now. So, it's like a fee for borrowing money.

Par, ent: Yes, exactly. Interest is the fee charged by the lender for allowing you to borrow their money.

Child: But why do they charge interest? Why can't they just let us borrow money for free?

Parent: Well, lenders charge interest to make money for themselves. They are taking a risk by lending money to someone, and the interest helps to make up for that risk. Also, interest rates can be affected by things like inflation and the economy's overall health.

Child: That makes sense. Is there a way to avoid paying interest?

Parent: Well, sometimes it's not possible to avoid paying interest, but you can try to minimize it. For example, if you pay off your credit card balance in full every month, you won't have to pay any interest. But if you only make the minimum payment, you'll pay more interest over time.

Child: Okay, I understand now. Thanks for explaining it to me.

Parent: You're welcome! Understanding interest is essential so you can make intelligent decisions about borrowing and lending money in the future.

CONVERSATIONS BETWEEN PARENTS AND CHILDREN: (INTEREST CALCULATION)

You have $100 in your savings account, and the bank offers a 5% annual interest rate. This means that the bank will pay you 5% of your original $100 at the end of the year if you don't withdraw any money from your account.

To calculate the interest, you can use the following formula:

Interest = Principal x Rate x Time

Principal: the original amount of money you have in your savings account ($100)

Rate: the annual interest rate in decimal form (5% = 0.05)

Time: the length of time in years (1 year)

So, the interest you will earn at the end of the year is as follows:

Interest = $100 x 0.05 x 1 = $5

This means you will have $105 in your savings account at the end of the year (the original $100 plus the $5 interest earned). It's important to remember that the interest rate and time can affect the amount of interest earned, so it's a good idea to check with the bank or use an online calculator to estimate the interest earned for a specific period.

GOOD DEBT VS. BAD DEBT

Good debt is a type of finance that can increase in value over time or generate income, such as a mortgage for a home or a student loan for education. These types of debts can be considered investments in your future financial well-being.

For example, a mortgage allows you to own a home, which can appreciate over time and potentially provide a return on investment if you sell it in the future. Similarly, a student loan can help you obtain higher education and potentially lead to a higher-paying job. Good debt can be seen as an investment in your future financial success.

Bad debt is a type of debt used to finance purchases that do not have the potential to increase in value or generate income, such as credit card debt used for unnecessary purchases or high-interest personal loans used for vacations or luxury items. These debts are often seen as a financial burden and can lead to financial difficulties if not appropriately managed.

Bad debt can be considered a poor financial decision as it does not contribute to your long-term financial well-being. It can harm it by accumulating high-interest charges. Overall, bad debt can be seen as a liability rather than an asset.

Here are some examples of bad debt:

Credit card debt purchases non-essential items like luxury goods, expensive meals, or vacations.

High-interest personal loans are used to finance a lifestyle beyond your means or to pay for unnecessary purchases.

With very high-interest rates, payday loans are often taken out by individuals struggling to make ends meet.

Car loans with high-interest rates or extended repayment terms lead to negative equity, meaning you owe more on the car than it is worth.

Retail store credit cards with high-interest rates encourage you to buy more than you can afford.

Comparison of Good Debt vs. Bad Debt,

The main difference between good and bad debt is the potential return on investment. Good debt is used to finance purchases that can increase in value or generate income, such as a home mortgage or student loan. Therefore, these debts can be seen as investments in your future financial well-being, potentially leading to a higher net worth.

On the other hand, bad debt is used to finance purchases that do not have the potential to increase in value or generate income, such as credit card debt used for luxury items or high-interest personal loans used to finance a lifestyle beyond your means. Therefore, bad debt can be seen as a financial burden that accumulates high-interest charges and does not contribute to your long-term financial success.

In summary, good debt is an investment in your future financial well-being, while bad debt is a liability that can lead to financial difficulties if not appropriately managed. Therefore, knowing the potential risks and benefits of different debt types and using them responsibly to essential our financial goals is essential.

Here are some tips for teaching kids about the differences between good and bad debts:

Start by explaining the concepts of good and bad debt in simple terms. Then, use examples that your child can relate to, such as a mortgage for a home or a car loan for a vehicle.

Emphasize the importance of responsible borrowing and the potential risks of taking on too much debt. Explain how high-interest rates and fees can quickly accumulate and lead to financial difficulties.

Encourage your child to ask questions and be curious about different types of debts. Help them understand the potential benefits and drawbacks of each type of debt, and encourage them to consider whether a purchase is worth taking on debt.

Model responsible borrowing behaviour by demonstrating how you manage your debts and finances. Discuss your financial decisions with your child and explain how you prioritize spending and saving.

Consider using real-life examples to illustrate the differences between good and bad debts. For example, show your child how investments in education, a home, or a business can lead to long-term financial success, while impulsive or unnecessary purchases can lead to financial difficulties.

Encourage your child to build good habits by using credit responsibly, paying bills on time, and avoiding excessive debt. Help them understand the importance of a good credit score and how it can impact their ability to borrow money in the future.

CONVERSATIONS BETWEEN PARENTS AND CHILDREN: (GOOD DEBT AND BAD DEBT)

EXAMPLE -1:

Parent: Do you know what debt means?

Child: No, I don't.

Parent: Well, debt is when you borrow money from someone or a company and have to pay it back later. Sometimes, this can be good, but other times, it can be harmful. Can you think of some examples of things people might borrow money for?

Child: Like buying a car or a house?

Parent: Yes, those are called good debt. It's called good debt when you borrow money to buy a house or a car. That's because you're investing in something that will increase in value over time and that you'll use for a long time.

Child: What about borrowing money for something else?

Parent: Sometimes people borrow money for things they don't need, like expensive clothes or toys. This is called bad debt because it doesn't create value and can lead to financial trouble if you can't repay it.

Child: So, it's like good debt is when you borrow money for something important, and bad debt is when you borrow money for something unimportant?

Parent: That's right! Good debt can help you build your future and make smart investments, while lousy debt can hold you back and cause problems. It's essential to understand the differences to make good choices about borrowing money in the future.

EXAMPLE -2:

Parent: Hey Buddy/Princess, we discussed good and bad debt.

Child: Good debt is for buying essential things like a house or a car, and bad debt is for buying things we don't need.

Parent: That's right. I'm going to give you another example. Let's say you wanted to go to college when you're older. That's a good thing.

Child: Yes, I want to go to college!

Parent: Great! Attending college can be expensive, so many people take out student loans to help pay for it. But if you study hard and graduate, you'll have more opportunities and be able to earn more money in the future. That's an investment in your future, and it's a good debt.

Child: Oh, I see. But what about borrowing money to buy a new video game console or toy?

Parent: Well, buying things like that is not a good investment. You'll enjoy playing with them for a while, but eventually, you'll get bored, or they'll break. If you borrow money to buy something like that, it's bad debt because you're not getting any value from it over time. Plus, you'll have to pay back more than you borrowed because of interest fees.

Child: I understand now. It's essential to be smart about

borrowing money and only do it for things worth it in the long run.

Parent: Exactly! Good job, Buddy/Princess!

EXAMPLE -3:

Parent: Do you remember discussing good and bad debt?
Child: Good debt is for buying things that will help us in the future, like a house or education. Bad debt is for buying things we don't need, like toys or junk food.
Parent: That's right! Here's another example: you're saving up to buy a new bike and have enough money to buy a cheap one that might break easily. But you also have the option to wait and save more money to buy a more expensive, higher-quality bike that will last longer. Which option is a better use of your money?
Child: It's better to save up more and buy the better bike.
Parent: That's a great choice! Sometimes it's better to wait and save up more money to buy something of better quality that will last longer, instead of buying something cheap that might break quickly and you'll have to replace it sooner. That's an example of good debt.
Child: So, is buying an expensive bike good debt too?
Parent: Not necessarily. If the bike is too expensive and you can't afford it, it's not a good idea to go into debt to buy it. Finding a balance and only taking on debt you can afford is essential, bringing long-term value to your life.

MANAGING DEBT RESPONSIBLY

Managing debt responsibly means using debt in a way that allows you to meet your financial obligations while still living within your means. It involves creating a budget and a plan for paying off debt promptly, making timely payments, avoiding unnecessary debt, and maintaining a good credit score. Essentially, it uses debt in a way that does not create financial stress or hardship.

Here are some examples of managing debt responsibly:

Paying off high-interest debt first: If you have multiple debts with different interest rates, it is essential to prioritize paying off the debt with the highest interest rate first. By doing so, you will reduce the amount of interest you pay overtime and save money in the long run.

Making payments on time: Late payments can result in penalties, fees, and damage to your credit score. By making payments on time, you can avoid these negative consequences and maintain good credit.

Creating a budget: A budget can help you track your income and expenses, identify areas where you can reduce spending, and allocate funds toward paying off debt.

Avoiding unnecessary debt: Before taking on any new debt, consider whether it is necessary and whether you can afford to make the payments. Taking on unnecessary debt can lead to financial stress and hardship.

Maintaining a good credit score: A good credit score can help you qualify for lower interest rates and better loan terms. To maintain a good credit score, make timely payments, keep credit card balances low, and avoid opening too many new credit accounts.

Managing debt irresponsibly can have serious consequences, including

Damage to Credit Scores: Late payments, missed payments, and defaulting on loans can negatively impact credit scores. This can make it difficult to obtain credit in the future and may result in higher interest rates and fees.

Increased Debt: Failure to make timely payments can result in additional fees, interest charges, and penalties. This can increase the debt owed and make it even more challenging to pay off.

Legal Action: In extreme cases, lenders may take legal action to collect unpaid debts. This can result in wage garnishment, property liens, and even bankruptcy.

Stress and Anxiety: Financial problems can be incredibly stressful, leading to anxiety, depression, and other mental health issues.

Strained Relationships: Financial problems can also strain relationships, particularly with family members and close friends who may have loaned money to the individual.

It is essential to teach kids the importance of managing debt responsibly to avoid these consequences and ensure a healthy financial future.

Teaching kids to manage debt responsibly is an important lesson that can help them avoid financial problems in the future. Here are some tips on how to teach kids about managing debt responsibly:

Start with the basics: Explain to kids what debt is and how it works. Then, teach them the importance of paying bills on time and avoiding late fees.

Use real-life examples: Show kids how debt works in real life by using examples from your own experiences or those of family members and friends. For example, you could explain how you paid off a car loan or a mortgage.

Teach budgeting skills: Help kids develop good budgeting habits by teaching them how to create and stick to a budget. Encourage them to save money and prioritize paying off debt.

Discuss credit scores: Explain the importance of maintaining a good credit score and how it can affect their ability to get loans or credit in the future.

Encourage responsible spending: Teach kids to avoid unnecessary debt by encouraging responsible spending habits. Explain the difference between needs and wants, and help them understand the consequences of overspending.

Lead by example: As a parent, modelling responsible financial behaviour is essential. Show your kids how to manage debt responsibly by making timely payments, keeping credit card balances low, and avoiding unnecessary debt.

Use age-appropriate language: Use appropriate language and examples for your child's age and understanding. Keep the conversation simple and easy to understand.

By teaching kids these skills early on, they will be better prepared to manage debt responsibly as adults.

CONVERSATIONS BETWEEN PARENTS AND CHILDREN: (IMPORTANCE OF MANAGING DEBT RESPONSIBLY)

EXAMPLE -1:

Parent: Hey, Buddy/Princess, do you know what debt is?

Child: Yes, it's when you borrow money from someone and have to repay them.

Parent: That's right. And when you borrow money, it's essential to manage it responsibly. Do you know what I mean by that?

Child: Not really.

Parent: When you borrow money, you must ensure you can pay it back on time and in full. If you can't, you'll have to pay extra interest charges, which can be expensive.

Child: Oh, I see.

Parent: Being responsible with your money is essential so you don't have too much debt. If you have too much debt, it can be hard to pay for the things you need, like a house or a car, and you'll have to pay even more interest charges.

Child: That sounds scary.

Parent: It can be, but if you manage your debt responsibly, you can avoid those problems. You can start by only borrowing what you need and ensuring you can pay it back on time. And if you do have debt, make sure you're making your payments on time rather than spending what you can afford.

Child: Okay, I understand. I'll make sure to be responsible with my money.

Parent: That's great to hear! If you have any questions, just let me know.

EXAMPLE -2:
Parent: Have you ever heard about responsibly managing debt?
Child: No, what is that?
Parent: Sometimes people borrow money to buy things they can't afford, like a car or a house. That's called debt. But managing it responsibly means paying it back on time and not taking on too much debt.
Child: Why is that important?
Parent: If you don't pay back your debts on time, you'll get charged extra money called interest, which can add up and make it harder to pay back what you owe. And if you take on too much debt, it can be hard to pay it all back, and you might have to give up things you need, like food or a place to live.
Child: That doesn't sound nice.
Parent: It can be. That's why it's important only to borrow what you can afford to pay back and always to make your payments on time. That way, you'll build a good credit score, which will help you get better deals on loans and credit cards in the future.
Child: Oh, I see. So it's like being responsible with money.
Parent: Exactly. It's essential to make good choices with your money and not get over your head with debt.

EXAMPLE -3:

Sure, here's another example conversation between a parent and a child on the importance of managing debt responsibly:
Parent: Hi, sweetie! Do you know what debt is?
Child: Hmm, it's when you owe someone money.
Parent: That's right! Debt is when you borrow money and then have to pay it back. There's something called good debt and bad debt. Can you think of an example of good debt?
Child: Um, is it when you borrow money to buy a house?
Parent: Yes, that's one example of good debt. What about bad debt?
Child: Is it when you borrow money to buy toys?

Parent: Yes, that's a good example. When you borrow money to buy things you don't need or can't afford, and if you don't pay back your debts on time, it can cause many problems. For example, you can owe more money because of interest charges, damaging your credit score.

Child: What's a credit score?

Parent: A credit score is a number that tells people how responsible you are with borrowing and paying back money. Suppose you manage your debt responsibly and make your payments on time. But if you manage your debt well, your credit score can improve, and it can be hard to borrow money in the future.

Child: Wow, I didn't know debt was so important!

Parent: Yes, it's essential to be responsible with money, including managing debt responsibly. It's okay to borrow money sometimes, but you should always make sure you can afford to pay it back and that you're borrowing for something important.

TEACHING KIDS ABOUT LOANS

A loan is a financial transaction in which one party (the lender) agrees to provide money, property, or assets to another party (the borrower) in exchange for future repayment That's lousy debt when the principal amount, plus interest or fees.

Loans can be used for various purposes, such as funding a business, purchasing a home or a car, paying for education or medical expenses, or consolidating debt. We can obtain loans from banks, credit unions, online lenders, or other financial institutions.

Here are some examples of different types of loans:

Student loans: Many students take out loans to pay for their college education. These loans must be repaid after graduation, often with interest.

Mortgages: A mortgage is a loan used to purchase a home. Homebuyers typically make a down payment and then borrow the remaining amount from a lender. The borrower must repay the loan with interest over a set period, usually 15-30 years.

Car loans: People who want to buy a car but need more cash upfront may take a car loan. The borrower repays the loan over a set period with interest.

Personal loans: Some people take out loans to pay for unexpected expenses, such as medical bills or home repairs. The borrower repays the loan over a set period with interest.

Business loans: Entrepreneur and business owners may take out loans to start or expand their businesses. We must repay these loans with interest.

PROS OF A LOAN

Access to funds: Loans can access funds that may not be available through other means, such as credit cards or savings.

Affordability: Loans can offer affordable interest rates and repayment terms, making it easier for borrowers to manage their finances.

Convenience: Loans can be convenient because we can obtain them quickly and easily in many cases.

Credit building: If borrowers make timely payments on their loans, they can help build their credit scores, which can benefit future borrowing.

CONS OF A LOAN

Debt accumulation: Loans can lead to debt accumulation if borrowers are not careful about managing their finances and repaying the loan on time.

Interest payments: Loans typically require borrowers to pay interest, which can add up over time and increase the total cost of the loan.

Repayment periods: Loans require borrowers to repay the loan over a set period, which can create financial stress if the borrower cannot make the payments on time.

Risk of default: If a borrower cannot make loan payments, there is a risk of default, which can have severe consequences for their credit score and financial well-being.

Teaching kids about the different types of loans can be done by following these steps:

Introduce the concept of loans: Explain to your child that a loan is a sum of money someone borrows and must repay with interest.

Explain different types of loans: Discuss the different types of loans, such as student loans, mortgages, car loans, personal loans, and business loans. Provide examples of each type of loan and explain why someone might take out that type of loan.

Discuss the risks and benefits of loans: Help your child understand that loans can be helpful in some situations but can also be risky. Discuss the benefits and drawbacks of taking out a loan, such as interest rates and repayment terms.

Use real-life examples: Show your child examples of loan documents and explain the terms and conditions. You can also use real-life examples from your experience, such as a mortgage or car loan, to help your child understand how loans work.

Encourage responsible borrowing: Teach your child the importance of responsible borrowings, such as borrowing only what they can afford and making timely payments.

Practice making loan payments: Finally, you can teach your child about making loan payments by having them practice calculating loan payments and creating a plan for paying off a hypothetical loan.

CONVERSATIONS BETWEEN PARENTS AND CHILDREN:
(IMPORTANCE OF UNDERSTANDING ABOUT LOANS)

EXAMPLE -1:
Parent: Hey, do you know what a loan is?
Child: Not really. Is it like borrowing money from someone?
Parent: That's right! It's when you borrow money from a bank

or lender, and you have to pay it back with interest. Do you know what interest is?

Child: No, I don't.

Parent: Interest is an extra amount of money you must pay for what you borrowed. It's like a fee for borrowing money.

Child: Oh, I see. Why would someone need to borrow money?

Parent: Sometimes, people need to borrow money for essential things like buying a house or car or paying for college. But it's important to understand that loans come with benefits and risks.

Child: What are the benefits?

Parent: The benefits of loans are that they can provide access to funds you may not have otherwise and help you build credit if you make your payments on time.

Child: What are the risks?

Parent: The risks of loans are that you must make your payments on time to avoid damaging your credit score and ending up owing more money than you borrowed because of interest charges. That's why it's essential to be responsible when borrowing money and to make sure you can pay it back on time.

Child: Okay, I understand. Thank you for explaining it to me!

Parent: You're welcome. If you have any questions about loans or borrowing money, please ask me. It's essential to understand how to manage your money responsibly.

EXAMPLE -2:

Parent: Have you ever heard of a student loan?

Child: No, what's that?

Parent: It's a type of loan that students can take out to pay for college. Sometimes college can be expensive, so many students need help paying for it.

Child: Oh, okay. So how does it work?

Parent: A student loan is like any other, specifically designed for college students. You can borrow money from a bank or the government to pay for tuition, books, and other college expenses. Then you have to pay the money back with interest after you graduate.

Child: Why would someone want to take out a student loan?

Parent: College can be essential for getting a good job and making a good salary, but only some have enough money to pay for it upfront. That's where student loans come in - they can help make college more affordable and accessible for more people.

Child: But what are the risks?

Parent: The risks are that if you take out too much money or don't make your payments on time, you could end up with a lot of debt that can be hard to pay off. It's important only to borrow what you need and plan how to repay it after graduation.

Child: Okay, I think I understand. Thanks for explaining it to me.

Parent: You're welcome. It's essential to know about different types of loans and how they work so you can make intelligent decisions about your finances.

EXAMPLE -3:

Parent: Have you ever heard of a mortgage?

Child: No, what's that?

Parent: A mortgage is a loan people take to buy a house. Do you remember when we bought our house?

Child: Yeah, I remember.

Parent: We got a mortgage from the bank to help us pay for the house. We had to pay back the loan over many years, with interest.

Child: Oh, I see. But why would you need a loan to buy a house?

Parent: Houses can be costly, and most people need more money saved up to buy one outright. So they take out a mortgage to help them pay for it. It's like borrowing money from the bank and then paying it back over time.

Child: But what happens if you can't pay it back?

Parent: That's a good question. If you can't make your

mortgage payments, the bank can foreclose on your house, taking it away from you. That's why it's important only to borrow what you can afford and to make your payments on time.

Child: I see. So taking out a mortgage is a big responsibility.

Parent: Yes, it is. That's why it's essential to understand how mortgages work and ensure you're ready to take on that responsibility before buying a house.

INVESTING FOR KIDS

Introducing Children to the World of Investing

The stock market is filled with individuals who know the price of everything, but the value of nothing. Teach your kids to be investors, not just speculators.

Warren Buffett

Investing is crucial to building wealth and securing one's financial future. As a parent or guardian, it is essential to teach kids about investing, and the various options available are essential. The earlier kids learn about investing, the better they will make informed financial decisions. In this chapter, we will explore the world of investing and provide practical tips on introducing kids to the concept of investing.

Understanding the Basics of Investing: The first step in introducing kids to investing is to help them understand the basics of investing. This includes concepts such as risk and reward, diversification, and investment options such as stocks, bonds, and mutual funds. It is essential to explain these concepts in simple terms so that kids can understand them to begin to grasp the fundamentals of investing.

Choosing the Right Investments: Once kids have a basic understanding of investing, the next step is to help them choose suitable investments. This involves looking at different investment options and analysing their potential risks and rewards. Again, it is essential to involve kids in the decision-making process and encourage them to ask questions and do their research. By involving kids in decision-making, they will learn to make informed financial decisions independently.

Teaching Kids to Be Patient: Investing is a long-term process that requires patience and discipline. Therefore, it is essential to teach kids the value of patience when investing is essential. Kids need to understand that investing is not a get-rich-quick scheme but a long-term process that requires time and dedication. By instilling patience and discipline in kids, they will be more likely to stick with their investment plans and reap the rewards in the long run.

Introducing kids to investing is essential in preparing them for their financial future. By understanding the basics of investing, choosing suitable investments, and learning to be patient, kids can develop a solid foundation for their financial future. In addition, as a parent or guardian, being patient and supportive throughout the process is important so kids can feel confident and empowered to make informed financial decisions independently.

Investing is an essential aspect of financial literacy that can help children build wealth and achieve their financial goals. While it may seem like a complex and intimidating topic, it is essential to teach kids about investing early on to set them up for success in the future.

UNDERSTANDING THE BASICS OF INVESTING

Investment refers to putting money, time, or effort into something to gain a profit or advantage in the future. It can take various forms, such as buying stocks, bonds, mutual funds, real estate, or starting a business venture. The ultimate goal of investing is to generate a return on the investment over time.

Investing is allocating resources, usually money, to generate a profit or benefit in the future. The main goal of investing is to grow wealth over time by putting money into assets that have the potential to increase in value.

There are various types of investments, including stocks, bonds, mutual funds, real estate, and alternative investments like cryptocurrency and precious metals. Each type of investment has its own set of risks and potential rewards.

Investing involves a certain level of risk, and there is no guarantee of returns. However, by diversifying investments and understanding the basic principles of investing, individuals can mitigate risks and potentially reap significant benefits over the long term.

TYPES OF INVESTMENTS

Several types of suitable investments include:

Stocks: Investing in stocks is one of the most common ways to invest. Stocks are shares of ownership in a company. Investing in them means you can make money through capital appreciation (the stock price going up) and dividends (a portion of the company's profits paid to shareholders).

Bonds: Bonds are essentially loans that you make to companies or governments. When you invest in bonds, you earn interest and receive the entire principal back when the bond matures.

Mutual Funds: A mutual fund is an investment that pools money from multiple investors to purchase a portfolio of stocks, bonds, or other securities. This diversifies the risk across many different investments.

Real Estate: Real estate can be a good investment for long-term growth. You can invest in a rental property, commercial property, or even in Real Estate Investment Trusts (REITs), companies that own and operate income-generating real estate properties.

Exchange-Traded Funds (ETFs): ETFs are like mutual funds but trade like stocks. They track an index or group of assets, giving investors broad exposure to a particular market or sector.

Certificates of Deposit (CDs): CDs are low-risk investments where you deposit money for a set amount of time at a fixed interest rate. When the CD matures, you receive your original investment plus interest.

These are just a few examples of suitable investments, and it's essential to research and consult with a financial advisor before making any investment decisions.

TEACHING KIDS ABOUT INVESTMENTS

Teaching kids about investments can be done in a few steps:
Start with the basics: Explain to the child what an investment is and how it works. Examples include:
- Buying stocks in a company.

- Investing in a mutual fund.
- Buying a rental property.

Discuss the advantages of investing: Talk about how investments can help grow money over time and the benefits of compound interest. Explain that investing can also help beat inflation and build wealth.

Discuss the risks: Be honest with the child about the risks of investing. For example, explain that there is always a possibility of losing money and that investments can be affected by changes in the economy or stock market.

Encourage research: Encourage the child to research different types of investments and to understand the risks and potential rewards.

Start small: If the child is interested in investing, start with small amounts of money and track the progress over time.

It's important to note that children should always have the guidance and supervision of an adult when investing.

ADVANTAGES AND DISADVANTAGES OF INVESTMENTS

When discussing the advantages and disadvantages of investments, here are a few key points to consider:

Advantages:

- Potential for higher returns than keeping money in a savings account.
- It can help build wealth over time through compound interest.
- It can help beat inflation.
- It can provide a source of passive income.
- Diversification can help spread risk.

Disadvantages:

- Investments can be risky, and we can permanently lose money.
- Some investments require much knowledge and research to make informed decisions.
- Market fluctuations and changes in the economy

can impact investment values.
- Fees and expenses can eat into returns.
- Some investments may not be as liquid as others, making it difficult to access funds when needed.

CONVERSATIONS BETWEEN PARENTS AND CHILDREN: (INVESTMENTS)

EXAMPLE -1:

Parent: Hey, Buddy/Princess, do you know what an investment is?

Child: No, I have no idea.

Parent: An investment is something you buy or put money into with the expectation that it will grow in value or provide you with a return in the future.

Child: Oh, I see. Can you give me an example?

Parent: Sure, one example is buying stock in a company. If you buy a share of stock, you become a part owner of that company. If the company does well, and the stock price goes up, the value of your investment goes up too.

Child: That sounds interesting. What are some other types of investments?

Parent: There are also bonds, a type of loan to a company or government. You lend them money, and they pay you interest on that loan. Real estate is another type of investment where you buy a property and rent it out or sell it later for a profit.

Child: What are some advantages of investing?

Parent: One advantage is that it can help you grow your wealth over time. By investing your money wisely, you can earn more than you would by saving it in a bank account. Additionally, investments can provide a source of passive income, which means you earn money without doing much work.

Child: That sounds great! But are there any disadvantages?

Parent: Yes, there are. Investing always comes with some risk. Some investments are riskier than others, and there is always a chance that you could lose money instead of making it.

Therefore, research is essential and only invests money you can afford to lose.

Child: Okay, I understand. Thanks for explaining it to me, Dad/Mom.

Parent: You're welcome, Buddy/Princess. It's never too early enough to start learning about money and investing.

EXAMPLE -2:

Parent: Hey, have you ever heard of the word "investments"?

Child: No, what does it mean?

Parent: Well, investing means putting your money into something with the hope of making more money in the future.

Child: Oh, okay. But is it okay to put your money into something you need clarification on?

Parent: Yes, it can be risky. But if you do it smartly, you can make more money than you would by keeping it in a savings account. It's all about finding suitable investments that work for you and your goals.

Child: What are some suitable investments?

Parent: There are many different types of investments. Some people like to invest in stocks, which means buying a small part of a company and hoping that the company grows and becomes more valuable. Other people invest in real estate, which means buying property and renting it out to make money. And some people invest in bonds, like loans to companies or governments, and they pay you back with interest.

Child: Hmm, that sounds interesting. But how do you know which one is right for you?

Parent: That's a great question. It all depends on your goals and your risk tolerance. Some investments are riskier than others, but they also have the potential for higher returns. So it's essential to research and talk to a financial advisor before investing.

Child: Okay, thanks for explaining that to me. I need to learn more about investments before investing my money.

Parent: It's essential always to be informed before making any financial decisions.

EXAMPLE -3:
Parent: Have you ever heard of the word "investment"?
Child: No, what does it mean?
Parent: Well, it's like when you put your money into something with the hope of making more money in the future. For example, you have $10 and want to use it to make even more money. So you could put that $10 into a piggy bank and save it or use it to buy something you think will be worth more, like a rare toy.
Child: Oh, I get it. But what are some other things I could invest in?
Parent: There are lots of things you can invest in, like stocks, bonds, or even real estate. But it's important to remember that investing always carries some risk, and there's no guarantee you'll make money. That's why it's essential to research and make informed decisions.
Child: Hmm, I see. So, what are the advantages of investing?
Parent: One of the most significant advantages is that it allows you to make more money than you would by saving it in a piggy bank. And if you choose your investments wisely, you can also make your money work for you while you sleep, which means you could be earning money even when you're not actively doing anything.
Child: That sounds pretty cool. But what are the disadvantages?
Parent: As I mentioned before, investing always carries some risk. That means that you could lose money instead of making money.
Additionally, some investments require a lot of money, which is only possible for some.
Child: I see. So what should I do if I want to start investing?
Parent: Well, it's always a good idea to talk to a trusted adult and research to ensure you understand the risks and potential

rewards of different types of investments. And remember, it's essential only to invest money you can afford to lose and always make informed decisions based on your financial goals and circumstances.

CHOOSING THE RIGHT INVESTMENTS

A suitable investment is an investment that is expected to provide a return on the invested capital over time. It can also be considered an investment expected to appreciate or generate income. In addition, the suitable investment should align with the investor's goals, time horizon, and risk tolerance.

For example, investing in stocks can be a suitable investment for someone with a long-term investment horizon and willing to take on a higher level of risk in exchange for potentially higher returns. On the other hand, investing in bonds can be a suitable investment for someone with a shorter-term investment horizon and looking for a more stable source of income.

Ultimately, we should make a suitable investment after careful consideration of one's financial goals and risk tolerance and after conducting thorough research and analysis to determine the potential risks and returns of the investment.

Choosing a suitable investment can depend on various factors such as personal financial goals, risk tolerance, investment horizon, and market conditions.

Here are some steps to help choose the suitable investment:

Define your financial goals: Determine what you want to achieve from your investment, whether saving for retirement, buying a house, or starting a business.

Understand your risk tolerance: Assess your risk tolerance and determine how much risk you will take to achieve your financial goals.

Consider your investment horizon: Decide how long you will invest your money. If you have a long-term horizon, you can consider investing in stocks or mutual funds, whereas, for a short-term investment, you may consider fixed-income securities.

Research your investment options: Do your research and gather information about different investment options such as stocks, bonds, mutual funds, ETFs, and real estate.

Diversify your portfolio: It is essential to diversify your portfolio to reduce risk. We can achieve this by investing in different asset classes and sectors.

Consult a financial advisor: Seek the advice of a financial advisor who can guide you on investment options that align with your financial goals and risk tolerance.

By following these steps, you can choose the suitable investment to help you achieve your financial goals while managing your risk.

CONCEPT OF CHOOSING THE SUITABLE INVESTMENT

Explaining the concept of choosing the suitable investment for a child can be simplified using the following steps:

Start by explaining the concept of investing: You can start by explaining what investing means and how it differs from spending. Let your child know that investing is the process of putting money into something with the expectation of earning a profit in the future.

Explain the importance of choosing a suitable investment: Once your child understands the concept of investing, you can explain the importance of choosing a suitable investment. Tell them that choosing a suitable investment can help them earn more money while choosing the wrong investment can result in a loss of money.

Discuss the different types of investments: There are several types of investments, such as stocks, bonds, mutual funds, and real estate. Explain each type of investment to your child in simple terms and how they work.

Consider your child's goals: Ask them about their goals and

what they want to achieve with their investments. Then, depending on their goals, you can help them choose a suitable investment that aligns with their objectives.

Teach them to research: Explain to your child that research is essential to choosing a suitable investment. Encourage them to read up on different investment options, compare the risks and returns, and seek guidance from a financial advisor.

Emphasize the importance of diversification: Teach your child about diversifying their investments. Encourage them to invest in various investments to spread out their risk.

Explain the concept of risk: Help your child understand that every investment comes with a certain level of risk. Teach them how to assess the risk in different types of investments and make informed decisions based on their risk tolerance.

Teach them to track their investments: Once your child has made an investment, teach them how to track it regularly. Show them how to read investment statements, monitor performance, and adjust if necessary.

Encourage patience: Investing is a long-term game, and teaching your child the value of patience is essential. Explain that investments take time to grow, and they shouldn't panic if they experience short-term losses.

By following these steps, you can help your child understand the importance of choosing a suitable investment and how to make informed decisions that align with their goals.

CONVERSATIONS BETWEEN PARENTS AND CHILDREN:
(IDENTIFYING THE RIGHT INVESTMENT)

EXAMPLE -1:

Parent: Hi, Buddy/Princess! Do you know what an investment is?

Child: Yes, it's like putting your money into something to make more money, right?

Parent: That's right! But it's also essential to choose a suitable investment so that your money can grow and be safe. Do you want to learn more about that?

Child: Yes, please!

Parent: Great! Let's start with understanding your goals. Why do you want to invest your money?

Child: Well, I want to save money for a big trip to Disney World with my family next year.

Parent: Okay, that's a good goal. We need to find a suitable investment to help you reach that goal. We need to consider the risks and the returns of different investment options.

Child: What are risks and returns?

Parent: Good question! Risks are the chances that you might lose money, and returns are the profits you make from the investment. Some investments have high risks but can bring higher returns, while others are safer but offer lower returns.

Child: Oh, I get it. How do we choose the suitable investment for my goal?

Parent: We can start by looking at safe investments with a steady rate of return, like a savings account or a certificate of deposit. Or, we could also look at mutual funds or stocks that have the potential for higher returns but come with more risk. It all depends on your risk tolerance and your goals.

Child: I see. So, it's essential to consider the investment options' risks and returns and choose the one that best matches my goal and risk tolerance.

Parent: Exactly! And remember, it's always good to talk to a financial advisor or research before making investment decisions.

Child: Thanks, Mom/Dad! I'm excited to start investing and saving for our trip to Disney World!

EXAMPLE -2:

Parent: Hey, Buddy/Princess! Do you remember the piggy bank we got you last month?

Child: Yes, I do! It's almost complete now.

Parent: That's great! What can we do with the money you saved up in there?

Child: What can we do?

Parent: We can invest it! Do you know what investing means?

Child: No, not really.

Parent: Investing means putting your money into something that can help you earn more. If we buy some company shares, and the company does well, our shares will increase, and we can sell them for a profit.

Child: Oh, I get it now!

Parent: But we must be careful when choosing where to invest our money. We must research and ensure we choose the suitable investment to give us a good return.

Child: How do we do that?

Parent: We can start by looking at options like stocks, bonds, mutual funds, and real estate. We must consider how much risk we are willing to take, how much we can afford to invest, and how long we are willing to wait for a return. It's essential to choose something that matches our goals and our budget.

Child: That makes sense.

Parent: Remember, it's not a good idea to put all our eggs in one basket is not a good idea. We should spread our investments across different options to keep all our money if one doesn't do well.

Child: Okay, I'll keep that in mind. Thanks for explaining it to me, Mom/dad!

EXAMPLE -3:

Parent: Hey, Buddy/Princess, do you know what investing is?

Child: Not really. Can you explain it to me?

Parent: Sure, investing means putting your money into something with the hope of making more money in the future. There are different types of investments, and they can be short-term or long-term.

Child: What do short-term and long-term mean?

Parent: Short-term investments are those where you can get your money back with some extra earnings. For example, putting your money in a savings account or buying a bond that matures in a year or two is a short-term investment.

Child: And what is a long-term investment?

Parent: A long-term investment is where you invest your money for a more extended period, usually five years or more. The idea is to let your money grow over time to have more money. Some examples of long-term investments are stocks, real estate, or investing in your retirement.

Child: That sounds interesting, but how do I know which is better?

Parent: Well, that depends on your financial goals. If you want to save money for something you want to buy soon, like a new video game or a bike, then a short-term investment would be better. But if you're thinking about the future, like buying a car or going to college, a long-term investment could help you save money in the long run.

Child: Okay, I understand. Thanks for explaining it to me, Mom/Dad!

Parent: Anytime, Buddy/Princess. Remember, investing is a great way to grow your money, but choosing the suitable investment for your financial goals is essential as constantly investing responsibly.

TEACHING KIDS TO BE PATIENT

Patience is key in finance because many financial decisions involve waiting for the right time to move or for investments to mature. Rushing into a decision can often result in losses or missed opportunities. In addition, financial goals such as saving for retirement or paying off debt can take a long time to achieve, requiring consistent effort over an extended period.

Patience lets individuals focus on their goals and stick to their financial plans, even during market fluctuations or unexpected events. It also helps to avoid emotional decision-making and allows for a more rational and thoughtful approach to financial matters. Overall, patience is an essential virtue for achieving long-term financial success.

Having patience is vital in investments for several reasons.

Firstly, investments, especially long-term investments, require time to grow and generate returns. As a result, it is common for investments to experience fluctuations in value in the short term. However, over the long term, quality investments tend to provide steady returns that can compound over time.

Secondly, patience is essential in avoiding impulsive decisions that could lead to financial losses. Investors who need more patience may be tempted to buy or sell investments based on short-term market trends or news headlines, which could lead to losses if the market changes direction. Patience allows investors to make more thoughtful and informed decisions based on long-term trends and fundamentals.

Thirdly, having patience is essential in achieving financial goals. Whether saving for retirement or a significant purchase, investing with patience allows investors to stay committed to their financial goals and not get discouraged by short-term market movements.

Patience is crucial for successful investing, as it allows investors to weather short-term volatility, avoid impulsive decisions, and stay committed to long-term financial goals.

IMPORTANCE OF PATIENCE IN INVESTMENTS

Here are some points explaining the importance of patience in investments:

Avoiding impulsive decisions: Patience allows you to carefully think through your investment decisions without being swayed by emotions or short-term market fluctuations.

Long-term investments: Long-term investments have historically provided higher returns than short-term investments, but they require patience to realize these ages.

Overcoming setbacks: All investments have ups and downs. Patience helps weather the storms and stay committed to your investment strategy, even with temporary setbacks.

Building wealth: Building wealth through investments takes time and consistent contributions. Patience allows you to stick with your investment plan and reap the rewards of compound interest over time.

Learning from mistakes: Patience allows you to learn from your mistakes and adjust your investment strategy accordingly. Unfortunately, rushing into investments can lead to costly mistakes that we could have avoided with a more patient approach.

Patience is essential in investments, allowing you to make informed decisions, ride out market volatility, and reap long-term growth benefits.

HOW TO TEACH A KID ABOUT THE IMPORTANCE OF HAVING PATIENCE IN INVESTMENTS

Here's an explanation of how to teach a kid about the importance of having patience in investments:

Start with the basics: Before diving into investing and patience, ensure your child understands basic financial concepts like saving, budgeting, and interest. Once they understand these concepts, it will be easier to understand the importance of patience in investing.

Use real-life examples: Share with your child stories about people who have made successful investments by being patient. Explain how those people made investment decisions and how their patience paid off in the long run.

Discuss the risks and rewards of investing: Teach your child that investing is not a guaranteed way to make money and involves risks. Explain that having patience means being willing to weather short-term losses in the hope of long-term gains.

Encourage them to set long-term goals: Help your child set long-term financial goals and explain how having patience in their investments can help them achieve them. This could be saving for a car, a down payment on a house, or college tuition. **Let them make their own investment decisions:** As your child ages, encourage them to start making their own investment decisions with their own money. Let them experience the ups and downs of the market and help them learn from their mistakes. This will help them develop the patience needed to succeed as an investor.

Remember to keep the language age-appropriate and tailor your teaching approach to your child's learning style. With time and guidance, your child can learn the value of patience in investing and become a responsible and successful investor.

CONVERSATIONS BETWEEN PARENTS AND
CHILDREN: (PATIENT IN INVESTMENTS)

EXAMPLE -1:

Parent: Hey, Buddy/Princess, do you know what it means to be patient?

Child: Not really; what does it mean?

Parent: It means waiting calmly for something to happen, even if it takes a long time. Is that an important trait to have?

Child: Yeah, I guess so.

Parent: That's right. It's essential when it comes to investing your money. Sometimes, when you invest your money, you might have no results later. It might take a while for your investment to grow.

Child: Why does it take so long?

Parent: Well, sometimes the value of the investment might go up and down over time. But if you wait patiently and don't panic when things don't go as planned, you can still come out on top in the long run.

Child: But what if I need the money right away?

Parent: That's a good question. That's why it's essential only to invest money that you don't need right away. If you need the money for something short-term, keeping it in a savings account or somewhere safe where it won't lose value is best.

Child: Oh, I see. So patience is essential when investing so you can let your money grow over time.

Parent: Exactly. And if you stay patient and stick to a sound investment plan, you'll likely see your money grow more than if you just kept it in a savings account.

EXAMPLE -2:

Parent: Have you ever heard the phrase "patience is a virtue"?

Child: Yeah, I think so. It means that it's good to be patient, right?

Parent: That's right! And it's essential when it comes to investing your money. Of course, when you invest your money, you want it to grow over time, but sometimes the value of your investment might go up and down, which can be stressful.

Child: So what do you do?

Parent: You must remember that investing is a long-term game. It's essential to be patient and not make rash decisions based on short-term changes in the market. For example, if the value of your investment goes down, it might be tempting to sell it right away and cut your losses. But if you're patient and give it some time, it might recover and grow in value.

Child: Oh, I see. So it's essential to think long-term and not worry about short-term changes.

Parent: Exactly! And remember, the longer you hold onto your investments, the more time they have to grow in value. So being patient can pay off in the end.

Child: Okay, that makes sense. I'll remember to be patient when I invest my money.

Parent: That's great to hear. Investing can be a great way to build wealth over time, but doing it thoughtfully and patiently is essential.

EXAMPLE -3:

Parent: Have you heard the phrase "Good things come to those who wait?"

Child: Yeah, I've heard it before.

Parent: That phrase is very relevant when it comes to investing. Investing is a way to make your money grow over time, but it requires patience. If you try to make a quick profit by buying and selling stocks rapidly, you'll likely lose money instead.

Child: Why is that?

Parent: Because the stock market is unpredictable in the short term. Prices can go up or down rapidly based on news or rumours, and it's almost impossible to predict what will happen next. But if you're patient and hold onto your investments for a more extended period, you're much more likely to see a positive return on your investment.

Child: So, you're saying that if I want to make money with investments, I must wait a long time?

Parent: That's right. You have to be willing to wait for your investments to grow. That's why it's essential to start investing early, so you have more time for your money to grow. And remember, patience isn't just crucial for investing; it's an important life skill too.

GIVING BACK

Teaching Children about Charitable Giving (Philanthropy) & Charitable Giving.

No one has ever become poor by giving.

Anne Frank

As parents, we must teach our children the importance of giving back to society. It is essential to teach them to be empathetic towards others and to understand the value of helping those in need. In this chapter, we will explore the importance of Charitable Giving (Philanthropy) and how to teach children about charitable giving.

WHY TEACHING CHILDREN ABOUT CHARITABLE GIVING (PHILANTHROPY) IS IMPORTANT:

Charitable Giving (Philanthropy) is donating time, money, and resources to help those in need. Teaching children about Charitable Giving (Philanthropy) helps them to become more empathetic, compassionate, and responsible citizens. It also instils values such as generosity and kindness that can help shape their character for the rest of their lives.

WAYS TO TEACH CHILDREN ABOUT CHARITABLE GIVING:

Start small: Encourage your children to donate a portion of their pocket money to a charity they choose. This could be as simple as donating a few dollars to a local animal shelter or food bank.

Volunteer: Volunteering as a family can be a great way to teach children about the importance of giving back. Find a local charity that aligns with your family's values and volunteer your time together.

Donate items: Encourage your children to donate gently used items such as clothing, books, or toys to a local charity.

Lead by example: Children often learn by example, so model charitable behaviour yourself. Talk about the charities you support and why they are essential to you.

TEACHING CHILDREN ABOUT THE

IMPACT OF THEIR GIVING:

It is essential to help children understand the impact of their giving. Talk to them about how their donations can make a difference in the lives of others. Show them photos and videos of the people or animals they are helping, and explain how their contributions can help improve their lives.

Teaching children about Charitable Giving (Philanthropy) and charitable giving is integral to building their financial literacy. By instilling values such as generosity and kindness, we can help shape our children into responsible and empathetic citizens. In addition, by encouraging them to give back to society, we can help them understand the value of helping others in need.

WHY TEACHING CHILDREN ABOUT CHARITABLE GIVING (PHILANTHROPY) IS IMPORTANT

Charitable Giving (Philanthropy) refers to giving one's time, money, or resources to help others, often focusing on improving the well-being of others or society. It typically involves donating to charitable organizations or causes, volunteering time or skills, or advocating for positive change.

The goal of Charitable Giving (Philanthropy) is to positively impact society by addressing social problems, promoting social justice, or advancing important causes such as education, health care, and the environment.

CHARITABLE GIVING (PHILANTHROPY) IS ESSENTIAL FOR MANY REASONS:

Social Impact: Charitable Giving (Philanthropy) can create social change and positively impact the world. By supporting causes and organizations aligning with one's values, Charitable Giving (Philanthropy) can address societal issues and improve the world.

Community Building: Charitable Giving (Philanthropy) can unite people around a common cause, building stronger communities and fostering a sense of social responsibility.

Personal Fulfilment: Giving back through Charitable Giving (Philanthropy) can provide a sense of personal fulfilment and purpose. Knowing that one has made a difference in the world can be a source of great satisfaction.

Legacy: Charitable Giving (Philanthropy) allows individuals to create a lasting legacy that can benefit future generations. By essentializing important causes, individuals can leave a positive mark on the world that will endure beyond their lifetimes.

Charitable Giving (Philanthropy) is essential because it allows individuals to impact the world positively, build stronger communities, find personal fulfilment, and create a lasting legacy.

CHARITABLE GIVING (PHILANTHROPY) EXAMPLES

Here are some examples of Charitable Giving (Philanthropy) that we can explain to kids:

Donating to a charity: Children can be encouraged to donate a portion of their allowance to a charity they choose. For example, they can donate to an animal shelter, a children's hospital, or a disaster relief fund.

Volunteering: Kids can participate in volunteering activities such as cleaning up a park, visiting a nursing home, or serving food at a shelter. This helps them understand the value of giving back to their community.

Fundraising: Children can organize fundraising events such as a bake sale, lemonade stand, or charity run. The money raised can be donated to a cause they care about.

Sharing: Children can be taught the importance of sharing their resources with others who are less fortunate. For example, they can donate their old clothes, books, or toys to needy people.

Random acts of kindness: Encourage children to perform small acts such as helping an older person carry groceries, holding a door open for someone, or complimenting a friend. This helps them understand the value of giving without expecting anything in return.

These are just a few examples of philanthropic activities that children can engage in. By encouraging them to participate in these activities, they will develop a sense of empathy and compassion towards others and the world around them.

RELATED ESTABLISHMENTS

Here are some examples of Charitable Giving (Philanthropy) related establishments:

Bill and Melinda Gates Foundation: Founded by Microsoft co-founder Bill Gates and his wife, Melinda Gates, this is one of the largest philanthropic organizations in the world. It focuses on global health and development, education, and climate change.

Oprah Winfrey Foundation: Established by media mogul Oprah Winfrey, this foundation supports a variety of causes, including education, health care, and the arts.

Ford Foundation: Founded by Henry Ford and his son Edsel in 1936, this foundation supports various causes, including human rights, education, and economic development.

Michael J. Fox Foundation: Established by actor Michael J. Fox, this foundation is dedicated to finding a cure for Parkinson's disease.

The Giving Pledge: Started by Warren Buffett and Bill and Melinda Gates, this is a commitment by some of the world's wealthiest individuals and families to give away the majority of their wealth to address society's most pressing problems.

Malala Fund: Founded by Nobel Peace Prize laureate Malala Yousafzai, this organization advocates for girls' education and provides resources to help girls worldwide access education.

Robin Hood Foundation: Based in New York City, this foundation fights poverty by funding organizations that provide education, job training, and other services to people in need.

Heifer International: This organization fights hunger and poverty by providing livestock and other resources to people in developing countries.

Make-A-Wish Foundation: This organization grants wishes to children with life-threatening medical conditions, providing them and their families with hope, strength, and joy.

Habitat for Humanity: This organization builds homes for needy people, focusing on providing safe and affordable housing for low-income families.

HOW TO TEACH KIDS ABOUT CHARITABLE GIVING (PHILANTHROPY)

Teaching kids about Charitable Giving (Philanthropy) and giving can be a great way to instil important values like empathy and generosity. Here are some tips on how to teach kids about Charitable Giving (Philanthropy):

Lead by example: Children learn by observing the behaviour of adults around them. So, if you want your kids to be philanthropic, led by example. Involve them in your charitable activities and explain why you are doing what you are doing.

Talk about it: Start a conversation with your kids about Charitable Giving (Philanthropy) and why it's essential. Use age-appropriate language and examples that they can relate to.

Let them choose: Encourage your kids to pick a cause or charity they are passionate about. Then, give them the freedom to choose and support their decision.

Give back as a family: Participate in charity events or volunteer together. This can be a great way to bond while doing good for others.

Set an example with an allowance: Teach kids about budgeting and saving by giving them an allowance and encouraging them to save a portion for charitable giving.

Make it fun: Make giving and charity a fun activity for kids by involving them in fundraising events or organizing a charity drive.

Teaching kids about Charitable Giving (Philanthropy) can be a great way to foster empathy, generosity, and a sense of community.

CONVERSATIONS BETWEEN PARENTS AND CHILDREN: (CHARITABLE GIVING)

EXAMPLE -1:

Parent: Hey, Buddy/Princess, do you know what Charitable Giving (Philanthropy) means?

Child: No, I don't.

Parent: Charitable Giving (Philanthropy) is giving back to others by donating your time, money, or resources. It's a way to help those less fortunate or struggling with difficult situations.

Child: Oh, I understand. So, how does Charitable Giving (Philanthropy) help people?

Parent: When you practice Charitable Giving (Philanthropy), you are making a positive impact in someone else's life. For example, you can donate money to organizations that help provide food and shelter to people experiencing homelessness or support education for underprivileged children. These acts of kindness can make a big difference in someone's life.

Child: That sounds great! How can I practice Charitable Giving (Philanthropy)?

Parent: There are many ways to practice Charitable Giving (Philanthropy), such as volunteering at a local charity, donating a portion of your allowance to a cause you care about, or organizing a fundraiser for a community in need. It's all about finding a cause you are passionate about and doing what you can to help.

Child: I would like to help too! Can we find a charity to donate to together?

Parent: Absolutely! Let's do some research and find a cause that you care about. Remember, even small acts of kindness can make a big difference.

EXAMPLE -2:
Parent: Hey, Buddy/Princess, remember when we volunteered at the local food bank last month?
Child: Yes, it was fun. We got to help lots of people.
Parent: That's right! Did you know many people are less fortunate than us and need our help?
Child: How can we help them?
Parent: One way we can help is by giving to charity. Charitable Giving (Philanthropy) is giving money, time, or resources to those in need.
Child: Oh, I see. But why is it important to give?
Parent: It's important to give because it helps others who are in need. We may not realize it, but we are fortunate to have everything. Giving to those in need shows gratitude for what we have and helps improve the world.
Child: I want to help too. How can I get involved in Charitable Giving (Philanthropy)?
Parent: There are many ways you can get involved. We can donate to a charity together, volunteer at a local shelter, or even start our fundraising campaign for a cause we believe in. But, most importantly, we do what we can to help those in need.

EXAMPLE -3:
Parent: Have you heard about the concept of Charitable Giving (Philanthropy)?
Child: No, what is it?
Parent: Charitable Giving (Philanthropy) is when people give their time, money, or resources to help others in need. It's all about being generous and giving back to society.
Child: That sounds interesting. Why is it important?
Parent: Well, many people in the world don't have the things we do. They may need more food, clothing, or a safe living place. Charitable Giving (Philanthropy) helps to make their

lives better and helps them to feel cared for.

Child: How can I help with Charitable Giving (Philanthropy)?

Parent: There are many ways you can get involved with Charitable Giving (Philanthropy). You can donate money or goods to a charity, volunteer at a shelter or food bank, or even do something nice for someone else. It's all about thinking of others and doing what you can to improve their lives.

Child: That sounds like a good thing to do. Can we donate some of our old toys to a charity?

Parent: Absolutely! That's a great idea. We can discuss which charity we want to support and how we can make a difference together.

WAYS TO TEACH CHILDREN ABOUT CHARITABLE GIVING

Charitable giving refers to donating money or resources to a charitable organization or cause to promote social good, address community needs, and support organizations that serve the public interest.

Charitable giving can take many forms, including monetary donations, in-kind gifts, volunteering time or services, or participating in fundraising events. The goal of charitable giving is to make a positive impact on the lives of others and improve the world in some way.

Charitable giving is essential to life because it allows individuals to contribute to causes and organizations they are passionate about and positively impact the world. Charitable giving helps to support communities, promote positive social change, and provide aid and resources to those in need. It also helps individuals feel a sense of purpose and fulfilment, as they can give back to society and make a difference in the lives of others.

Charitable giving can also positively impact an individual's finances, as donations to qualified charities are typically tax-deductible. Charitable giving can create a more compassionate and equitable society and improve the well-being of individuals and communities.

EXAMPLES OF CHARITABLE GIVING

Here are some examples of charitable giving:

Donating money to a non-profit organization: One of the most common forms of charitable giving is making a financial contribution to a non-profit organization that supports a cause you care about. This could be a local food bank, animal shelter, or international relief organization.

Volunteering time and skills: Charitable giving doesn't always have to involve money. You can also give back by volunteering your time and skills to a non-profit organization. For example, you could tutor children at an after-school program, help build homes with a local Habitat for Humanity chapter, or provide pro bono legal services to a community organization.

Donating goods: Another way to give back is by donating items you no longer need to a charitable organization. This could include clothing, furniture, or household items. Many non-profits also accept donations of canned goods and other non-perishable food items.

Supporting a friend or family member in need: Charitable giving can also take the form of helping out a friend or family member experiencing financial or personal hardship. This could involve offering a place to stay, helping to pay for medical bills, or providing emotional support during a difficult time.

Participating in fundraising events: Finally, you can support charitable causes by participating in fundraising events. This could include running a 5K race to support a cancer research organization or participating in a charity auction to raise money for a local school.

WAYS OF TEACHING IMPORTANCE OF CHARITABLE GIVING

Teaching kids about charitable giving can instil values of generosity, kindness, and empathy in them. Here are some ways to teach kids about the importance of charitable giving:

Lead by example: Children often learn by watching their parents. So, show them how you give back to the community. For example, you can involve them in volunteering activities, donate to charity, or sponsor a child's education.

Explain the concept of giving: Start by explaining the concept of giving and how it can help others. Then, use simple examples to help your child understand the impact of their actions on the community.

Let them choose a cause: Encourage your child to choose a cause they are passionate about. It can be helping people experiencing homelessness, educating underprivileged children, or caring for animals.

Make giving a habit: Set aside a small amount of money for your child to donate to their chosen cause regularly. This can help them build the habit of giving and feel the satisfaction of helping others.

Celebrate their giving: When your child donates to charity or volunteers their time, celebrate their actions. Praise and encourage them for their efforts and let them know how proud you are of them.

Create a giving jar: Create a jar where your child can put loose change or extra money they receive. Once the jar is full, donate the money to a charity of your child's choice.

Share stories: Share stories of people who have made a difference in the world through charitable giving. This can inspire your child to make a positive impact on the world.

Teaching kids about charitable giving can help them develop empathy and social responsibility. It can also help them feel a sense of purpose and fulfilment by making a positive difference in the lives of others.

CONVERSATIONS BETWEEN PARENTS AND CHILDREN: (CHARITABLE GIVING)

EXAMPLE -1:

Parent: Hey, have you ever heard of "charitable giving?"
Child: No, what does it mean?
Parent: Charitable giving is when people donate their time, money, or resources to help others in need. It's a way to give back to your community and positively impact the world.
Child: That sounds cool! Can I do it too?
Parent: Of course! There are lots of ways that you can participate in charitable giving. For example, you can donate your old clothes or toys to a local charity, volunteer at a food bank or animal shelter, or even organize a fundraiser with your friends to raise money for a good cause.
Child: Wow, I never thought about doing that before. But how can my small contributions make a difference?
Parent: Every little bit counts! Even small donations or acts of kindness can significantly impact someone's life. Plus, when we all work together, we can make an even more significant difference and help create a better world for everyone.
Child: That's amazing! I want to start giving back right now.
Parent: I'm proud of you! It's important to remember that charitable giving is not only about helping others but can also bring you joy and fulfilment.

EXAMPLE -2:
Parent: Hey, Buddy/Princess! Do you know what charity means?
Child: No, what is it?
Parent: Well, charity means helping others who are in need. It's a way of giving back to the community.
Child: Oh, that sounds nice! How can I help?
Parent: There are many ways to help. For instance, you can donate your old toys and clothes to a charity that helps needy children. You can also volunteer at a local food bank or animal shelter.
Child: I have a lot of toys that I don't play with anymore. Can we donate them?
Parent: Of course! We can find a charity that collects toys for

children who don't have any. How does that sound?

Child: Great! I want to help other kids have fun too.

Parent: That's very kind of you, Buddy/Princess. You know, giving to others makes us feel good too. It's a win-win situation.

Child: I can't wait to start giving back!

EXAMPLE -3:

Sure, here's another example conversation between a parent and a child about Charitable Giving:

Parent: Hey, Buddy/Princess, do you know what charitable giving is?

Child: Is it like giving money to people who need it?

Parent: That's right! Charitable giving is when you give money, time, or resources to people who are in need. Why do you think it's essential to do that?

Child: Hmm, I'm still determining.

Parent: Well, think about it this way - many people in the world don't have enough food, a safe place to live, or access to healthcare. Charitable giving is a way to help those people and make their lives better.

Child: Oh, I see. We should help them if we can.

Parent: Yes, exactly! And it's not just about helping others; it can also make us feel good. But, again, this is because they are helping someone else and can make us happy and proud of ourselves for doing something good.

Child: That makes sense. Can we do some charitable giving too?

Parent: Of course! There are lots of ways we can give back. For example, we could donate some of our old clothes to a shelter or give some money to a charity that helps sick kids. How does that sound?

Child: That sounds great! Let's do it!

TEACHING CHILDREN ABOUT THE IMPACT OF THEIR GIVING

In finance, giving can refer to various forms of charitable

donations or philanthropic activities. It involves voluntarily providing financial or material resources to individuals or organizations in need without expecting anything in return. Giving in finance can take many forms, such as donating to charities, supporting social causes, or investing in socially responsible companies. It is essential to building a sustainable and equitable society, as it promotes compassion, empathy, and generosity toward others.

EXAMPLES OF GIVING

Here are a few examples of giving that can be taught to kids:

Donating clothes and toys to charity: Kids can go through their belongings and choose items in good condition but no longer needed. We can donate these items to a charity that helps children in need.

Helping out in the community: Children can volunteer their time and energy to help out in the community. They can participate in activities like cleaning up a local park, serving food at a soup kitchen, or helping at a senior centre.

Fundraising for a cause: Kids can organize a fundraising event for a cause they care about, like raising money for a children's hospital or a local animal shelter.

Donating a portion of their allowance: Children can be encouraged to set aside a portion to donate to a charity of their choice.

Random acts of kindness: Children can be taught to be kind and compassionate to others by performing small acts of kindness, like holding the door open for someone or giving a compliment.

These examples teach the value of giving but also help instil essential life skills like empathy, kindness, and responsibility.

IMPORTANCE OF GIVING

Here are some ways to teach kids about the importance of giving in their life:

Start with age-appropriate activities: For younger kids, you can start with simple activities like donating toys or clothes to those in need. Older kids can volunteer at a local charity or organize a fundraiser for a cause they care about.

Talk about the impact: Help your child understand the impact their giving can have on someone's life. Share stories about how their giving can make a difference to others.

Lead by example: Kids learn a lot from watching their parents. If you make giving a priority in your own life, your child is more likely to follow in your footsteps.

Encourage empathy: Help your child understand what it's like to be in someone else's shoes. Encourage them to think about how they would feel if they were in a difficult situation and how they would want others to help them.

Teach gratitude: Help your child appreciate what they have and the opportunities they have been given. Encourage them to give back to others as a way of showing gratitude.

Make it fun: Giving doesn't have to be a chore. Encourage your child to get creative with their giving, such as organizing a charity bake sale or hosting a charity sports game.

Focus on the process, not just the outcome: While making a difference in someone's life is essential, giving can be just as rewarding for your child. So help them focus on the positive feelings they get from helping others rather than just the result.

CONVERSATIONS BETWEEN PARENTS AND
CHILDREN: (IMPORTANCE OF GIVING)

EXAMPLE -1:

Parent: Do you remember when we donated your old toys to the children's home last month?

Child: We gave away all the toys I don't play with anymore.

Parent: Exactly! That was a great example of giving. It means sharing what we have with those who might not have as much as we do. It could be our time, our possessions, or even our money.

Child: But why is giving meaningful?

Parent: Giving to others can make us feel good about ourselves and help improve the world. Sometimes, people face difficult times and need a little extra help. When we give, we can make a difference in their lives.

Child: Oh, I see. We can help others by giving them what they need.

Parent: That's right! We can donate food to the local food bank, clothes to the homeless shelter, or even sponsor a child's education. By giving, we can help create a positive impact on the lives of others.

Child: That sounds great! I want to give too!

Parent: That's wonderful, sweetie! Remember, it's not about how much you give but the act of giving itself that matters. Every little bit counts, and we can all make a difference uniquely.

EXAMPLE -2:

Parent: Hey, have you ever heard about the joy of giving?

Child: Giving? Do you mean, like, giving someone a present or something?

Parent: Yes, that's one way of giving. But there are other ways too. For example, you can give your time, talents, or money to help others.

Child: Why is giving so important?

Parent: Well, giving can significantly impact the lives of others, especially those who are struggling. And when you give, you also feel good about yourself and become more grateful for what you have.

Child: I see. But I'm just a kid. How can I give to others?

Parent: There are many ways. You can donate some of your toys or clothes that you no longer need to a charity. You can volunteer at a local shelter or food bank. You can even organize a fundraiser to raise money for a cause you care about.

Child: That sounds like a lot of work. But I want to try it.

Parent: That's great to hear! Remember, giving doesn't have to be a big gesture. Even a small act of kindness can make a difference.

EXAMPLE -3:
Parent: Do you remember when we talked about sharing our toys with others and how it makes them happy?
Child: Yes, I remember.
Parent: That's giving. In the same way, we can also give things like our time, money, or things we no longer need to people who need them.
Child: How can we give others money or things we don't need?
Parent: We can donate money to organizations that help people who are in need. And for things we no longer need, we can donate them to charity organizations or even directly to people who might need them.
Child: Oh, I see. But why is it important to give?
Parent: Giving is essential because it helps us to care for others and to make the world a better place. It also makes us feel good and happy to help others, just like sharing our toys with friends can make us happy too.

PRACTICAL MONEY SKILLS

Preparing Kids for Real-World Financial Situations

The more you learn, the more you earn.

Warren Buffett

In today's world, financial literacy is becoming increasingly important. Children need to be taught practical money skills to help them navigate the complex financial landscape they will encounter as they grow older. This chapter will explore practical money skills that parents can teach their children to help prepare them for real-world financial situations.

Budgeting: One of the most crucial practical money skills children need to learn is budgeting. Children should be taught to set financial goals and create a budget to help them achieve them. This section will explore how other parents can teach their children to create and stick to a budget.

Banking: Another crucial practical money skill is banking. Children should be taught about different types of bank accounts, how to deposit and withdraw money, and how to use a debit card. This section will explore how parents can teach their children about banking.

Shopping: Children also need to learn how to be savvy shoppers. They should be taught to compare shops, read labels, and understand how advertising can influence their buying decisions. This section will explore how parents can teach children to be savvy shoppers.

Credit Cards: Credit cards can be a valuable financial tool but can lead to debt if not used responsibly. Children should be taught how credit cards work, how to pay them off in full each month, and how to avoid high-interest rates and fees. This section will explore how parents can teach their children about credit cards.

Identity Theft and Scams: Children must be taught about the dangers of identity theft and scams. They should be taught how to protect their personal information, recognize scams, and what to do if they become a victim of identity theft or a scam. This section will explore how parents can teach their children about identity theft and scams.

Bargaining or Negotiations: Children should know about bargaining or negotiations because it is an important life skill that can help them in various situations. By understanding bargaining or negotiations, children can develop valuable skills that will serve them well throughout their lives, promoting cooperation, understanding, and positive communication.

Teaching children practical money skills is essential for preparing them for real-world financial situations. By teaching children about budgeting, banking, shopping, credit cards, and identity theft and scams, parents can help their children develop the skills they need to make sound financial decisions.

BUDGETING

Budgeting is creating a plan to manage your income and expenses over a certain period, usually a month or a year. It involves estimating your income, identifying your fixed and variable expenses, prioritizing your spending, and finding ways to save money. Budgeting aims to ensure that you spend within your means and can achieve your financial goals, such as paying off debt, saving for retirement, or making a significant purchase.

EXAMPLES OF BUDGETING SKILLS

Here are some examples of good budgeting skills:

Setting financial goals: Identifying your goals before creating a budget is essential. This could be anything from saving for a down payment on a house to paying off credit card debt. Then, having clear goals, you can create a budget to help you achieve them.

Creating a realistic budget: A realistic budget should be based on your current income and expenses. It's essential to yourself about your spending habits and to create a budget that you can realistically stick to.

Tracking your expenses: To create a budget, you must accurately understand your current spending habits. Keep track of all your expenses, including small purchases like coffee or snacks, for at least a month. This will give you a better idea of where your money is going and where you can cut back.

Prioritizing expenses: Once you know where your money is going, prioritize your expenses. This means ensuring that your basic needs like rent, utilities, and food are covered before spending on discretionary items like entertainment or shopping.

Saving for emergencies: A reasonable budget should include a savings plan for unexpected expenses like car repairs or medical bills. Having an emergency fund can help you avoid debt when something unexpected happens.

Revising your budget regularly: Your financial situation will change over time, so it's essential to revisit it regularly to ensure it works for you. For example, if you get a raise or start a new job, you may need to adjust your budget to reflect your new income.

Sticking to your budget: Creating a budget is only the first step. To be successful, you need to stick to it. This means avoiding impulse purchases and cutting back on expenses when necessary. It also means being disciplined about saving and avoiding debt.

HOW TO TEACH KIDS ABOUT THE IMPORTANCE OF GOOD BUDGETING SKILLS

Teaching kids about good budgeting skills can be a valuable lesson that will help them throughout their life. Here are some tips for teaching kids the importance of good budgeting skills:

Start with the basics: Teach your child to identify their needs and wants and differentiate between them. Help them understand that needs, such as food, clothing, and shelter, are necessary for their well-being, while wants are nice to have but not essential.

Set an example: Show your child how to manage money responsibly by setting a good example yourself. Talk to them about your budgeting process, and involve them in some of the decisions you make.

Give them an allowance: Giving your child an allowance can help them learn to manage money in a safe environment. Help them allocate their allowance to saving, spending, and donating.

Involve them in family budgeting: Bring your child into the family budgeting process by involving them in discussions about money. Teach them how to track spending and encourage them to develop ideas for saving money.

Use real-life examples: Use real-life examples to help your child understand the importance of budgeting. For example, when you go grocery shopping, show them how you compare prices and make choices based on your budget.

Encourage saving: Encourage your child to save money by setting goals and tracking progress. For example, if they want to buy a new toy, help them figure out how much they need to save each week to reach their goal.

Make it fun: Budgeting doesn't have to be boring. Find ways to make it fun by using games and activities to teach your child about money management.

Overall, teaching your child good budgeting skills is vital in helping them develop into responsible and financially-savvy adults.

CONVERSATIONS BETWEEN PARENTS AND
CHILDREN: (BUDGETING SKILLS)

EXAMPLE -1:
Parent: Hey, Buddy/Princess, do you know what budgeting means?

Child: No, what does it mean?

Parent: Well, budgeting means planning how to spend your money. It's like creating a plan for your money.

Child: Oh, okay. Why is it important?

Parent: Great question! It's important because it helps you ensure you have enough money to pay for the things you need and want while also ensuring you spend only a little.

Child: Can you give me an example?

Parent: Sure. You get $10 a week as an allowance. You could spend all of it on toys or candy immediately, but then you wouldn't have any money left for anything else you might want or need, like new clothes or books. So, if you budget your money, plan to spend $5 on toys or candy, and put $5 into your savings account, you can still buy the things you want and need.

Child: Oh, I see. So budgeting helps me save money?

Parent: That's right! And it also helps you learn to be responsible with your money, an essential skill.

Child: Okay, I want to learn more about budgeting!

Parent: Great, we can start by making a budget together and deciding how to spend your allowance.

EXAMPLE -2:

Parent: Hi, sweetie! How was school today?

Child: It was good, Mom. We learned about saving money in our math class.

Parent: That's great! Do you remember what we talked about last week when we discussed budgeting?

Child: Yeah, it's about planning how much money we have and how we spend it, right?

Parent: Yes, that's right! And do you know why it's essential to have good budgeting skills?

Child: So, we have enough money?

Parent: That's one reason! It's also important because it helps us ensure we have enough money for the things we need, like groceries and bills, and for the things we want, like a new toy

or a family vacation.
Child: Oh, I see.
Parent: It also helps us save money for things we might need, like college or a car.
Child: Hmm, I never thought about that.
Parent: Good budgeting skills can make a big difference in our lives, and it's never too early to start learning. So, are you ready to start making your budget for your allowance?
Child: Yeah, that sounds like a good idea!

EXAMPLE -3:
Parent: I wanted to talk to you about budgeting.
Child: Budgeting? What's that?
Parent: Well, budgeting is when you plan how to spend your money. It's like planning your money before you spend it.
Child: Oh, I see. Why is it important?
Parent: It's important because it helps you ensure you have enough money for the things you need, like food, clothes, and a place to live. It also helps you save money for things you want, like toys or games.
Child: Okay, how do I start budgeting?
Parent: First, you should consider what you must buy every week or month, like lunch at school or allowance. Then, you can list how much you'll need for each thing. After that, you can think about how much money you'll have to spend and ensure you only spend that much.
Child: That sounds like a good idea. I want to save up for a new game, so I'll try budgeting my money.
Parent: Great, I'm glad you're interested in budgeting. It's an essential skill to have, and it will help you in the future when you have even more things to pay for.

BANKING

Banking refers to accepting deposits, lending funds, and providing financial services to customers. Banks are financial institutions that manage money, provide loans, and offer other financial services such as checking and savings accounts, credit cards, and investments.

Banks play a crucial role in the economy by providing a secure place to deposit money, offering loans to businesses and individuals, and facilitating the flow of money throughout the economy.

Banking services refer to the range of financial products and services banks offer their customers. The types of services offered may vary depending on the bank.

MOST COMMON BANKING SERVICES

Deposit Accounts: Deposit accounts, allowing customers to deposit their money safely and securely. Examples of deposit accounts include savings accounts, checking accounts, and money market accounts.

Loans: Banks offer a variety of loans to their customers, including personal loans, car loans, mortgages, and business loans. Loans are provided at an interest rate and are paid back over a set period.

Credit cards: Credit cards are issued by banks and allow customers to purchase on credit. Customers pay back the amount owed, interest, and fees over time.

Debit cards: Debit cards are linked to a customer's bank account and allow them to make purchases or withdraw cash directly from their account.

Online banking: Most banks offer online banking services that allow customers to access their accounts, pay bills, transfer money, and check their account balances from a computer or mobile device.

Investment services: Some banks offer investment services such as mutual funds, stocks, and bonds to help customers grow their wealth.

Insurance services: Many banks also offer insurance services such as life insurance, home insurance, and car insurance.

Overall, banking services are designed to help customers

manage their finances and achieve their financial goals.

HOW TO TEACH KIDS ABOUT BANKING SERVICES

Teaching kids about banking services can be done through practical activities and games that demonstrate the concepts in a fun and interactive way. Here are some ideas:

Play "Bank" at home: Set up a pretend bank with a cash register and play money. Teach your child how to make deposits and withdrawals, count change, and keep track of their account balance.

Go on a field trip: Take your child to a local bank or credit union and give them a tour. Talk to them about the different banking services, such as savings accounts, checking accounts, loans, and ATMs.

Create a budget: Help your child create a budget for their allowance or any money they earn from doing chores. This can teach them the importance of managing their money and making wise financial decisions.

Teach them about credit: Discuss with your child the concept of credit and how it works. For example, explain how loans and credit cards work and how to pay bills on time to avoid fees and penalties.

Use online resources: There are many online resources available that can help teach kids about banking and money management, such as interactive games and activities, educational videos, and informative articles.

Overall, teaching kids about banking services can help them develop good financial habits and make informed decisions about their money as they grow older.

CONVERSATIONS BETWEEN PARENTS AND CHILDREN: (BANKING AND BANKING SERVICES)

EXAMPLE - 1:
Parent: Hey, Buddy/Princess, do you know what a bank is?
Child: Umm, I think so. It's a place where people keep their

money, right?

Parent: Yes, that's right. But banks offer many other services too. For example, have you heard of ATMs?

Child: Yes, I have seen them. You can withdraw money from them.

Parent: Correct. Banks also offer services like savings accounts, where you can save money and earn interest. And they offer loans, which you can use to buy a car or a house.

Child: Oh, I see. That sounds useful.

Parent: Yes, it is. And it's essential to understand how banks work and what services they offer so that you can make intelligent financial decisions as you grow up.

EXAMPLE -2:

Parent: Do you know what a debit card is?

Child: Yes, it's like a plastic card you can use to buy things, right?

Parent: That's right. And it's linked to your bank account, so the money comes out of your account when you use the card.

Child: Oh, I get it.

Parent: Using a credit card is like borrowing money from the bank. You have to pay it back with interest.

Child: Interest?

Parent: Yes, it's a fee that you have to pay for borrowing the money. That's why it's essential to use credit cards responsibly and only spend money you know you can repay.

Child: I see. So it's like borrowing money from the bank, but you have to pay them extra.

Parent: Exactly. And that's why it's essential to understand how credit cards work and to use them responsibly.

EXAMPLE -3:

Parent: Do you know what a bank statement is?

Child: No, I've never heard of it.

Parent: Well, it's like a report that your bank sends you every month. It shows all your transactions with your account that month, like deposits, withdrawals, and purchases.

Child: Oh, I see. That's like a report card for your money.

Parent: Yes, exactly. And it's important to review your bank statement every month to ensure there are no mistakes or fraudulent charges on your account.

Child: Fraudulent charges?

Parent: Yes, sometimes bad people will try to steal your money by using your account information to make purchases. So it's essential to monitor your account and immediately report anything suspicious to the bank.

Child: Okay, I will remember that.

EXAMPLE -4:

Parent: Hey, have you ever wondered what happens to your money when you deposit it in the bank?

Child: Not really; I know I can withdraw it later.

Parent: Yes, that's right. But there's more to banking than just depositing and withdrawing money. Banks offer many different services that can help you manage your finances better. For example, you can use a savings account to earn interest on your money or a checking account to pay your bills.

Child: Oh, I didn't know that. Can you explain more about these services?

Parent: Sure, we can go to the bank together, and I can show you how it works. You can also ask the bank employees any questions you have about banking. Understanding these services is essential because they can help you make smart financial decisions in the future.

EXAMPLE -5:

Parent: Do you know what a credit card is?

Child: It's a card you use to buy things, right?

Parent: Yes, that's right. But do you know how it works? When you use a credit card, you borrow money from the bank. Then, you have to pay back that money with interest.

Child: Oh, I didn't know that.

Parent: That's why it's essential to use credit cards responsibly. It would be best if you only spent what you can afford to pay back and pay your bills on time. If you don't, you could avoid ending up with a lot of debt and damage your credit score.
Child: Okay, I understand.

EXAMPLE -6:

Parent: You know how we must pay monthly bills, like electricity and water?
Child: Yeah.
Parent: We can pay those bills online using our bank account. It's called online banking.
Child: Really? How does that work?
Parent: We have to log into our bank account on the computer or phone, and then we can pay the bills from there. It's convenient because we can't attend the in-person bill payment center.
Child: Oh, I see. That's cool.
Parent: Yes, it is. And there are many other services that banks offer, like loans and mortgages. So it's essential to understand these services to make informed financial decisions in the future.

These conversations can help kids understand the basics of banking and financial literacy and set them on a path toward making intelligent financial decisions as they grow up.

SHOPPING

Shopping refers to browsing, selecting, and purchasing goods or services from stores or online platforms. It is an everyday activity where individuals acquire items they need or desire.
We can shop for necessities such as food and clothing or luxury items such as jewellery and electronics. We can do the act of shopping in person at physical stores or virtually through online marketplaces. It is a significant part of modern consumer culture and can impact personal finances.

MODES OF SHOPPING

There are several modes of shopping available today. Here are a few:

In-Store Shopping: Customers visit a physical store to browse and purchase products in this mode. This shopping mode allows customers to touch and feel the products before purchasing them.

Online Shopping: This mode allows customers to shop for products from the comfort of their homes using the Internet. Customers can browse online stores, select their desired products, and pay online.

Mobile Shopping: Mobile shopping uses mobile devices such as smartphones and tablets. Customers can use mobile shopping apps or mobile-optimized websites.

Social Media Shopping: Social media platforms such as Facebook, Instagram, and Pinterest have integrated shopping features that allow customers to browse and purchase products directly from the platform.

Subscription-Based Shopping: In this mode of shopping, customers subscribe to a service that delivers products to them regularly. This can include products such as food, beauty products, and clothes.

Curb side Pickup: This shopping mode allows customers to order products online and pick them up at a designated location without entering a physical store.

Click and Collect: In this shopping mode, customers order products online and collect them in-store at a designated pickup location.

Pop-Up Shops: Pop-up shops are temporary retail spaces that allow customers to browse and purchase products for a limited time. These can be physical or virtual.

Personal Shopping: Personal shopping is a service some retailers provide where a dedicated salesperson helps customers find and purchase products that suit their needs and preferences.

Augmented Reality Shopping: Augmented reality shopping uses technology to allow customers to try on and visualize products virtually before making a purchase.

HOW TO TEACH KIDS ABOUT SHOPPING

Teaching kids about shopping can be a fun and interactive experience. Here are some ways to approach it:

Play store: Set up a play store at home with toys or household items and give your child play money to "buy" items. This can help them understand the concept of buying and selling.

Grocery shopping: Take your child to the grocery store and involve them. Teach them how to compare prices, read labels and make decisions.

Online shopping: Show your child how to shop online safely and securely. Explain the difference between online and in-store shopping, and help them understand the benefits and drawbacks of each.

Budgeting: Teach your child how to budget for their purchases.

Help them understand the concept of saving for something they want and prioritize their spending.

Charity shopping: Take your child to a charity shop or thrift store and explain the concept of donating and reusing items. Show them how their purchase can help others and the environment.

Shopping manners: Teach your child good shopping manners, such as being polite to salespeople, not touching items they don't intend to buy, and thanking the cashier.

By involving your child in these activities and conversations, you can help them develop a healthy and responsible attitude towards shopping.

INTELLIGENT SHOPPING

Teaching kids about intelligent shopping is a great way to help them become financially responsible adults. Here are some tips for teaching kids about smart shopping:

Make a list: Teach your child to make a shopping list before heading to the store. This will help them avoid impulse buying and stay within their budget.

Compare prices: Encourage your child to compare the prices of different products before purchasing. Teach them to look for deals and discounts to get the best value for their money.

Avoid brand names: Teach your child to avoid purchasing brand names when generic or store-brand products are just as good. This can save them a lot of money over time.

Shop online: Online shopping can be a great way to save money. Teach your child to compare prices online before making a purchase.

Wait for sales: Teach your child to wait for sales before making big purchases. This can save them a lot of money over time.

Use cash: Encourage your child to use cash instead of credit cards when shopping. This will help them avoid overspending and racking up credit card debt.

Set a budget: Teach your child to set a budget before shopping. This will help them stay within their means and avoid overspending.

Teach them about taxes: Teach your child about sales tax and how it affects the cost of goods. This will help them understand the importance of budgeting for taxes.

Involve them in shopping: Involve your child in the shopping process, such as making a list, comparing prices, and finding deals. This will help them learn valuable shopping skills and become more financially responsible.

Lead by example: Finally, led by example. Be an intelligent shopper and demonstrate the importance of smart shopping to your child through your actions.

TRAPS IN SHOPPING

Teaching kids about the traps in shopping is essential to help them become aware and make smart shopping decisions. Here are some tips on teaching kids about shopping traps:

Talk about advertising: Explain to kids that advertising is designed to make people want things they may not necessarily need or want in the first place. Show them examples of advertisements and ask them to think critically about what the ad is trying to sell and why.

Discuss peer pressure: Explain to kids that sometimes they may feel pressure to buy things because their friends have them or because they think it will make them more popular. Help them understand that it's okay to say no and decide what they want to buy is okay.

Teach the difference between wants and needs: Help kids understand that there is a difference between things they want and things they need. Talk about prioritizing needs over wants and how this can help them make better shopping decisions.

Demonstrate comparison shopping: Take your child when you shop and show them how to compare prices and look for sales or deals. Teach them to compare prices at different stores or online before purchasing.

Explain credit and debt: Help kids understand that buying things on credit can lead to debt and financial trouble in the future. Explain that it's essential only to buy things they can afford to pay for with cash.

These shopping trips teach kids to make intelligent and responsible shopping decisions.

EXAMPLES FOR CHEATING IN SHOPPING

There are several ways in which consumers can be cheated while shopping. Here are a few examples:

Deceptive pricing: This is when the seller displays one price but charges a different price at the time of payment. For example, we may advertise a product for sale at $10, but at the time of payment, the seller may charge an additional $5 as "taxes" or "shipping and handling fees."

False advertising is when the seller makes false claims about the product to entice consumers to buy it. For example, a seller may claim that a product can cure a particular disease when there is no scientific evidence to support this claim.

Hidden charges: This is when the seller charges hidden fees that the consumer is unaware of at the time of purchase. For example, a seller may advertise a product for $20 but charge an additional $10 for "processing fees" at the time of payment.

Substandard products: This is when the seller sells products of poor quality or do not meet the advertised specifications. For example, a seller may advertise a product as "new" but sell a used or refurbished product instead.

To teach a child about the traps in shopping, it's important to discuss these concepts with them and provide real-life examples to help them understand.

You can also encourage them to read product reviews, compare prices at different stores, and ask questions before purchasing to avoid falling victim to these traps.

CONVERSATIONS BETWEEN PARENTS
AND CHILDREN: (SHOPPING)

EXAMPLE -1:

Parent: Hey, do you want to come with me to the store today?

Child: Yeah, sure!

Parent: Great! I wanted to talk to you about something important. Sometimes, stores use tricks to make us spend more money than necessary. They might put candy and toys near the checkout or use bright colors to make us notice things we don't need. Do you understand what I'm saying?

Child: I think so.

Parent: Okay. When we go to the store, I was hoping you could pay attention to what we need and try to focus on other things. And if you see something you want, we can put it on a list and decide later if it's something we need. Sound good?

EXAMPLE -2:

Parent: We're going shopping for school supplies today. I want to ensure we get everything we need without spending too much money. Do you want to help me make a list?

Child: Yeah, that sounds fun!

Parent: Great. So, we need pencils, erasers, notebooks, and other things. And when we get to the store, we will look for sales and deals to help us save money. Do you know what a sale is?

Child: It's when things cost less than usual, right?

Parent: Exactly! So we will look for those and find what we need for a reasonable price. And if we can't find something on our list, we can always return it.

EXAMPLE -3:

Child: Mom, can I buy this toy? It's cool!

Parent: Let's take a look at it. Hmm, it was expensive. Do you have enough money saved up to buy it?

Child: Not really, but I want it.

Parent: I understand. But sometimes, we must choose what we spend our money on. So, for example, if we buy this toy, we might need more money for other things we need later. And we may regret spending so much money on something that's not that important. So let's think about it for a little while and decide later if it's something we want to buy it.

These conversations can teach kids about being intelligent shoppers and making wise choices with their money.

EXAMPLE -4:

Parent: Hey, Buddy/Princess, you spent all your allowance on toys last week. Do you know that there are innovative ways to shop and save money?

Child: Really? How?

Parent: For example, you can wait for sales or use coupons to get discounts. You can also compare prices of the same item at different stores before buying.

Child: Oh, I see. That makes sense.

Parent: Remember, just because something is on sale doesn't mean you have to buy it. You should always ask yourself if you need it and if it fits your budget.

EXAMPLE -5:

Parent: Let's shop for your new school clothes. Before we go, I want to teach you some intelligent shopping skills.

Child: Okay, what are they?

Parent: First, let's list what you need so we don't buy unnecessary items. Then, we can check online for any deals or coupons for the stores we're going to. Finally, we can compare prices of the same items at different stores to ensure we get the best deal.

Child: Wow, I never thought about doing all of that before shopping.

Parent: These skills will help you save money and make you a smarter shopper.

EXAMPLE -6:

Parent: I saw you bought some candy with your money. Do you know that sometimes stores make candy look bigger than it, so you'll buy it?

Child: Really? That's not fair!

Parent: Yes, it's a trick called "packaging deception." That's why reading the labels and looking at the item's weight is essential to ensure you get what you pay for.

Child: Okay, I'll remember to check the labels next time.

CREDIT CARDS

Credit cards are financial tools that allow individuals to borrow money from a lender, typically to make purchases. Unlike debit cards, which draw from funds in a linked bank account, credit cards extend a line of credit that must pay paid back with int. We can use credit cards for various transactions, including in-person purchases, online shopping, and bill payments. Many credit cards also offer rewards programs that allow users to earn points or cashback for making purchases; we can redeem them for benefits like travel, merchandise, or statement credits.

Using a credit card responsibly can help individuals build, which is essential in obtaining loans, renting apartments, and even getting their specific jobs. However, misusing credit cards can lead to debt and financial hardship essential for individuals, especially young people, to understand the responsibilities and potential risks of using credit cards. In addition, education about budgeting, interest rates, and payment due dates can help individuals use credit in an innovative, intelligent, and responsible manner.

PROS AND CONS

Here are some key points to help kids understand credit cards and their pros and cons:

A credit card is like a small loan that you can use to buy things and pr them off later. But unlike a loan from a bank, you usually don't have to pay interest if you pay off your credit card balance in full each month.

Credit cards are convenient because you don't have to carry cash around. Instead, you can use them to buy things online or over the phone. But if you're not careful, it's easy to overspend and end up with a lot of debt.

Credit cards come with fees, like annual, late, and interest charges. So it's essential to understand how these work to avoid them.

To use a credit card responsibly, you should always pay your balance in full each month and only use your credit card to buy things you can afford. You should also track your spending and ensure you stay within your budget.

Finally, it's essential to protect your credit card information from fraud and theft is essential. Don't share your credit card number or security code with anyone; always ensure the websites you use to purchase are secure.

Overall, credit cards can be a helpful tool if used responsibly. But it's essential to understand how they work and how to avoid the potential pitfalls that come with them.

Credit cards can be a convenient tool for making purchases and managing your finances, but like any financial product, they have pros and cons. Here are some advantages and disadvantages of using a credit card:

PROS:

Convenience: Credit cards allow you to purchase without carrying cash or writing checks. They are widely accepted and can be used for online and in-store purchases.

Rewards: Many credit cards offer rewards such as cashback, points, or miles for purchases made with the card. We can redeem these rewards for merchandise, travel, or statement credits.

Building credit: Using a credit card responsibly can help you build a positive credit history and improve your credit score.

Consumer protection: Credit cards offer more excellent consumer protection than cash or debit cards. If you are the victim of fraud or a billing error, you can dispute the charge and withhold payment until the issue is resolved.

CONS:

High-interest rates: Credit cards often have high-interest rates, which can lead to significant debt if you carry a balance from month to month.

Fees: Some credit cards charge annual fees, late fees, balance transfer fees, and other charges that can add up quickly.

Overspending: Credit cards can make it easy to overspend and accumulate debt beyond what you can afford to pay back.

Credit damage: Using a credit card irresponsibly, such as making late payments or maxing out your credit limit, can harm your credit score and make it more difficult to obtain credit in the future.

It's essential to carefully consider the advantages and disadvantages of using a credit card and use them responsibly to avoid potential financial problems.

CONVERSATIONS BETWEEN PARENTS AND
CHILDREN: (CREDIT CARDS)

EXAMPLE -1:

Parent: Have you ever heard of a credit card?

Child: No, what is it?

Parent: A credit card is like a small plastic card that allows you to buy things without using cash. When you use a credit card, you borrow money from the bank and have to pay it back later with interest.

Child: Interest?

Parent: Yes, interest is like a fee you have to pay for borrowing the money. It's like when you borrow a toy from your friend and have to give it back with an extra toy as a thank you.

Child: Oh, I see.

Parent: So, when you use a credit card, you have to be careful not to spend more than you can afford to pay back. If you don't pay it back on time, you'll have to pay more interest.

Child: That doesn't sound good.

Parent: No, it's not. But if you use a credit card responsibly and pay it off in full every month, it can help you build a good credit history and improve your credit score, which is essential for things like getting a loan or renting an apartment.

Child: Okay, I think I understand.

Parent: Great! And always remember to use a credit card wisely and only buy things you need or can afford to pay back.

EXAMPLE -2:

Parent: Hey, Buddy/Princess, have you ever heard of a credit card?

Child: No, what's that?

Parent: A credit card is a small plastic card that you can use to buy things instead of cash or a debit card.

Child: Oh, that sounds cool! How does it work?

Parent: When you use a credit card to buy something, you borrow money from the bank or company that gave you the card. Then at the end of the month, you have to pay back the money you borrowed, plus some extra fees and interest.

Child: Hmm, that doesn't sound very clear.

Parent: Yeah, it can be if you must be more careful. That's why it's essential only to use a credit card if you know you can repay what you borrowed. And if you can't pay it back on time, you could end up with even more fees and interest, which can add up quickly.

Child: Okay, I see. Should I be careful and only use a credit card when necessary?

Parent: Exactly! Having a credit card to build up your credit score is good, but you always want to use it responsibly and ensure you can pay it back on time.

EXAMPLE -3:

Parent: Hey, Buddy/Princess, do you know what a credit card is?

Child: Um, I think so. It's like a plastic card people use to buy things, right?

Parent: That's right! But there's a bit more to it than that. For example, when you use a credit card, you borrow money from the bank to pay for your purchases. And then, at the end of the month, you have to pay the bank back what you borrowed, plus any interest or fees.

Child: Oh, I get it. So it's like getting a loan to buy stuff?

Parent: Exactly! And credit cards can be beneficial for emergencies or big purchases you can't afford to pay for all at once. But it's essential to be careful with them and only use them for things you can afford to pay back.

Child: Okay, I think I understand. But what happens if you don't pay the bank back on time?

Parent: Well, that's where it can get tricky. If you don't pay your credit card bill on time, the bank can charge you extra fees and interest, making it even harder to pay off what you owe. And if you keep missing payments, it can hurt your credit score, making it harder for you to get loans or credit in the future.

Child: Wow, I didn't know that! So it's essential to be responsible with credit cards.

Parent: That's right. Like anything else, it's all about using them wisely and making sure you can pay back what you borrow.

IDENTITY THEFT AND SCAMS

Theft: Theft is a criminal act of taking someone else's property without their permission or consent. It can include taking money, jewellery, electronics, or other belongings.

Theft can also include intangible items like intellectual property or confidential information. The severity of the theft can vary from a minor offense, such as taking a small item from a store without paying for it, to more serious offenses, such as burglary or robbery, which involve the use of force or threat of violence.

Scams: Scams are fraudulent schemes or activities designed to deceive and cheat people for personal gain. Scams can take various forms, including phishing scams, investment scams, identity theft, charity scams, lottery scams, and many others. In addition, scammers often use social engineering tactics and exploit vulnerabilities in technology to trick people into giving away their personal information or money.

Phishing scams, for example, involve sending fake emails or text messages that appear to be from a legitimate source, such as a bank or a government agency. The message may ask the recipient to click on a link or provide their login credentials, allowing the scammer to steal their information.

Investment scams often involve promising high returns on investments that do not exist or are too good to be true. Identity theft scams may involve stealing personal information, such as social security or credit card numbers, for fraudulent activities.

Charity scams may involve pretending to be a reputable charity and asking for donations, but the money is never used for charitable purposes. Lottery scams may involve telling people they have won a large sum but must pay a fee to claim the prize.

It is essential to be aware of scams and protect yourself, such as not giving out personal information to unknown sources and verifying the legitimacy of offers before providing any money or personal information.

HOW TO TEACH KIDS ABOUT THEFT

Teaching kids about knowing theft is essential to keep them safe and aware of their surroundings. Here are some tips for parents:

Start with the Basics: Explain to children what theft is in simple terms. Help them understand that theft is taking something that doesn't belong to them without permission and is considered wrong and against the law.

Discuss Ownership and Respect: Teach children the concept of ownership and the importance of respecting other people's belongings. Explain that everyone has the right to own and enjoy their possessions, and asking for permission before using or taking something that belongs to someone else is essential.

Use Real-Life Examples: Share age-appropriate examples of theft to help children understand its consequences and impact on individuals and communities. You can discuss scenarios like taking someone's toy without asking, shoplifting, or stealing money from someone's wallet.

Teach Empathy and Perspective: Encourage children to consider how theft can make others feel. Help them develop empathy by asking questions like, "How would you feel if someone took your favourite toy without asking?" This helps children understand the emotional impact of theft on others and encourages them to treat others' belongings with care and respect.

Discuss Consequences: Explain that theft is morally wrong and has legal consequences. Help children understand that stealing can result in punishment, damage relationships, and harm their reputation. Teach them that honesty and respecting others' property are essential values.

Encourage Open Communication: Create a safe and open environment for children to ask questions and express their thoughts. Encourage them to talk about any experiences or concerns related to theft. This allows for meaningful discussions and provides an opportunity to address any misconceptions.

Set a Good Example: Children learn by observing their parents and caregivers. Be a positive role model by demonstrating honesty, respect for other's property, and ethical behaviour. Show them that it is always better to ask for permission and treat others' belongings carefully.

Remember, teaching about theft is an ongoing process, and it's essential to reinforce these values consistently. By instilling a sense of respect, empathy, and understanding, you can help children develop a solid moral compass and make ethical choices throughout their lives.

HOW TO TEACH KIDS ABOUT SCAMS

Teaching kids about different types of scams can be tricky, but keeping them safe from online predators and fraudsters is essential. Here are some tips to help you teach your kid the importance of knowing different types of scams:

Start with the basics: Explain to your child what scams are and why they're dangerous. Ensure they understand that scammers use deception to trick others out of money, information, or other valuable things.

Discuss common scams: Talk to your child about some of the most common scams, such as phishing scams, lottery scams, and social media scams. Use real-life examples to illustrate how these scams work and the harm they can cause.

Encourage open communication: Let your child know they can always come to you if they receive a suspicious email, text message, or phone call. Ensure they understand that it's essential to talk to a trusted adult before responding to requests for personal information.

Teach them to be cautious: Teach your child to be cautious when sharing personal information online or with strangers. For example, ensure they know not to click links or download attachments from unknown sources.

Emphasize the importance of privacy: Explain to your child the importance of keeping personal information private, including their name, address, phone number, and social security number.

Practice good online habits: Encourage your child to practice good online habits, such as using strong passwords, logging out of accounts when they're done, and avoiding public Wi-Fi networks.

Stay up-to-date: Stay informed about the latest scams and frauds, and share this information with your child. By staying up-to-date on the latest scams, you can help your child avoid becoming a victim.

By teaching kids the importance of knowledge about theft and scams, you can help them develop a sense of responsibility and respect for others and keep them safe from potential harm.

CONVERSATIONS BETWEEN PARENTS AND CHILDREN: (THEFT AND SCAMS)

EXAMPLE -1:
Parent: Hey, Buddy/Princess, do you know what theft means?
Child: No, what is it?
Parent: Theft is when someone takes something that doesn't

belong to them without permission. It's like when someone takes your toy without asking you first.

Child: Oh, I get it. That's not fair.

Parent: That's right. It's not fair, and it's against the law. That's why it's important to always ask for permission before taking something that doesn't belong to you.

Child: I always ask first, but what if someone takes something from me?

Parent: If someone takes something from you without your permission, that's theft. You should always tell a grown-up you trust if someone takes something from you or sees someone taking something that doesn't belong to them.

Child: Okay, I'll remember that.

Parent: It's essential to know about theft and how to protect yourself from it is essential. It would be best to learn about scams and how to avoid them so you don't become a victim.

Child: What are scams?

Parent: Scams are when people trick you into giving them money or personal information. They might pretend to be someone they're not, like a bank or a government agency, and ask you to give them your credit card or social security number. You should only give that information to people if you're sure they're who they say they are.

Child: Wow, I didn't know that. Thanks for telling me, Mom/ Dad.

Parent: Of course, Buddy/Princess. It's essential to be aware of these things to protect yourself and your money.

EXAMPLE -2:

Parent: Hey, have you heard of scams before?

Child: No, what is that?

Parent: Scams are when someone tricks you into giving them your money or personal information. For example, someone might call you, say they're from your bank, and ask for your account number and password. Then, they can take your money from your account if you give it to them.

Child: Oh no, that doesn't sound nice. How can I protect myself from scams?

Parent: The first step is to be cautious and never give out your personal information over the phone or the Internet. If someone asks for your information, you should verify their identity by calling the company or bank directly. You should also talk to another trusted adult or me if you need clarification.

Child: Okay, I'll remember that. What are some other common scams that I should watch out for?

Parent: There are many different types of scams out there, like email scams, lottery scams, and investment scams. It's essential to be aware of these scams and know how to spot them. Then, we can look up some examples together and discuss staying safe.

Child: Sounds good; thanks for telling me about this!

EXAMPLE -3:

Parent: Hey, Buddy/Princess, I wanted to talk to you about something important. Have you ever heard of something called a scam?

Child: No, what's that?

Parent: A scam is when someone tries to trick you into giving them money or personal information. There are many types of scams, and they can happen online, on the phone, or even in person.

Child: How do they trick you?

Parent: They might pretend to be someone else, like a bank or the government, and ask you to give them your personal information, like your name, address, or social security number. Or they might try to sell you something that doesn't exist or isn't worth what they charge.

Child: That doesn't sound good.

Parent: No, it's not. That's why it's essential to be aware of different types of scams and always to be cautious when someone you don't know asks you for money or personal

information. If you ever feel unsure or uncomfortable, asking for help from a trusted adult, like a teacher or me, is okay.
Child: Okay, I'll remember that. Thanks for telling me, Mom/Dad.

BARGAINING OR NEGOTIATIONS

Bargaining is a negotiation process between two or more parties, typically intending to reach an agreement or settlement on a specific matter. In bargaining, each party tries to gain the most favourable outcome while also trying to satisfy the other party's interests to some degree.

Bargaining can occur in various settings, such as business deals, labor negotiations, or buying and selling goods or services. It involves a back-and-forth exchange of offers, counteroffers, and compromises until both parties agree that they are willing to accept.

EXAMPLES OF BARGAINING

Here are some examples of bargaining that parents can use to teach their kids:

Cleaning their room: Parents can teach their kids to negotiate on cleaning their room by agreeing to let them have extra playtime or screen time after they complete their chores.

Eating vegetables: Parents can teach their kids to negotiate on eating vegetables by allowing them to choose which vegetable they want to eat or how they want it prepared.

Doing homework: Parents can teach their kids to negotiate on doing homework by agreeing to give them a break after completing a certain amount of work or allowing them to choose the order in which they complete their assignments.

Sharing toys: Parents can teach their kids to negotiate by setting clear expectations and rules around sharing and allowing them to choose which toys they are willing to share.

Going to bed: Parents can teach their kids to negotiate on going to bed by allowing them to choose a specific bedtime within certain limits or agreeing to read a different story or sing a song before bed.

EXAMPLES OF BARGAINING IN REAL LIFE

Flea market: Bargaining is often a common practice at flea markets, where buyers negotiate with sellers to get a better price on items like clothing, furniture, and collectibles.

Car dealership: Car dealerships are another place where bargaining is standard, as buyers negotiate with salespeople over the price of a car, financing terms, and other incentives.

Salary negotiations: In the workplace, employees may negotiate with their employer over salary, benefits, and other compensation.

Home renovations: When renovating a home, homeowners may bargain with contractors over the price of materials, labour costs, and project timelines.

Rent negotiation: Tenants may negotiate rent prices, lease terms, and conditions like maintenance or repairs with landlords.

HOW TO TEACH KIDS ABOUT BARGAINING
OR NEGOTIATION

Teaching kids about bargaining or negotiation can be a valuable life skill that can help them in various situations, such as buying or selling goods, making deals, resolving conflicts, etc. Here are some tips on teaching kids about bargaining or negotiation:

Start with simple examples: Explain what bargaining or negotiation means and provide simple examples that children can relate to. For instance, you could explain how they can bargain with their siblings over who gets to choose the TV show or which game to play.

Practice in a safe environment: Encourage your kids to practice bargaining in a safe environment where no real stakes are involved, such as during a pretend-to-play session or a role-playing game. This can help them build confidence and improve their negotiation skills.

Teach them to listen and understand the other party's perspective: Bargaining or negotiation is not just about getting what you want, understanding the other party's needs, and finding a mutually beneficial solution. Teach your kids to listen actively and ask questions to understand the other person's point of view.

Role model good negotiation skills: Kids learn by example, so it's important to model good negotiation skills yourself. This can include negotiating with your kids respectfully and fairly or discussing how you negotiate deals at work or with friends.

Encourage creativity and problem-solving: Encourage your kids to think creatively and develop solutions that benefit both parties. For instance, they could offer extra chores in exchange for a toy they want or suggest a compromise that meets their needs.

Emphasize the importance of respect and fairness: Lastly, it's important to emphasize the importance of being respectful and fair when negotiating. Teach your kids to be polite, use good manners, and always try to find a solution that benefits both parties. This can help them build positive relationships and earn respect from others.

CONVERSATIONS BETWEEN PARENTS AND
CHILDREN: (BARGAINING OR NEGOTIATIONS)

EXAMPLE -1:

Parent: Have you ever heard the term "bargaining" or "negotiating"?

Child: No, what does it mean?

Parent: Bargaining or negotiating is when two or more people try to agree. It's like making a deal with someone to get what you want.

Child: Oh, okay. What's so important about it?

Parent: Well, it's an essential skill because you'll use it

throughout your life, whether trying to buy something, sell something, or get a better deal. It's also a way to communicate and understand people's needs and wants.

Child: How can I learn how to bargain or negotiate?

Parent: You can start by practicing with little things like negotiating how much screen time you get or trying to get a better deal on something you want to buy. Remember to be respectful, listen to the other person's perspective, and try to devise a solution that works for both of you.

Child: Okay, I'll try that. Thanks, Mom/dad!

EXAMPLE -2:

Parent: Do you remember when we visited the farmer's market last week?

Child: Yeah, I remember. We got some delicious fruits and veggies.

Parent: That's right.

Do you remember how the vendors were selling their products?

Child: They told us the prices, and we paid for what we wanted.

Parent: That's true, but did you notice that some vendors were open to negotiating prices?

Child: No, I overlooked that.

Parent: Sometimes vendors offer a lower price if you buy in bulk or negotiate with them. Understanding the art of bargaining or negotiating is essential because it can help you save money and get a better deal.

Child: Oh, I see. So, bargaining is like trying to get a better deal on something?

Parent: Exactly. It's about finding a way to compromise and reach an agreement that benefits both parties.

Child: That's interesting. How can I learn how to bargain or negotiate?

Parent: You can start by practicing with small things like negotiating how much allowance you get or trying to get a better deal on a toy you want to buy. Remember to be respectful, listen to the other person's perspective, and always try to find a win-win solution.

Child: Okay, I'll try that. Thanks, Mom/dad!

EXAMPLE -3:

Parent: Have you ever wanted to buy something, but it was too expensive?

Child: Yeah, I have. I wanted that new video game, but it was too expensive.

Parent: That's understandable. Did you know that sometimes you can negotiate the price with the store or seller?

Child: Really? How can I do that?

Parent: You can ask if there's any way they can offer a discount or if they can give you a better deal. It's called bargaining or negotiating. It's a way to communicate with people and find a solution for both parties.

Child: I didn't know that. How can I learn more about bargaining or negotiating?

Parent: You can start by practicing with small things like negotiating how much allowance you get or trying to get a better deal on a toy you want to buy. Remember to be respectful and polite when negotiating and always try to find a fair solution.

Child: Okay, I'll try that. Thanks for teaching me about bargaining, Mom/dad!

FINANCIAL LITERACY AT SCHOOL

Making the Most of Financial Education (Something that we MISS most of the TIME)

Financial literacy is not an option, it's a necessity. It's the language of the world of money, and kids need to be fluent in it.

Suze Orman

Financial literacy is a vital life skill that empowers individuals to make informed financial decisions. While the importance of financial literacy is widely recognized, there is often a significant gap in financial education provided in schools. This chapter aims to shed light on the significance of financial literacy at school and the missed opportunities for effective financial education. It explores the potential benefits, challenges, and strategies for maximizing school financial education.

THE IMPORTANCE OF FINANCIAL LITERACY AT SCHOOL

Young people face numerous financial challenges in an increasingly complex and financially driven world. They must understand budgeting, saving, investing, credit, and debt management to navigate their financial lives successfully. Unfortunately, many young adults enter the real world without a solid foundation in financial literacy, which can lead to financial stress, poor decision-making, and long-term financial difficulties. Integrating financial education into the school curriculum becomes crucial in addressing this gap.

BENEFITS OF FINANCIAL EDUCATION AT SCHOOL

Empowering Students: Financial education equips students with the knowledge and skills to take control of their financial well-being. It empowers them to make informed decisions, set financial goals, and develop healthy financial habits early on.

Long-term Financial Security: By learning about budgeting, saving, and investing, students can establish a solid financial foundation that sets them on a path toward long-term financial security. They gain the tools necessary to build wealth, plan, and make sound financial choices.

Real-life Application: Financial education provides practical skills that students can apply immediately and throughout their lives. It prepares them to manage personal finances, handle financial emergencies, and make informed spending, saving, and investing choices.

Financial Independence: Financial education promotes independence and self-sufficiency by equipping students with financial knowledge and skills. It helps them develop the confidence and capability to navigate their financial lives independently, reducing their reliance on others for financial support.

CHALLENGES TO FINANCIAL EDUCATION IN SCHOOLS

Despite the evident benefits, there are challenges to implementing effective financial education in schools. Some of these challenges include:

Lack of Curriculum Integration: Financial education often struggles to find a place in the already packed school curriculum. It is often perceived as an additional subject rather than an essential life skill that cuts across various disciplines.

Teacher Training and Expertise: Many educators may lack the necessary training and expertise to teach financial literacy effectively. Providing adequate training and support to teachers is crucial in delivering quality financial education.

Limited Resources: Financial education programs may face resource constraints, such as budget limitations and a lack of appropriate teaching materials. Access to up-to-date resources and tools is essential for engaging and effective financial education.

Strategies for Implementing Financial Literacy in Schools:
To ensure the most effective financial education in schools, several strategies can be implemented:

Integration Across Subjects: Embedding financial education concepts across multiple subjects allows for seamless integration into the existing curriculum. For example, math classes can include budgeting and compound interest lessons, while social studies classes can explore economic concepts.

Engaging Teaching Methods: Employing interactive and hands-on teaching methods, such as simulations, games, and real-life scenarios, enhances student engagement and understanding. Practical experiences can help students grasp financial concepts more effectively.

Partnerships and Collaboration: Schools can collaborate with financial institutions, community organizations, and volunteers to provide additional resources and expertise. Partnerships can bring guest speakers, organize workshops, and offer real-world experiences to enhance financial education.

Ongoing Assessment and Evaluation: Regular assessment and evaluation of financial education programs allow schools to measure their effectiveness and identify areas for improvement. Continuous refinement ensures that financial education remains relevant and impactful.

BUILDING ON FINANCIAL LITERACY OUTSIDE OF SCHOOL

Parental Involvement: Parents play a crucial role in complementing financial education taught at school. They can actively engage in conversations about money, involve children in household budgeting, and provide real-life examples of financial decision-making.

Financial Literacy Resources: Various resources available outside of school can enhance financial literacy. Online platforms, books, podcasts, and mobile apps offer interactive tools and educational content tailored to different age groups, allowing children to explore financial concepts at their own pace.

Savings and Allowance: Encouraging children to save money early helps instil the habit of saving and teaches them the value of money. Providing them with a regular allowance and discussing how to allocate their funds into spending, saving, and giving categories can cultivate responsible financial behaviour.

Financial Role Models: Exposing children to positive financial role models can inspire and motivate them to develop good financial habits. This can be done through discussions about successful entrepreneurs, philanthropists, or family members demonstrating responsible financial practices.

Real-World Experiences: Allowing children to have real-world experiences with money, such as accompanying parents during shopping trips, visiting banks, or participating in community activities, helps them understand the practical aspects of finance and develop practical money management skills.

Entrepreneurial Opportunities: Encouraging children to explore entrepreneurial endeavours, such as starting a small business or participating in fundraising, provides hands-on experience in financial decision-making, budgeting, and managing profits and expenses.

Financial Goal Setting: Teaching children about setting financial goals and creating action plans to achieve them helps them develop a sense of purpose and responsibility. It also teaches the importance of delayed gratification and long-term planning.

Volunteer and Philanthropic Activities: Engaging children in volunteer and philanthropic activities expose them to the concept of giving back to society and understanding the impact of money beyond personal financial goals. It cultivates empathy, generosity, and an understanding of social responsibility.

Media and Entertainment: Engaging with age-appropriate financial media and entertainment, such as movies, TV shows, and books, can offer valuable learning opportunities. Selecting content that addresses financial themes, responsible spending, and the consequences of financial decisions can facilitate discussions and reinforce financial literacy concepts.

Continued Learning: Financial education is an ongoing

process. Encouraging children to stay curious, seek new information, and engage in lifelong learning about personal finance ensures they stay informed about emerging financial trends, products, and strategies.

By combining financial education at school with active involvement outside the classroom, children can develop a solid foundation in financial literacy and gain the necessary skills and knowledge to navigate their financial futures successfully.

THE IMPORTANCE OF FINANCIAL LITERACY AT SCHOOL

Financial literacy is an essential life skill that empowers individuals to make informed financial decisions, manage money effectively, and achieve financial well-being. As society becomes increasingly complex and financially interconnected, the need for comprehensive financial education has never been greater. One crucial avenue for promoting financial literacy is through schools, where students can receive structured and systematic instruction in financial concepts, skills, and behaviours. Here, we explore the importance of financial literacy at school and its impact on students' present and future financial well-being.

EQUIPPING STUDENTS WITH ESSENTIAL LIFE SKILLS

Financial literacy education equips students with practical skills and knowledge essential for navigating the complexities of the modern world. It gives them the tools to budget effectively, manage debt, save for the future, and make informed spending, investing, and financial planning decisions. By teaching students about personal finance at an early age, schools empower them to become financially responsible adults capable of achieving their financial goals.

Fostering Financial Independence: Financial literacy education at school fosters financial independence among students. It teaches them the importance of earning, saving, and managing money. By developing a solid understanding of financial concepts such as income, expenses, budgeting, and saving, students become less reliant on others for financial support and more capable of taking control of their financial lives. This fosters a sense of empowerment and self-sufficiency.

Countering Financial Illiteracy: Financial illiteracy is a pervasive problem with severe consequences for individuals and society. Without adequate financial literacy education, individuals may fall prey to predatory lending practices, accumulate unmanageable debt, make poor investment decisions, and fail to plan for their long-term financial well-being. By providing financial education in schools, we can counter financial illiteracy and equip students with the knowledge and skills to make sound financial decisions, avoid common financial pitfalls, and secure their financial futures.

Promoting Economic Stability: A financially literate society will likely experience economic stability and growth. When individuals understand how to manage their money effectively, they are better positioned to contribute to the economy. Financially literate individuals are more likely to save, invest, and make wise financial decisions, which can stimulate economic activity and promote sustainable economic growth. By imparting financial literacy skills to students, schools contribute to building a financially capable workforce and fostering economic stability in the long run.

Breaking the Cycle of Financial Insecurity: Financial literacy education can play a crucial role in breaking the cycle of financial insecurity. By teaching students the importance of financial planning, budgeting, and saving, schools provide them with the knowledge and tools to make sound financial decisions and break free from the cycle of living pay check to pay check. Financially literate individuals are better equipped to build wealth, secure their financial future, and pass on these essential skills to future generations.

Empowering Students to Make Informed Decisions: In

today's digital age, students are bombarded with advertising, complex financial products, and an overwhelming amount of information about money. Financial literacy education empowers students to analyse financial information critically, evaluate the validity of marketing claims, and make informed decisions based on their financial goals and values. It cultivates consumer awareness and helps students become savvy consumers capable of protecting themselves from financial scams and making wise financial choices.

Enhancing Career Readiness: Financial literacy is relevant to personal finance and plays a significant role in career readiness. Many jobs require employees to manage finances, understand employee benefits, and make decisions about retirement planning. By providing financial literacy education at school, students gain the skills necessary to navigate these aspects of their professional lives confidently. It equips them with the knowledge to negotiate salaries and understand workplace benefits.

THE CONSEQUENCES OF NOT HAVING FINANCIAL EDUCATION IN SCHOOL

In today's complex and ever-changing financial landscape, the absence of comprehensive financial education in schools can significantly affect individuals, communities, and society. Without access to proper financial education, students are left ill-equipped to make informed financial decisions and face numerous life challenges. Here, we explore the consequences of not having financial education in school and the far-reaching impact it can have.

Increased Financial Vulnerability: One of the most immediate consequences of not having financial education in school is increased financial vulnerability. Without the knowledge and skills to manage money effectively, individuals are more likely to fall into debt, struggle with budgeting, and make poor financial choices. This vulnerability can lead to financial stress, a cycle of living pay check to pay check, and an inability to build a solid financial foundation.

Lack of Basic Financial Skills: Financial education gives individuals the fundamental skills to navigate everyday financial tasks. Without this education, individuals may lack basic financial skills such as budgeting, saving, and managing credit. As a result, they may struggle to meet their financial obligations, accumulate debt, and face challenges in achieving their financial goals.

Limited Understanding of Financial Concepts: Financial concepts and terms can be complex and overwhelming, especially for those without formal financial education. Without exposure to financial education in school, individuals may lack a solid understanding of interest rates, investments, compound interest, and risk management concepts. This limited understanding can hinder their ability to make informed financial decisions and effectively plan for their future.

Increased Susceptibility to Financial Fraud and Scams: Financial illiteracy makes individuals more vulnerable to financial fraud and scams. Without a solid understanding of financial concepts, individuals may be easily swayed by deceptive financial practices, predatory lending schemes, or fraudulent investment opportunities. This lack of knowledge can result in substantial financial losses and long-lasting negative impacts on individuals' financial well-being.

Inadequate Retirement Planning: Retirement planning is a critical aspect of long-term financial security, yet many individuals without financial education fail to plan for retirement adequately. Without the knowledge of retirement savings options, investment strategies, and the power of compound interest, individuals may find themselves unprepared for retirement, relying solely on limited social security benefits, and facing financial hardships in their later years.

Limited Economic Growth and Stability: The absence of

financial education in schools can have a broader economic impact. Financially illiterate individuals may struggle to manage their finances, leading to reduced consumer spending, increased reliance on social welfare programs, and limited economic growth. Without a financially literate population, societies may experience economic instability and face challenges in building sustainable economic futures.

Generational Impact: The consequences of not having financial education in schools can have a generational impact. Without the knowledge and skills gained from financial education, individuals may struggle to pass on sound financial practices to their children, perpetuating a cycle of financial illiteracy and insecurity. This lack of intergenerational financial literacy can limit opportunities for upward mobility and hinder the overall financial well-being of future generations.

The absence of financial education in schools can have far-reaching consequences for individuals and society. Without access to proper financial education, individuals face increased financial vulnerability, limited financial skills, a lack of understanding of critical financial concepts, susceptibility to fraud and scams, inadequate retirement planning, and hindered economic growth. It is crucial to recognize the importance of financial education in schools and work towards implementing comprehensive financial literacy programs to empower individuals with the knowledge and skills needed for financial success.

THE ROLE OF SCHOOLS IN PROVIDING FINANCIAL EDUCATION

Schools play a vital role in shaping our children's future, not just academically but also in preparing them for real-world challenges. One critical aspect of their development is financial education. The role of schools in providing financial education is paramount, as it equips students with essential knowledge and skills to navigate the complex world of personal finance. Here, we delve into the significance of schools in delivering financial education and its impact on students' lives.

Empowering Students with Financial Literacy: Financial literacy is the foundation of sound financial decision-making and responsible money management. Schools have a unique opportunity to empower students by providing them with the necessary knowledge and skills to understand financial concepts, make informed financial choices, and develop healthy financial habits. By incorporating financial education into the curriculum, schools ensure that students graduate with a solid financial foundation that can benefit them throughout their lives.

Filling the Gap in Home-Based Financial Education: Not all students have access to financial education at home. In many households, discussions about money matters are limited, and children may not receive adequate guidance on managing finances. Schools bridge this gap by offering structured financial education programs that give students the tools to navigate financial challenges and independently make informed decisions. By providing this education, schools empower students to take control of their financial future and break the cycle of financial illiteracy.

Teaching Practical Life Skills: Financial education in schools goes beyond theoretical knowledge. It equips students with practical life skills essential for their future success. By teaching topics such as budgeting, saving, investing, and understanding credit, schools enable students to develop financial independence and responsibility. These skills are beneficial for personal financial management and entrepreneurship, career development, and overall economic well-being.

Promoting Financial Well-Being: Financial stress can significantly impact a student's overall well-being and academic performance. By providing financial education, schools aim to alleviate this stress and promote financial well-being among students. When students understand how to manage their money effectively, make informed choices, and plan for their future, they experience greater financial security and peace of mind. This, in turn, positively influences their academic performance, mental health, and overall quality of life.

Preparing Students for a Complex Financial Landscape: The financial landscape continuously evolves, with new technologies, investment options, and financial products emerging regularly. Schools that offer financial education prepare students for this complexity by teaching them about emerging trends, digital banking, online security, and the potential risks and opportunities in the financial world. By staying ahead of the curve, schools ensure students have the knowledge and skills to navigate the ever-changing financial landscape confidently.

Fostering Responsible Citizenship: Financial education in schools goes beyond personal finance. It also fosters responsible citizenship by helping students understand their financial decisions' broader economic and social implications. By teaching concepts such as responsible consumption, ethical investing, and the impact of financial choices on society and the environment, schools cultivate socially conscious individuals who contribute positively to their communities.

Building a Strong Foundation for the Future: Financial education in schools provides students with a strong foundation for their future endeavours. Whether students pursue higher education, start their businesses, or enter the workforce, the financial skills they acquire in school will serve them well. By developing a financially literate generation, schools contribute to society's overall economic growth and stability.

Schools play a crucial role in providing financial education to students. By empowering students with financial literacy, filling the gap in home-based financial education, teaching practical life skills, promoting financial well-being, preparing students for a complex financial landscape, fostering responsible citizenship, and building a solid foundation for the future, schools set students on a path towards financial success and a brighter future. Schools must continue to prioritize and expand financial education programs to ensure that all students have the opportunity to develop the skills they need to thrive in an increasingly complex financial world.

EXAMPLES OF HOW SCHOOLS CAN PROVIDE FINANCIAL EDUCATION TO STUDENTS:

Incorporating Financial Literacy into the Curriculum: Schools can integrate financial literacy topics into mathematics, social studies, or economics. Teachers can design lessons and activities that incorporate real-life financial scenarios, budgeting exercises, and discussions on personal finance concepts.

Dedicated Financial Education Courses: Schools can offer dedicated financial education courses as part of the curriculum. These courses can cover various topics such as budgeting, saving, investing, understanding credit, consumer rights, and financial planning. They can be offered as elective courses or integrated into the mandatory curriculum.

Guest Speakers and Workshops: Schools can invite guest speakers, such as financial advisors, bankers, or professionals from the finance industry, to conduct workshops and seminars on financial literacy. These experts can provide valuable insights, share real-world experiences, and offer practical tips to students.

Simulated Financial Experiences: Schools can organize simulations or interactive activities replicating real-world financial scenarios. For example, students can participate in stock market simulations, entrepreneurship projects, or budgeting challenges. These hands-on experiences allow students to apply their knowledge and learn from practical situations.

Financial Literacy Clubs and Programs: Schools can establish financial literacy clubs or programs where students can come together to learn and discuss personal finance topics. These clubs can organize workshops, competitions, and group activities that promote financial learning and encourage peer-to-peer knowledge sharing.

Partnerships with Financial Institutions: Schools can collaborate with local banks, credit unions, or other financial institutions to provide educational resources and expertise. These partnerships can result in workshops, field trips to financial institutions, internship opportunities, or access to online financial literacy platforms.

Integration of Technology: Schools can leverage technology to enhance financial education. Online platforms, mobile applications, and educational software can provide interactive lessons, virtual simulations, and engaging educational content that students can access inside and outside the classroom.

Parent Involvement: Schools can encourage parental involvement in financial education by organizing parent workshops or providing resources for parents to engage in financial discussions with their children at home. This collaboration between schools and parents reinforces financial literacy education and extends its impact beyond the school environment.

Community Outreach Programs: Schools can initiate community outreach programs that promote financial literacy beyond the classroom. For example, students can organize financial literacy workshops for community members or participate in initiatives that educate underserved populations about personal finance.

Continuous Professional Development for Educators: Schools can invest in professional development opportunities for educators to enhance their knowledge and skills in teaching financial literacy. This can include workshops, conferences, or online courses tailored to educators.

By implementing these strategies, schools can effectively provide comprehensive financial education to students, equipping them with the necessary skills and knowledge to make informed financial decisions and thrive in their personal and professional lives.

CHALLENGES TO FINANCIAL EDUCATION IN SCHOOLS

Financial education is crucial in preparing students for their future financial well-being. However, several challenges hinder the effective implementation of financial education in schools. Understanding these challenges is essential to address them and ensure that students receive the necessary knowledge and skills to navigate the complex world of personal finance.

Lack of Priority: One of the significant challenges is the lack of priority given to financial education in school curricula. Schools often prioritize core academic subjects, leaving little room for financial education. This results in inadequate time and resources allocated to teaching financial literacy.

Limited Teacher Training: Many teachers may lack the necessary training and expertise to teach financial education effectively. They might not have received formal education or professional development in personal finance, making it challenging to deliver comprehensive financial education to students.

Curriculum Constraints: School curricula are often crowded with numerous subjects and learning objectives, leaving little flexibility to incorporate financial education. Competing priorities and a full curriculum can make it difficult to dedicate sufficient time and attention to financial literacy.

Lack of Standardized Curriculum: The absence of a standardized financial education curriculum across schools can lead to inconsistencies in the depth and quality of financial education provided. Without clear guidelines and benchmarks, ensuring that students receive consistent and comprehensive financial literacy instruction becomes challenging.

Financial Education Resources: Access to high-quality and up-to-date financial education resources can be limited. Schools may struggle to find appropriate textbooks, educational materials, or digital resources that align with their curriculum and cater to the needs of diverse student populations.

Engagement and Relevance: Engaging students in financial education can be challenging, as personal finance topics may seem distant or irrelevant to their immediate lives. Making financial education relatable and applicable to their everyday experiences is crucial to sustaining student interest and participation.

Evaluation and Assessment: Measuring the effectiveness and impact of financial education programs can be complex. Assessing students' financial knowledge and behaviour change requires suitable evaluation methods and tools. Limited guidance and resources for evaluation make it challenging to determine the success of financial education initiatives.

Parental Involvement and Support: Engaging parents in reinforcing financial education at home can be challenging. Limited parental knowledge or interest in personal finance can hinder the continuity of financial education and its practical application outside the classroom.

Evolving Financial Landscape: The financial landscape continually evolves, with new financial products, technologies, and economic conditions emerging. Keeping up with these changes and providing relevant and up-to-date financial education can be challenging for schools.

Limited Time and Resources: Schools often face time and resource constraints, making investing in financial education initiatives difficult. Limited budgets, competing priorities, and administrative pressures can hinder the allocation of adequate resources for comprehensive financial education programs.

Addressing these challenges requires a multi-faceted approach involving policymakers, educators, parents, and the wider community. Collaboration between stakeholders, increased funding for financial education initiatives, teacher training programs, curriculum development, and partnerships with financial institutions and organizations can help overcome these challenges and ensure financial education becomes integral to every student's educational journey. By addressing these challenges, we can empower the next generation with the knowledge and skills needed for their financial well-being.

STRATEGIES FOR IMPLEMENTING FINANCIAL LITERACY IN SCHOOLS

Implementing financial literacy in schools is crucial for equipping students with the knowledge and skills to make informed financial decisions. To effectively integrate financial literacy into the curriculum, schools can adopt various strategies that promote comprehensive and engaging financial education for students. Here are some key strategies for implementing financial literacy in schools:

Curriculum Integration: Integrate financial literacy across various subject areas, such as mathematics, social studies, and consumer sciences. By embedding financial concepts and skills into existing curriculum frameworks, students can see the practical applications of financial knowledge in real-life contexts.

Early Introduction: Start introducing financial literacy concepts at an early age. Develop age-appropriate lessons and activities that gradually build students' understanding of money, saving, budgeting, and other fundamental financial concepts. This early exposure sets a strong foundation for lifelong financial competence.

Practical Experiences: Provide students with hands-on,

experiential learning opportunities. For example, organize simulations, financial challenges, or entrepreneurship projects that allow students to apply financial concepts in practical scenarios. This approach helps students develop critical thinking, problem-solving, and decision-making skills in financial contexts.

Guest Speakers and Experts: Invite financial professionals, bankers, entrepreneurs, or community members with expertise in personal finance to share their knowledge and experiences with students. Guest speakers can provide real-world insights and inspire students to explore different financial pathways.

Interactive Technology: Utilize interactive technology tools and resources to enhance student engagement and understanding. Incorporate financial literacy apps, online simulations, and educational websites that offer interactive lessons, games, and quizzes. This tech-based approach appeals to students' digital literacy skills and keeps them actively involved in their financial learning.

Personal Finance Projects: Assign personal finance projects or assignments that require students to research and analyse topics like budgeting, investing, or managing debt. These projects encourage independent learning, critical thinking, and problem-solving skills while allowing students to explore personal finance topics that resonate with their interests and aspirations.

Collaborations and Partnerships: Establish partnerships with financial institutions, community organizations, or non-profit agencies specializing in financial education. Collaborations can provide access to resources, expertise, and funding for financial literacy programs, workshops, or events. This also helps students connect classroom learning with real-world financial institutions and services.

Teacher Professional Development: Invest in professional development programs that enhance educators' knowledge and skills in financial literacy instruction. Training opportunities, workshops, and certifications can equip teachers with the tools and strategies to effectively teach financial concepts, engage students, and address their needs.

Parent Involvement: Engage parents and guardians in the financial education process by organizing workshops, seminars, or family-oriented activities. Encourage parents to reinforce financial concepts at home and discuss money-related topics with their children. This collaboration strengthens the continuity of financial education and expands the impact beyond the school setting.

Ongoing Evaluation and Improvement: Regularly assess the effectiveness of financial literacy programs and make necessary adjustments based on student feedback and outcomes. Collect data on student knowledge, attitudes, and behaviours related to finance to measure the program's impact and identify areas for improvement.

By implementing these strategies, schools can create a robust and comprehensive financial literacy program that empowers students to become financially responsible and confident individuals. Financial literacy education equips students with essential life skills that support their personal and financial well-being, enabling them to successfully make informed decisions and navigate the complexities of the financial world.

BUILDING ON FINANCIAL LITERACY OUTSIDE OF SCHOOL

While financial literacy education in schools is crucial in equipping students with fundamental knowledge about money management, it is equally important to build on this foundation outside the classroom. Building financial literacy skills outside of school helps students reinforce their learning, apply concepts to real-life situations, and develop a deeper understanding of personal finance. Here are some critical strategies for building on financial literacy outside of school:

Family Involvement: Parents and guardians play a significant role in fostering financial literacy skills in children. Engage in regular conversations about money, budgeting, saving, and spending with your child. Encourage them to set financial goals and make informed decisions about their allowances or earnings. Involve children in family financial activities, such as budget planning or grocery shopping, to provide hands-on experience and practical lessons.

Educational Resources: Leverage various educational resources outside school to supplement financial literacy learning. Encourage your child to read books, watch videos, or listen to podcasts focused on personal finance. Many websites and apps offer interactive games and activities that engagingly teach financial concepts. These resources provide additional reinforcement and expand your child's knowledge beyond what is covered in school.

Financial Apps and Tools: Introduce your child to financial apps and online tools designed specifically for young learners. These platforms often simulate real-world financial scenarios and offer interactive experiences that teach budgeting, saving, and investing. Some apps even allow children to manage virtual bank accounts or set financial goals, providing a practical and hands-on learning experience.

Savings and Budgeting:

- Encourage your child to practice saving and budgeting by giving them opportunities to earn and manage money.
- Help them set up savings accounts and teach them the importance of setting financial goals and tracking their progress.
- Assist them in creating a budget for their income and expenses, instilling a sense of responsibility and discipline in managing their financial resources.

Entrepreneurial Ventures: Encourage your child's entrepreneurial spirit by supporting small business ideas or ventures. Whether it's a lemonade stand, handmade crafts, or a service-based project, these experiences teach children the value of hard work, financial responsibility, and business running. They also foster creativity, problem-solving, and critical thinking skills.

Volunteer and Community Engagement: Engage your child in volunteer activities that promote financial literacy within the community. Participate in financial literacy workshops, community events, or initiatives to educate children and families about money management. By actively participating in these activities, children gain a deeper understanding of financial concepts and develop a sense of social responsibility.

Role Modelling: Be a positive role model regarding financial behaviours and decision-making—display responsible money habits, such as budgeting, saving, and avoiding impulsive purchases. Involve your child in financial discussions and decision-making processes when appropriate, helping them understand the thought processes behind financial choices.

Real-Life Experiences: Take advantage of everyday situations to teach financial lessons. For example, involve your child in grocery shopping and discuss price comparisons, discounts, and the importance of making informed choices. Teach them about interest when saving money or borrowing from a bank. These practical experiences connect financial literacy concepts and the real world.

Workshops and Programs: Explore workshops and programs offered by local organizations, libraries, or financial institutions that focus on financial literacy for children. These programs often provide structured learning opportunities, hands-on activities, and expert guidance, further enhancing your child's financial knowledge and skills.

Continuous Learning: Encourage your child to maintain a curious mindset and continue their financial learning journey. Support them in seeking out additional resources, attending seminars, or joining online communities focused

These extracurricular activities and programs can help students develop critical financial skills and knowledge they can use.

PARENTAL RESPONSIBILITY

Creating a Family Culture of Financial Responsibility

The best inheritance a parent can give to their children is a few minutes of their time each day to talk about money.

Dave Ramsey

A s parents, we play a crucial role in teaching our children about financial responsibility. Our actions and behaviours significantly impact how our children perceive money and their spending habits. By creating a family culture of financial responsibility, we can equip our children with the necessary skills and values to make wise financial decisions.

Modelling Good Financial Behaviour:
Children learn by example; parents are their primary role models. This section will discuss the importance of modelling good financial behaviour to teach our children how to handle money responsibly. It will explore ways to establish and maintain a family budget, save for emergencies, and plan for long-term financial goals.

Teaching Kids About Money:
This section will discuss practical ways to teach children about money. It will explore how to introduce children to earning, saving, and spending. Additionally, it will discuss the importance of teaching children the value of money and the difference between wants and needs.

Developing Good Financial Habits:
The earlier children learn good financial habits, the better equipped they will be to make wise financial decisions. This section will explore ways to help children develop good financial habits such as budgeting, saving, and investing. Additionally, it will discuss how to teach children about debt and credit and how to use them responsibly.

Creating a Family Culture of Financial Responsibility:
Creating a family culture of financial responsibility involves more than just teaching our children about money. It requires a deliberate effort to instil values such as hard

work, responsibility, and self-discipline. This section will discuss practical ways to create a family culture of financial responsibility, including setting expectations, establishing consequences, and involving children in family financial decisions.

Teaching our children about financial responsibility is one of the most important things we can do as parents. By modelling good financial behaviour, teaching kids about money, developing good financial habits, and creating a family culture of financial responsibility, we can equip our children with the skills and values they need to make wise financial decisions.

MODELING GOOD FINANCIAL BEHAVIOR

Modelling good financial behaviour as a parent is crucial for instilling healthy money habits in your children. Children learn by observing their parents, and your actions and attitudes towards money significantly shape their financial beliefs and behaviours. Here are some key points to consider when it comes to modelling good financial behaviour for kids as a parent:

Practice Open and Honest Communication: Create an environment where money is openly discussed. Engage in age-appropriate conversations about the importance of money, budgeting, saving, and spending. Share your financial values and experiences with your children. By fostering open and honest communication, you help children develop a positive mindset toward money and build a foundation for their financial understanding.

Set Financial Goals as a Family: Involve your children in setting financial goals relevant to the whole family. This could include saving for a vacation, a particular purchase, or a future expense. Discuss the steps needed to achieve those goals and involve your children in decision-making. Working together towards shared financial goals teaches them the value of planning, saving, and collaborative effort.

Create and Follow a Budget: Demonstrate the importance of budgeting by creating a family budget. Involve your children in the process of allocating funds for different expenses. Show them how to prioritize needs over wants and make conscious spending decisions. Adhering to a budget teaches children about responsible money management and the importance of living within means.

Save and Practice Delayed Gratification: Encourage your children to save money regularly. Set up a savings account and teach them to put aside some of their earnings or allowances. Discuss the concept of delayed gratification and the rewards of saving for future goals. By modelling saving behaviour, you instil in them the value of patience, self-discipline, and long-term financial planning.

Demonstrate Responsible Spending: Show your children how to make responsible spending choices. Discuss the difference between needs and wants and encourage them to think critically before purchasing. Teach them to compare prices, read reviews, and consider the long-term value of their purchases. By modelling responsible spending habits, you help them develop good decision-making skills and avoid impulsive buying behaviour.

Practice Frugality and Resourcefulness: Demonstrate the importance of frugality and resourcefulness in daily life. Show your children how to find cost-effective solutions, avoid unnecessary expenses, and maximize what they have. Teach them to prioritize experiences over material possessions and embrace the concept of minimalism. By practicing frugality, you instil in them a sense of resourcefulness, creativity, and financial independence.

Involve Children in Financial Tasks: Include your children in age-appropriate financial tasks. Let them accompany you to the bank, involve them in grocery shopping and budget planning, and assign them small financial responsibilities. This hands-on experience allows them to learn practical money management skills and develop a sense of ownership over their financial decisions.

Be Mindful of Your Financial Language and Attitudes: Pay attention to your language when discussing money and avoid negative or anxious attitudes. Instead, foster a positive mindset by emphasizing the possibilities and opportunities that come with financial management. Avoid derogatory comments about others' financial situations and encourage empathy and understanding.

Emphasize the Value of Giving: Teach your children about giving back to others. Engage in philanthropic activities as a family and encourage them to donate some of their money or time to charitable causes. By modelling generosity and empathy, you cultivate their understanding of the positive impact they can have on the lives of others.

Continuously Educate Yourself: As a parent, commit to ongoing financial education and self-improvement. Stay informed about personal finance, investment strategies, and responsible money management. By continuously expanding your financial knowledge, you can better guide and mentor your children in their financial journey.

Remember, children are constantly observing and learning from their parent's actions. By modelling good financial behaviour, you equip them with valuable skills and attitudes to serve them well.

TEACHING KIDS ABOUT MONEY

Teaching kids about money is an essential responsibility for parents. By providing them with a solid foundation in financial literacy, you empower your children to make informed decisions and develop healthy money habits. Here are some key points to consider when teaching kids about money as a parent:

Start Early: Introduce the concept of money at an early age. Even pre-schoolers can learn basic money skills, such as recognizing coins and understanding their values. Use play money or create simple activities to teach them about counting, saving, and spending.

Make it Practical: Encourage hands-on learning experiences. Give your children a small allowance or provide opportunities to earn money through age-appropriate tasks or chores. This allows them to practice budgeting, saving, and making choices about their own money.

Teach the Value of Money: Help your children understand the value of money by discussing how it is earned through work or exchanged for goods and services. Explain that money represents time and effort and that making choices about how to spend it is essential.

Introduce Basic Money Concepts: Gradually introduce fundamental money concepts as your children grow. Teach them about budgeting, saving, and the differences between needs and wants. Help them understand the concept of delayed gratification and the benefits of saving for future goals.

Encourage Saving: Instil the habit of saving in your children. Teach them to set goals and allocate a portion of their money towards savings. Provide them with a piggy bank or a savings account where they can deposit their money regularly. Celebrate their milestones as they reach their savings targets.

Practice Responsible Spending: Teach your children to make wise spending decisions. Discuss the importance of comparing prices, looking for discounts, and distinguishing between essential and non-essential purchases. Encourage them to think critically before purchasing and prioritize long-term value over instant gratification.

Introduce Basic Banking: Introduce your children to the concept of banking. Take them to the bank and show them how money is deposited, withdrawn, and saved. Teach them about bank accounts, interest, and the benefits of saving in a secure financial institution.

Be Transparent About Family Finances: While maintaining appropriate boundaries, involve your children in discussions about family finances. Help them understand how money is allocated for household expenses, savings, and investments. This transparency helps them develop a realistic understanding of financial responsibilities and the importance of budgeting.

Teach the Pitfalls of Debt: Explain the concept of debt to your children and its potential consequences. Emphasize the importance of living within one's means and avoiding unnecessary debt. Teach them about the impact of interest rates and the long-term implications of poor financial choices.

Lead by Example: The most impactful way to teach kids about money is to lead by example. Be mindful of your financial habits and attitudes. Demonstrate responsible money management, such as budgeting, saving, and making thoughtful purchasing decisions. Show them that financial responsibility is a lifelong practice.

Remember, teaching kids about money is an ongoing process. Encourage questions, provide guidance, and be patient as they navigate their financial journey. Equipping them with strong financial literacy skills empowers them to make informed decisions and lays the groundwork for a secure financial future.

We are not repeating the teaching methods about money because we have already covered them. However, avoiding redundancy and providing new and valuable information to our audience is essential. Additionally, revisiting the same topics repeatedly can lead to disengagement and boredom. Therefore, we will focus on new financial education topics and provide our readers with fresh insights and perspectives.

DEVELOPING GOOD FINANCIAL HABITS

Developing good financial habits is crucial for both children and adults alike. As a parent, you play a significant role in shaping your child's financial behaviours and attitudes. Instilling positive money habits from an early age sets them up for a lifetime of financial success. Here are some key points to consider when it comes to developing good financial habits as a parent:

Lead by Example: Children learn by observing their parents, so it's important to model good financial habits yourself. Show them responsible money management practices, such as budgeting, saving, and avoiding unnecessary debt. Let them see you making thoughtful spending decisions and prioritizing long-term financial goals.

Teach the Value of Money: Help your child understand the value of money by discussing how it is earned through work or exchanged for goods and services. Explain that money is a limited resource and needs to be used wisely. Encourage them to appreciate the effort into earning money and the importance of making intentional choices.

Establish Clear Financial Rules: Set clear guidelines and expectations around money. Teach your child about saving, spending, and giving. For example, encourage them to save a portion of their allowance or earnings, allocate a certain amount for spending, and consider donating to charity. By establishing these rules, you create a framework for responsible financial behaviour.

Encourage Saving: Instil the habit of saving in your child. Help them set savings goals, such as purchasing a desired toy or saving for a future expense. Provide them with a piggy bank or a savings account where they can deposit their money regularly. Celebrate their milestones and achievements as they reach their saving targets.

Teach Delayed Gratification: Help your child understand the concept of delayed gratification. Encourage them to consider the long-term benefits of saving and making thoughtful spending choices. Teach them to prioritize their needs over impulsive wants and consider the value and utility of their desires.

Involve Them in Financial Decisions: Include your child in age-appropriate financial discussions and decisions. For instance, explain the thought process behind the choices when planning a family budget or making a significant purchase. This involvement helps them develop a sense of responsibility and understand the trade-offs in financial decision-making.

Reinforce the Importance of Budgeting: Introduce your child to budgeting. Teach them how to create a simple budget by allocating money for different purposes, such as saving, spending, and giving. Encourage them to track their expenses and review their budget regularly. This practice fosters financial awareness and accountability.

Teach the Pitfalls of Impulse Buying: Help your child recognize the dangers of impulsive buying. Discuss the consequences of impulsive purchases and the importance of thinking before spending. Teach them to differentiate between needs and wants and to make informed choices based on their priorities and financial goals.

Encourage Entrepreneurial Skills: Foster an entrepreneurial mindset in your child by encouraging them to explore money-making opportunities. Help them brainstorm small business ideas or ways to earn money through simple tasks or services. This cultivates their entrepreneurial spirit and teaches them the value of hard work and initiative.

Provide Financial Education Resources: Utilize various resources to enhance your child's financial knowledge. Look for age-appropriate books, games, and online platforms that teach financial literacy. These resources can supplement your efforts in teaching them about money management and reinforce the importance of developing good financial habits.

Remember, developing good financial habits is an ongoing process. Be patient and supportive as your child learns and grows in their understanding of money. By instilling these positive financial habits, you empower them to make sound financial decisions, build a strong foundation for their future, and confidently navigate the complexities of the financial world.

CREATING A FAMILY CULTURE OF FINANCIAL RESPONSIBILITY

A family culture of financial responsibility refers to shared values, beliefs, and behaviours related to money management. It involves instilling positive financial habits, attitudes, and behaviours that promote responsible spending, saving, and investing. This culture can be established through open communication about money matters, setting financial goals as a family, involving children in financial decision-making, and modelling good financial practices.

When a family creates a culture of financial responsibility, it fosters an environment that values financial planning, education, and discipline. It also helps to reduce financial stress and conflict, as everyone in the family is on the same page regarding money matters. By working together towards shared financial goals, families can strengthen their bonds, improve their financial well-being, and create a legacy of financial responsibility for future generations.

HERE ARE SOME KEY POINTS TO CONSIDER WHEN IT COMES TO CREATING A FAMILY CULTURE OF FINANCIAL RESPONSIBILITY

Openly Discuss Finances: Start by having open and age-appropriate discussions about finances within the family. Share the importance of financial responsibility and how it impacts the family's well-being. Encourage your children to ask questions, express their thoughts, and actively participate in conversations about money matters.

Set Financial Goals as a Family: Engage your family in setting financial goals together. This could include saving for a family vacation, funding a college education, or achieving a specific financial milestone. Involving everyone in the goal-setting process fosters a sense of shared responsibility and encourages collaboration toward achieving those goals.

Create a Budget: Work together as a family to create a budget that reflects your financial priorities. Explain the concept of budgeting, income, and expenses to your children. Involve them in allocating funds for different categories such as groceries, bills, savings, and entertainment. This exercise helps them understand the value of money and the importance of making informed spending decisions.

Encourage Savings and Smart Spending: Teach your children the significance of saving money. Help them establish a savings plan, whether for short-term goals like purchasing a desired item or long-term goals like building an emergency fund. Encourage them to practice smart spending by comparing prices, looking for deals, and distinguishing between wants and needs.

Demonstrate Financial Responsibility: Lead by example and demonstrate financial responsibility in your own actions. Show your children how you make wise financial choices, track expenses, and save for the future. Avoid impulsive purchases or excessive debt, as these behaviours can undermine the message of financial responsibility you want to instil in your children.

Involve Children in Financial Decisions: Include your children in age-appropriate financial decisions. For instance, explain the reasoning behind your choices when planning a significant purchase or making financial trade-offs. Encourage them to contribute their thoughts and perspectives, fostering their financial decision-making skills and a sense of ownership.

Teach the Value of Work: Instil a strong work ethic in your children by assigning age-appropriate chores and tasks. Emphasize the relationship between work and money, teaching them that money is earned through effort and hard work. This helps them appreciate the value of money and encourages a responsible approach to earning and managing it.

Encourage Philanthropy: Introduce the concept of giving back to the community by engaging in philanthropic activities as a family. Encourage your children to donate a portion of their allowance or earnings to a cause they care about. This fosters a sense of empathy, gratitude, and social responsibility, alongside financial responsibility.

Provide Financial Education: Seek opportunities to enhance your children's financial knowledge. Utilize age-appropriate books, games, and online resources that teach financial literacy. Consider enrolling them in financial education programs or workshops designed for children. These resources complement your efforts in creating a family culture of financial responsibility.

Emphasize Long-Term Thinking: Teach your children the importance of long-term financial thinking. Help them understand concepts like saving for retirement or investing for the future. Encourage them to set long-term financial goals and develop strategies to achieve them. This mindset cultivates a sense of responsibility and planning for the future.

Creating a family culture of financial responsibility gives your children a solid foundation for managing their money wisely. Through open discussions, practical experiences, and leading by example, you empower them to develop good financial habits that will serve them throughout their lives. Remember, the lessons you impart as a parent today will shape their financial well-being for years.

DEVELOPING A SOLID FAMILY CULTURE OF FINANCIAL RESPONSIBILITY

Developing a solid family culture of financial responsibility is a valuable investment in your family's long-term financial well-being. Instilling good money habits and values from an early age sets the stage for future financial success.

Here are several ways in which a good family culture of financial responsibility can have long-term benefits

Financial Independence: A family culture emphasizing financial responsibility helps children develop the skills and mindset necessary to become financially independent adults. By teaching them about budgeting, saving, and smart spending, you equip them with the tools to manage their finances effectively. This fosters a sense of confidence and self-reliance when it comes to money matters.

Wealth Accumulation: Encouraging a culture of financial responsibility within your family can contribute to long-term wealth accumulation. By teaching your children the importance of saving, investing, and making wise financial decisions, you lay the groundwork for their future financial security. They will be better prepared to build wealth, make informed investment choices, and take advantage of opportunities for financial growth.

Debt Management: Financial responsibility includes teaching children about debt's potential risks and consequences. Educating them on responsible borrowing, the importance of credit scores, and the impact of interest rates empowers them to make informed decisions regarding debt management. This knowledge helps them avoid excessive debt and navigate financial challenges with confidence.

Financial Resilience: A family culture that promotes financial responsibility cultivates resilience in financial hardships. Children who have been taught about saving for emergencies and planning for the unexpected are better prepared to handle financial setbacks. They understand the importance of building an emergency fund and having a financial safety net, which can provide a sense of security and peace of mind during challenging times.

Generational Wealth: By instilling good financial habits and values in your children, you set the stage for generational wealth. A family culture of financial responsibility creates a positive wealth creation and preservation cycle. The knowledge and skills passed down from generation to generation empower future family members to continue building wealth, making wise financial decisions, and securing a solid financial future.

Improved Financial Decision-Making: A family culture that values financial responsibility helps children develop critical thinking and decision-making skills. They learn to evaluate financial options, weigh the pros and cons, and make informed choices based on their goals and values. These skills translate into better financial decision-making throughout their lives, leading to more favourable outcomes and increased financial stability.

Reduced Financial Stress: Financial responsibility within the family can significantly reduce financial stress. Children raised in an environment where money is managed responsibly and transparently are less likely to experience financial anxiety than adults. They are equipped with the skills to budget effectively, save for their goals, and avoid excessive debt, promoting a sense of financial security and well-being.

Positive Money Mindset: A family culture that promotes financial responsibility helps shape a positive money mindset in children. They develop a healthy relationship with money, understanding that it is a tool to achieve their goals and create opportunities rather than a source of stress or anxiety. This positive mindset influences their attitudes towards saving, investing, and wealth creation, setting them up for long-term financial success.

In conclusion, a good family culture of financial responsibility provides numerous long-term benefits. It empowers children to become financially independent, accumulate wealth, manage debt effectively, and navigate financial challenges with resilience. It sets the stage for generational wealth and improves financial decision-making skills. Moreover, it reduces financial stress and fosters a positive money mindset. By prioritizing financial responsibility within your family, you lay the foundation for a prosperous financial future for yourself and future generations.

CREATING A FAMILY LEGACY FOR MULTI-GENERATIONAL WEALTH BUILDING

Creating a family legacy for multi-generational wealth building involves strategic planning, financial education, and a shared commitment to long-term financial success. Families can set the stage for future generations to thrive financially by laying a solid foundation and instilling the correct values.

Building a family legacy for multi-generational wealth building is about more than just accumulating wealth—it's about ensuring that future generations have the knowledge, resources, and opportunities to continue growing and preserving that wealth. It requires proactive planning, open communication, and a focus on values beyond monetary gains. A strong family legacy not only leaves a financial inheritance but also imparts valuable lessons and a sense of responsibility toward managing and growing wealth for the benefit of future family members.

Creating a Shared Vision: The first step in building a family legacy is establishing a shared vision for multi-generational wealth building. It involves gathering family members, engaging in open discussions, and identifying the values and goals guiding the family's financial decisions. This shared vision is a compass, providing all family members with a sense of direction and purpose.

Financial Education and Mentorship: To ensure the success of future generations, financial education, and mentorship play a crucial role. By equipping family members with the knowledge and skills to make informed financial decisions, families empower them to navigate the complexities of wealth management. This can include educating younger family members on basic financial concepts, investment strategies, risk management, and the importance of diversification. Additionally, mentorship from experienced family members or financial advisors can provide guidance and support in making sound financial choices.

Establishing Structures and Governance: Families often establish structures and governance mechanisms to sustain multi-generational wealth building. These may include family offices, trusts, or holding companies that provide a framework for managing and preserving wealth. These structures offer tax advantages and asset protection and ensure that family values and long-term goals are upheld across generations. Clear governance policies, including decision-making processes, conflict resolution mechanisms, and succession plans, help maintain unity and continuity within the family's financial affairs.

Passing Down Values and Principles: Building a family legacy for multi-generational wealth goes beyond financial strategies —it involves passing down values and principles that promote responsible and ethical wealth management. Families can develop frameworks that emphasize the importance of philanthropy, social responsibility, and sustainable investing. By instilling a sense of stewardship and giving back to society, families can shape future generations to use their wealth for the betterment of both their own lives and the world around them.

Encouraging Entrepreneurship and Innovation: To foster wealth creation across generations, families can nurture an entrepreneurial spirit and encourage innovation. This may involve supporting family members' business ventures, providing seed funding for new ideas, or fostering an environment that promotes creativity and risk-taking. By nurturing entrepreneurship, families can empower future generations to generate wealth and create legacies.

Continual Communication and Adaptation: Building a family legacy for multi-generational wealth requires ongoing communication and adaptability. As family dynamics and economic landscapes change, regular family meetings, discussions, and reviews of financial strategies are essential.

Open and transparent communication helps address concerns, align goals, and adjust the family's wealth-building plans.

Building a family legacy for multi-generational wealth building is a journey that requires long-term commitment, collaboration, and shared values. Families can create a lasting legacy that extends far beyond monetary assets by focusing on financial wealth and imparting financial education, passing down values, and fostering entrepreneurship. By building a solid foundation and nurturing the next generations, families can ensure the preservation and growth of wealth while positively impacting their family and community.

BUILDING A FAMILY LEGACY THROUGH AN EXCELLENT FINANCIAL CULTURE

Another example of building a family legacy through an excellent financial culture is establishing a tradition of philanthropy or charitable giving within the family. We can achieve this by setting aside a portion of the family's income or assets to be donated to charitable causes that align with the family's values and priorities.

Examples of a Tradition of Money Philanthropy in Family for Generations:

Annual Giving Circle: Create an annual family giving circle where each member contributes a set amount. Together, the family researches and selects charitable organizations to support. Each year, a different family member presents their chosen cause and advocates for its support.

Charitable Matching Program: Establish a family charitable matching program where the family matches the charitable donations made by individual family members. This encourages and amplifies their contributions, creating a sense of unity and shared impact.

Philanthropic Birthday Celebrations: Instead of traditional birthday gifts, encourage family members to request donations to a chosen charity. Each family member selects a meaningful cause, and donations are made in their name as a birthday gift. This practice instils the importance of giving back during celebratory occasions.

Legacy Grants: Create a family legacy fund or endowment that provides grants to charitable organizations. Each generation is responsible for managing and distributing a portion of the fund, ensuring a continued impact in the areas of interest to the family.

Community Service Projects: Engage in regular community service projects where the family contributes their time and skills to local organizations or causes. This hands-on approach allows family members to see the impact of their efforts directly and fosters a sense of responsibility towards their community.

Scholarship Programs: Establish a family scholarship program that provides financial assistance to deserving students. The scholarship can be awarded based on specific criteria, such as academic achievement, community involvement, or financial need. This program helps create opportunities for educational advancement and empowers future generations.

Impact Investing: Explore impact investing as a family, where financial resources are invested in businesses or ventures that generate both financial returns and positive social or environmental outcomes. The family can make a difference through their financial decisions by aligning investments with their philanthropic values.

Multi-Generational Volunteering: Encourage multi-generational volunteering by participating together in volunteer activities. This can include serving meals at a local shelter, participating in environmental clean-up initiatives, or assisting in community development projects. Volunteering as a family reinforces the value of giving back and strengthens family bonds.

Donor-Advised Funds: Establish a family donor-advised fund that allows family members to contribute to a pooled fund. Together, the family can research and recommend grants to be distributed to various charitable causes. This collaborative approach ensures the family's philanthropic efforts are aligned and impactful.

Philanthropic Education: Organize regular family discussions or workshops on philanthropy and financial literacy. Involve guest speakers or experts in the field to educate family members about effective giving strategies, understand social issues, and evaluate charitable organizations' impact.

By establishing a tradition of philanthropy, the family can pass down a legacy of generosity and social responsibility to future generations. The family members can develop a deep sense of purpose and pride in their giving, and the impact of their contributions can be felt for years to come. This can be a powerful way to create a lasting family legacy beyond financial wealth and material possessions.

PREPARING KIDS FOR ADULTHOOD

Giving Them the Tools to Succeed Financially

By failing to prepare, you are preparing to fail.

Benjamin Franklin

s children grow older and become more independent, teaching them about financial responsibility becomes increasingly important. By teaching kids about money management and financial planning, parents can help their children to develop the skills they need to succeed financially as adults. This chapter will explore some of the most important financial skills parents can teach their children, from budgeting and saving to investing and credit management.

Budgeting and Saving: Teaching kids about budgeting and saving is essential to preparing them for adulthood. This section will explore strategies for helping kids develop good budgeting habits and cultivate a healthy savings mindset. We will cover topics such as setting financial goals, creating a budget, tracking expenses, and establishing a savings plan.

Investing for the Future: Investing is essential to building long-term financial stability. However, it is always early enough to start teaching kids about the basics of investing. This section will explore some simple strategies for introducing kids to investing, from opening a savings account or investing in a mutual fund to learning about stocks, bonds, and other investment vehicles.

Credit Management: Understanding how to manage credit is essential for financial success. This section will explore some strategies for teaching kids about credit management, from understanding credit scores and reports to building good credit habits and avoiding debt traps.

Real-World Financial Situations: As kids grow older, they will inevitably encounter a range of financial situations in the real world, from managing expenses in college to buying a car or a home. In this section, we will explore some practical strategies for preparing kids to navigate these situations confidently, including financing college, buying a car, and saving for a down payment on a home.

Parental Responsibility: Finally, this section will explore parents' vital role in teaching their children financial responsibility. From modelling good financial habits to setting clear expectations and providing ongoing guidance and support, parents can play a critical role in helping their children succeed financially as they prepare for adulthood.

By teaching kids about budgeting, saving, investing, credit management, and real-world financial situations, parents can help their children to develop the skills they need to succeed financially as adults. With the proper guidance and support, kids can learn to be financially responsible and to make intelligent financial decisions that will set them on the path to long-term financial stability and success.

BUDGETING AND SAVING: BUILDING A STRONG FINANCIAL FOUNDATION

Budgeting and saving are two fundamental pillars of financial success. They provide individuals and families with the tools and mindset to manage their money effectively, achieve their financial goals, and secure their future. By developing strong budgeting and saving habits, individuals can gain control over their finances, reduce financial stress, and pave the way for long-term financial stability. This write-up explores the importance of budgeting and saving and guides how to establish and maintain these essential financial practices.

THE IMPORTANCE OF BUDGETING

Budgeting is creating a plan for how you will allocate your income and expenses. It involves tracking your income, identifying expenses, and ensuring that your spending aligns with your financial goals. Here are some key reasons why budgeting is crucial:

Financial Awareness: Budgeting allows you to understand

your financial situation clearly. It helps you track where your money is going, identify areas of overspending, and make informed decisions about your finances.

Goal Setting: Budgeting enables you to set specific financial goals and allocate your resources accordingly. Whether saving for a down payment on a house, paying off debt, or planning for retirement, a budget helps you prioritize and work towards achieving your goals.

Debt Management: A budget serves as a powerful tool for managing debt. By allocating funds towards debt repayment and avoiding unnecessary expenses, you can accelerate your debt payoff and reduce financial stress.

Emergency Preparedness: Budgeting allows you to build an emergency fund, which acts as a safety net during unexpected financial challenges. Having savings set aside for emergencies provides peace of mind and helps you avoid debt when faced with unforeseen circumstances.

THE BENEFITS OF SAVING

Saving is setting aside a portion of your income for future use. It is a vital component of financial well-being and offers numerous benefits:

Financial Security: Saving provides a safety net during times of financial hardship. It helps you weather unexpected expenses, job loss, or medical emergencies without resorting to high-interest debt.

Goal Achievement: Saving enables you to work towards your long-term financial goals. Whether it's purchasing a home, funding your children's education, or retiring comfortably, saving allows you to accumulate the necessary funds over time.

Compound Interest: You can use compound interest by saving and investing early. Compound interest allows your savings to grow exponentially over time, amplifying the returns on your investments.

Freedom and Flexibility: Saving gives you the freedom and flexibility to make choices that align with your values and aspirations. It gives you the financial independence to pursue opportunities, take calculated risks, and enjoy life on your terms.

TIPS FOR EFFECTIVE BUDGETING AND SAVING

To establish and maintain effective budgeting and saving habits, consider the following tips:

Track your expenses: Keep a record of your income and expenses to clearly understand your spending patterns and identify areas where you can cut back.

Set realistic goals: Define your short-term and long-term financial goals and break them into achievable milestones. This will help you stay motivated and focused on your savings targets.

Create a budget: Develop one that aligns with your goals and priorities. Allocate your income towards essential expenses, savings, debt repayment, and discretionary spending.

Automate your savings: Set up automatic transfers from your checking account to your savings account. This way, you can save consistently without the temptation to spend the money elsewhere.

Prioritize saving: Treat saving as a non-negotiable expense. Aim to save a percentage of your income before allocating funds to other discretionary expenses.

Cut unnecessary expenses: Review your budget regularly and identify areas where you can reduce or eliminate expenses. Be mindful of impulse purchases and find ways to save on everyday expenses.

Seek professional advice: If you need assistance with budgeting and saving, consider consulting with a financial advisor. They can provide personalized guidance and help you create a tailored financial plan.

Budgeting and saving are vital components of financial success and security. By creating a budget, tracking your expenses, and prioritizing saving, you can take control of your finances, achieve your goals, and build a solid financial foundation. The discipline and habits developed through budgeting and saving will serve you well throughout your life, providing the financial stability and freedom to pursue your dreams and enjoy a more secure future.

STRATEGIES TO HELP KIDS DEVELOP GOOD BUDGETING HABITS

Developing good budgeting habits is a valuable skill that can set children on the path to financial success and responsible money management. Parents can empower kids to make informed financial decisions, set financial goals, and develop healthy spending and saving habits by teaching kids about budgeting early. This write-up presents practical strategies to help kids develop good budgeting habits, laying the foundation for a lifetime of financial well-being.

Start with the Basics: Introduce the concept of budgeting to children by explaining that it involves planning and managing money. Teach them the difference between needs and wants and encourage them to prioritize spending based on their values and goals. Use real-life examples to help them understand budgeting, such as allocating a portion of their allowance for different purposes like saving, spending, and giving.

Set Clear Financial Goals: Help children set clear financial goals that align with their interests and aspirations. Whether it's saving for a new toy, a special outing, or a long-term goal like funding their education, encourage them to articulate their goals and create a plan to achieve them. Break down larger goals into smaller, achievable milestones to keep them motivated and engaged.

Teach the Three Jars Method: The three jars method is

a simple and effective way to teach kids about budgeting. Provide three jars labelled "Save," "Spend," and "Give." Whenever children receive money, guide them to divide it into these jars based on their goals. This helps them understand the importance of saving for the future, spending wisely, and giving back to others.

Involve Kids in Family Budgeting: Invite children to participate in family budgeting discussions and decision-making. Explain the concept of income and expenses, involve them in setting a family budget, and discuss how money is allocated for various needs and wants. This involvement helps kids develop a sense of ownership and responsibility toward financial decisions.

Encourage Tracking and Record-Keeping: Teach children the importance of tracking their income and expenses. Provide them with a simple notebook or budgeting app where they can record their earnings and expenses. Regularly review these records together, discussing patterns, identifying areas for improvement, and celebrating their progress.

Foster Delayed Gratification: Help children understand the concept of delayed gratification, emphasizing the value of saving for something they truly desire. Encourage them to wait and save up for larger purchases rather than impulsively spending their money. This cultivates patience, discipline, and a stronger appreciation for what they acquire.

Provide Opportunities for Earning: Encourage children to earn money through age-appropriate tasks or chores. This helps them develop a strong work ethic, understand the relationship between effort and income, and instil a sense of responsibility toward managing their earnings.

Lead by Example: As a parent, be a positive role model by demonstrating responsible budgeting habits. Show children how you create and stick to a budget, save for goals, and make thoughtful spending choices. Involve them in discussions about household expenses and financial decisions, giving them a first-hand understanding of financial responsibility.

Teach Wise Spending: Encourage children to compare prices, seek discounts, and consider value for money when purchasing. Teach them to differentiate between needs and wants, prioritize essential expenses, and make informed spending choices that align with their budget and values.

Celebrate Financial Milestones: Recognize and celebrate financial milestones achieved by your children, such as reaching a savings goal or successfully budgeting for a specific expense. Reward their efforts and reinforce positive budgeting habits to motivate them to continue their financial journey.

By implementing these strategies, parents can help their children develop good budgeting habits early. Teaching kids about budgeting empowers them to make wise financial decisions, set and achieve goals, and build a strong foundation for their future financial well-being. With consistent guidance, support, and hands-on experience, children can cultivate lifelong budgeting skills to serve them well.

STRATEGIES FOR HELPING KIDS CULTIVATE A HEALTHY SAVINGS MINDSET

Instilling a healthy savings mindset in children is crucial for their long-term financial well-being. Parents can help kids develop responsible financial habits and build a strong foundation for their future by teaching kids the value of saving money early. This write-up presents practical strategies for helping kids cultivate a healthy savings mindset, fostering a lifelong habit of saving and financial security.

Start Early: Introduce the concept of savings to children at a young age. Teach them the importance of setting aside a portion of their money for the future and encourage them to save even small amounts regularly. Emphasize the idea that saving is not only about accumulating wealth but also about having a financial safety net and being prepared for future needs.

Set Savings Goals: Help children set tangible savings goals that are meaningful to them. Whether it's saving for a specific toy, a special outing, or a long-term goal like college or a dream vacation, encourage them to articulate their goals and create a plan to achieve them. Break down larger goals into smaller milestones to make the process more manageable and rewarding.

Use Savings Jars or Piggy Banks: Introduce physical savings jars or piggy banks as a visual and tactile way for children to save money. Label each jar with a specific savings goal, such as "Toy," "Charity," or "Future." Encourage them to deposit money regularly into these containers and watch their savings grow. This hands-on approach helps children understand the tangible impact of saving and reinforces the habit.

Teach Delayed Gratification: Help children understand the concept of delayed gratification and its connection to saving. Encourage them to resist impulsive spending and wait for something they genuinely want. Teach them that the satisfaction of achieving a savings goal and being able to purchase something they've worked for is far more rewarding than instant but fleeting gratification.

Match Savings Contributions: Consider implementing a savings matching program where you match a portion of your child's savings. For example, you contribute a certain percentage for every dollar they save. This boosts their savings, teaches them the value of external rewards, and motivates them to save even more diligently.

Encourage Saving through Earning: Link saving to earning opportunities for children. Encourage them to earn money through tasks or chores and incentivize them to save some of their earnings. This helps them understand the connection between effort, income, and saving. It also instils a sense of responsibility and ownership over their savings.

Teach the Power of Compound Interest: Introduce the concept of compound interest to older children. Explain how saving money earns interest over time; the longer they save, the more their money can grow. Illustrate this concept using simple examples or online tools designed for kids. This knowledge motivates them to save early and continue doing so consistently.

Make Saving Fun: Engage children in fun activities that promote saving. Create savings challenges, games, or competitions within the family or among friends. Reward their savings milestones with small incentives or special privileges. By associating saving with positive experiences, children are more likely to develop a positive attitude towards saving and view it as enjoyable.

Celebrate Savings Milestones: Celebrate and acknowledge your child's savings milestones. Recognize their achievements, whether reaching a certain dollar amount, saving for a specific goal, or consistently saving for a certain period. This boosts their confidence, reinforces the importance of saving, and encourages them to continue their savings journey.

Lead by Example: As a parent, be a role model for saving. Demonstrate responsible saving habits and openly discuss your saving goals and strategies with your child. Involve them in family discussions about budgeting and saving decisions, making them feel part of the financial decision-making process. Your actions and attitudes towards saving will significantly influence your behaviour.

By implementing these strategies, parents can help children cultivate a healthy savings mindset to set them up for a lifetime of financial security. Teaching children the value of saving, setting goals, delayed gratification, and the power of compound interest empowers them to make wise financial choices and develop a habit of saving that will benefit them throughout their lives. With consistent guidance and support, parents can shape their children's financial future and foster a strong foundation of financial well-being.

TOOLS AVAILABLE TO HELP WITH
BUDGETING AND SAVING FOR KIDS

In today's digital age, numerous tools and resources are available to assist parents in teaching their children about budgeting and saving. These tools make learning more interactive and engaging and provide practical tools for managing money. This write-up explores popular tools explicitly designed for kids to help them develop good financial habits and foster a sense of responsibility toward budgeting and saving.

Mobile Apps: Several mobile apps tailored for kids provide a user-friendly interface to track their expenses, set savings goals, and manage their money. These apps often incorporate gamification elements, making budgeting and saving a fun and interactive experience. Some popular options include:

> **Rooster Money:** This app allows kids to track their allowances, set savings goals, and learn about money management through various features like "Savings Goals" and "Allowance Manager."

> **Greenlight:** Greenlight is a comprehensive app that combines budgeting tools with a prepaid debit card for kids. Parents can set up chore lists, allocate funds, and monitor their child's spending habits.

Online Savings Platforms: Many banks and financial institutions offer online savings platforms specifically designed for kids. These platforms often have attractive features such as goal setting, visual progress trackers, and educational resources. Kids can deposit money, set savings goals, and watch their savings grow. Examples include:

> **Capital One Kids Savings Account:** This account includes an interactive savings tool that helps kids visualize their savings goals and track their progress. It also provides educational materials to enhance financial literacy.

> **FamZoo:** FamZoo is an online family banking system that allows parents to create virtual accounts for their kids. It offers features like budgeting, goal-setting, and

tracking spending habits.

Virtual Allowance Tools: Virtual allowance tools enable parents to digitize their child's allowance and provide a convenient way to allocate funds while teaching money management skills. These tools often include features like automated allowance transfers, spending limits, and savings options. Examples include:

> **BusyKid:** BusyKid is an online chore and allowance platform that helps parents assign chores and automate allowances. It also incorporates educational resources to teach financial responsibility.

> **ChoreCheck:** ChoreCheck is a chore and allowance management tool that enables parents to assign tasks, set automatic payments, and teach kids the value of earning money through their efforts.

Interactive Websites: Various websites offer interactive games, quizzes, and educational resources to teach kids about budgeting and saving. These platforms combine entertainment with learning, making financial education engaging and enjoyable. Examples include:

> **MoneyConfidentKids.com:** Developed by T. Rowe Price, this website offers interactive games, videos, and quizzes to educate kids about money concepts, budgeting, and goal setting.

> **PracticalMoneySkills.com:** Practical Money Skills is an educational website that offers free resources, games, and tools to teach kids about budgeting, saving, and responsible money management.

Traditional Methods: While digital tools are valuable, traditional methods like physical piggy banks, saving jars, and paper-based budgeting worksheets are still effective in teaching kids about budgeting and saving. These methods provide tangible and hands-on experiences that help children visualize their money and understand the basic concepts of budgeting and saving.

> **Piggy Banks:** Piggy banks have long been a

symbol of saving money. They provide a physical representation of saving and allow kids to see their money accumulate over time. Parents can encourage their children to save some of their allowances or earnings by depositing coins and bills into their piggy banks regularly. This hands-on approach helps kids understand the value of saving and delayed gratification.

Saving Jars or Envelopes: Similar to piggy banks, saving jars or envelopes can allocate money for different purposes. Parents can label jars or envelopes with categories such as "Savings," "Spending," and "Donations." Kids can distribute their money accordingly, emphasizing the importance of setting aside funds for specific goals, spending responsibly, and giving back to others. This method teaches children the principles of budgeting and prioritizing financial resources.

Budgeting Worksheets: Using paper-based budgeting worksheets is an effective way to introduce kids to budgeting. Parents can create simple budgeting templates that outline income sources, expenses, and savings goals. Children can then fill in the amounts and track their financial activities manually. This method helps kids understand the flow of money, identify areas where they can save or reduce expenses, and set realistic goals for their savings.

Allowance Management: Assigning an allowance to children allows them to practice budgeting and saving. Parents can establish guidelines on how the allowance should be allocated—for example, a particular portion for saving, a portion for spending, and potentially even a portion for charitable giving. Giving kids control over their money within set parameters teaches them to make choices and prioritize their financial resources.

Family Financial Discussions: Regular family discussions about finances can create a learning environment for kids. Parents can involve their children in discussions about budgeting, saving for family goals, and making financial decisions. This allows kids to observe and participate in real-life scenarios, providing practical lessons on money management and saving for future needs.

Role-Playing Games: Engage children in role-playing games where they can take on different financial roles. For example, parents can set up a pretend store at home, allowing children to act as shopkeepers and customers. This activity helps them understand the exchange of money, the value of goods and services, and the importance of budgeting within a simulated setting.

It's important to note that traditional methods can be combined with digital tools and resources to create a comprehensive approach to teaching kids about budgeting and saving. Traditional methods' tactile experience and visual representation complement digital tools' convenience and interactive nature, enhancing the learning process.

Parents can instil essential financial skills, values, and behaviours in their children by incorporating these traditional methods into their financial education efforts. The hands-on experiences, discussions, and practical exercises create a solid foundation for building strong financial habits and responsible money management skills that can last a lifetime.

The availability of tools and resources for teaching kids about budgeting and saving has dramatically expanded in recent years. Whether through mobile apps, online platforms, interactive websites, or traditional methods, parents can leverage these tools to make financial education more engaging and accessible for their children. By incorporating these tools into their financial lessons, parents can empower their kids to develop good financial habits, cultivate responsible money management skills, and lay a strong foundation for a financially secure future.

INVESTING FOR THE FUTURE: BUILDING WEALTH AND FINANCIAL SECURITY

Investing is a crucial aspect of personal finance that plays a significant role in building wealth and securing a financially stable future. While investing may seem complex or reserved for adults, introducing the concept to children early on can have profound long-term benefits. Teaching kids about investing helps them develop a mindset focused on long-term financial goals, making informed decisions, and understanding the potential for growing their money over time.

Investing is a powerful tool that empowers individuals to grow their money over time. By setting aside funds and strategically allocating them to various investment vehicles, individuals can increase their wealth, create financial security, and achieve their long-term goals. While investing may initially seem like a concept for adults, introducing children to the basics of investing can pave the way for a lifetime of financial success. Parents can equip their children with essential knowledge and skills to make sound financial decisions and take advantage of future wealth accumulation opportunities by instilling a solid understanding of investing early on.

BENEFITS OF INVESTING FOR THE FUTURE

Wealth Accumulation: Investing allows individuals to participate in the growth of various assets such as stocks, bonds, real estate, and mutual funds. Over time, these investments have the potential to generate returns that outpace inflation and increase one's overall net worth.

Financial Security: By investing for the future, individuals can build a financial safety net that provides stability and security during unexpected events or retirement. Investments can generate income, appreciate value, and provide a cushion in financial need.

Compound Growth: Compound growth is one of the most powerful concepts in investing. By reinvesting earnings and allowing investments to grow over extended periods, individuals can benefit from compounding returns, where their money works for them and generates additional income. Investing early allows for more significant time for compounding to work its magic.

Long-Term Goals: Investing helps individuals work towards their long-term financial goals, such as buying a home, funding education, starting a business, or retiring comfortably. It provides a means to accumulate the necessary funds over time, making those goals more achievable.

Financial Independence: Building a well-diversified investment portfolio can generate passive income, reducing dependence on a traditional 9-to-5 job. This financial independence offers individuals more flexibility and freedom to pursue their passions and live on their terms.

TEACHING KIDS ABOUT INVESTING

Start with the Basics: Introduce children to the fundamental concepts of investing, such as the importance of saving, setting financial goals, and understanding risk and reward. Explain how investments can grow over time and provide examples of successful investments.

Encourage Long-Term Thinking: Help children develop a long-term mindset when it comes to investing. Emphasize the importance of patience, consistency, and staying invested even during market fluctuations. Teach them that investing is a marathon, not a sprint.

Make It Tangible: Use real-life examples and relatable scenarios to explain investing concepts. For instance, discuss how purchasing shares of a company is like owning a piece of that company. Show them how their investments can grow by tracking and sharing investment progress.

Use Investment Simulators: Online investment simulators and games can provide an interactive and engaging way for children to learn about investing. These platforms allow them to practice making investment decisions risk-free, gaining hands-on experience and knowledge.

Demonstrate the Power of Compound Growth: Teach children about compound interest and how reinvesting earnings can lead to exponential growth. Illustrate how even small, consistent contributions can make a significant difference in the long run.

Investing for the future is essential to building wealth and ensuring financial security. By introducing children to investing and equipping them with the necessary knowledge and skills, parents can empower them to make sound financial decisions, set long-term goals, and take advantage of the potential for financial growth. Teaching kids about investing early on lays a foundation for a lifetime of financial success, independence, and creating a better future. By embracing the power of investing, children can develop a robust financial mindset and position themselves for a prosperous and secure future.

STRATEGIES FOR INTRODUCING KIDS TO INVESTING: BUILDING A STRONG FINANCIAL FOUNDATION

Introducing children to investing at a young age can lead them toward financial literacy and long-term wealth creation. By teaching kids about investing, parents can equip them with essential knowledge and skills to make informed financial decisions and understand the potential benefits of growing their money over time.

Here are some effective strategies for introducing kids to investing:

Start with the Basics: Begin by explaining investing in simple terms that children can grasp. Teach them that investing means putting money into something with the expectation of earning a return. Emphasize that investing is a way to make their money grow over time.

Teach the Value of Saving: Help kids understand the importance of saving before investing. Explain how saving money allows them to accumulate funds that can be used for various purposes, including investing. Encourage them to set savings goals and track their progress.

Introduce Different Investment Options: Teach children about investment vehicles, such as stocks, bonds, mutual funds, and savings accounts. Explain the essential characteristics and potential risks and rewards associated with each option. Use age-appropriate examples and analogies to make the concepts more relatable.

Invest Together: Encourage children to invest alongside you to deepen their understanding and involvement in the investment process. Consider setting aside a portion of their savings or allowance for joint investments. Involve them in decision-making by discussing investment options and analysing potential risks and rewards together. By investing together, children can gain hands-on experience, witness the outcomes of investment decisions, and develop a sense of ownership and responsibility.

Explore Real-Life Examples: Bring investing to life by discussing real-life examples of successful investments. Share stories of companies that have grown over time and their impact on their investors. Help children understand that investing in quality companies or assets can lead to potential returns and wealth accumulation.

Use Stock Market Simulators: Engage children in virtual stock market simulators or investment games designed for kids. These platforms allow them to experience the thrill of investing in a safe and controlled environment. They can learn how to research companies, make investment decisions, and track their portfolio's performance.

Invest in Familiar Brands: Encourage children to invest in companies they are familiar with, such as brands they use or products they enjoy. This familiarity can help spark their interest and make the investment process more relatable. However, emphasize the importance of diversification and not putting all their eggs in one basket.

Set Up an Investment Account: Consider opening a custodial investment account for your child. This can be a joint account where you and your child can contribute funds. Involve them in setting up the account, monitoring investments, and tracking progress.

Practice Patience and Long-Term Thinking: Teach children the value of patience and long-term thinking when investing. Emphasize that investing is not a get-rich-quick scheme but a long-term wealth-building strategy. Help them understand that investing requires discipline, resilience, and a focus on long-term goals.

Reinforce the Importance of Research: Teach children the significance of researching before making investment decisions. Help them understand the importance of evaluating companies, considering financial performance, and assessing market trends. Encourage critical thinking and decision-making skills.

Celebrate Milestones: When your child achieves investment milestones or reaches financial goals, celebrate their accomplishments. This positive reinforcement can reinforce their interest in investing and motivate them to continue learning and growing their financial knowledge.

Teach Risk Management: Help children understand that investing involves risks and that managing those risks is essential. Teach them the concept of diversification, which involves spreading investments across different asset classes to reduce the impact of any single investment's performance. Explain how diversification can help mitigate the risks associated with investing. Encourage them to consider their risk tolerance and long-term goals when making investment decisions. Teach them the importance of regular portfolio monitoring, adjusting investments when necessary, and seeking professional advice when needed.

Introducing kids to investing is a valuable opportunity to teach them about financial literacy and help them develop the skills needed for long-term financial success. By implementing these strategies, parents can lay the foundation for a lifetime of intelligent financial decision-making, wealth accumulation, and a proactive approach to managing their finances. Remember to adapt the strategies to suit your child's age and comprehension level, ensuring a gradual progression toward more complex investment concepts as they grow.

CREDIT MANAGEMENT

Credit management is an essential aspect of personal finance that involves effectively managing and using credit to meet financial goals while maintaining a healthy credit profile. It's crucial to teach children about credit management early on so they can develop responsible habits and make informed decisions about borrowing and using credit.

Here are some key points to cover when teaching kids about credit management:

Understanding Credit: Start by explaining what credit is and how it works. Help children understand that credit allows people to borrow money with the promise to repay it in the future, usually with interest. Discuss different types of credit, such as credit cards, loans, and mortgages, and how they can finance various needs and goals.

Responsible Borrowing: Emphasize the importance of responsible borrowing. Teach children that borrowing should only be done when necessary and within their means. Discuss the concept of interest rates and how they affect the total amount repaid over time. Encourage them to consider the long-term implications of borrowing and to make informed decisions based on their financial capabilities.

Building and Maintaining Good Credit: Teach children about building and maintaining a good credit history. Explain how responsible borrowing and timely repayments contribute to a positive credit score. Discuss the potential benefits of having a good credit score, such as more accessible access to loans, better interest rates, and favourable financial opportunities.

Credit Card Usage: If appropriate, introduce the topic of credit cards. Discuss how credit cards work, including paying off the balance in full each month to avoid interest charges. Explain how credit card statements work, the consequences of late payments, and the potential pitfalls of overspending and accumulating credit card debt.

Managing Debt: Teach children the importance of managing debt responsibly. Discuss strategies for repaying debt, such as creating a repayment plan, prioritizing high-interest debts, and avoiding excessive borrowing. Encourage them to seek help and advice if they struggle with debt.

Identity Theft and Fraud Awareness: Educate children about the risks of identity theft and fraud related to credit. Teach them the importance of safeguarding personal information, being cautious with online transactions, and regularly monitoring credit reports for suspicious activity.

By providing children with a solid understanding of credit management, you equip them with essential knowledge and skills to make informed financial decisions, avoid unnecessary debt, and build a strong foundation for their financial future.

STRATEGIES FOR TEACHING KIDS ABOUT CREDIT MANAGEMENT

Start with the Basics: Explain the concept of credit and its importance in everyday life. Help children understand that credit is borrowed money that needs to be repaid, usually with interest. Use relatable examples to illustrate how credit is used for purchases and how it affects one's financial well-being.

Introduce Needs vs. Wants: Teach children the difference between needs and wants regarding spending. Help them understand that using credit for needs, such as essential items or emergencies, may be more justified than using it for wants or impulse purchases. Encourage them to prioritize needs and make responsible spending decisions.

Set Clear Financial Goals: Teach children the value of setting financial goals and how credit management plays a role in achieving them. Help them identify short-term and long-term goals, such as saving for a specific purchase or planning for higher education. Discuss how responsible credit use can help them reach their goals faster while emphasizing the importance of avoiding unnecessary debt.

Explore Credit Scenarios: Engage children in discussions or hypothetical scenarios involving credit. Present situations where credit may be necessary or tempting, such as buying a car or financing a vacation. Encourage them to think critically about the pros and cons of using credit in each scenario, considering factors like interest rates, repayment terms, and potential risks.

Emphasize Credit Responsibility: Instil the importance of responsible credit behaviour. Teach children the significance of making timely payments, avoiding excessive borrowing, and maintaining a good credit history. Explain how missed or late payments can negatively impact credit scores and limit future financial opportunities. Emphasize the consequences of poor credit management, such as high-interest rates, difficulty obtaining loans, or limited access to financial resources.

Use Real-Life Examples: Share real-life examples of credit management, such as explaining how a mortgage works or discussing the process of applying for a loan. Help children understand the responsibilities and obligations associated with credit and the potential consequences of mismanaging it.

Practice Budgeting and Saving: Incorporate budgeting and saving exercises into their financial education. Teach children the importance of budgeting their income and expenses and setting aside savings for emergencies or future goals. Show them how proper budgeting and saving can reduce the need for credit or make credit more manageable when necessary.

Role-Play and Simulations: Engage children in interactive activities that simulate real-world credit situations. Role-play scenarios where they must make credit-related decisions, such as applying for a credit card or taking out a loan. Encourage them to analyse the potential outcomes and consider the long-term impacts of their choices.

Encourage Questions and Discussions: Create an open and supportive environment where children feel comfortable asking questions about credit management. Foster discussions about credit-related topics and current financial events. Use age-appropriate resources, such as books, videos, or online educational materials, to enhance their understanding.

Lead by Example: Be a positive role model for responsible credit management. Let children observe how you handle credit and debt, demonstrating responsible borrowing, regular bill payments, and prudent financial decision-making. Discuss your experiences, successes, and challenges related to credit, highlighting the lessons learned.

By implementing these strategies, you can empower children to develop healthy credit management habits from an early age. Emphasizing the consequences of poor credit management helps them understand the potential risks and motivates them to make responsible financial choices.

HERE ARE SOME EXAMPLES OF GOOD CREDIT HABITS:

Paying Bills on Time: Teach children the importance of paying on time, such as credit card or utility bills. Emphasize the significance of meeting payment due dates to avoid late fees and negative impacts on their credit history.

Avoiding Excessive Debt: Teach children to use credit responsibly and avoid accumulating excessive debt. Encourage them to think critically before making purchases on credit and consider whether they can afford to repay the borrowed amount in a timely manner.

Monitoring Credit Activity: Teach children about credit reports and credit scores. Explain how regularly monitoring their credit activity can help them identify any errors or fraudulent activity. Encourage them to review their credit reports at least once a year and understand how their financial behaviours can impact their credit scores.

Building a Positive Credit History: Explain to children that responsible credit use can contribute to building a positive credit history. Encourage them to establish credit early by using small credit accounts, such as secured credit cards or student loans, and making timely payments. Emphasize the long-term benefits of maintaining a good credit history for future financial opportunities.

Understanding Interest Rates: Teach children about interest rates and how they affect credit. Explain the concept of compound interest and how it can significantly increase the amount repaid if credit balances are not paid off promptly. Encourage them to compare interest rates when considering borrowing options and to choose the most affordable option.

Managing Credit Limits: Help children understand the concept of credit limits and how they should be managed. Explain that maxing out credit cards or consistently utilizing the entire credit limit can negatively impact their credit scores and make it harder to obtain future credit. Encourage them to keep their credit utilization ratio low by using a small portion of their available credit.

Communication with Creditors: Teach children the importance of open communication with creditors. If they face financial difficulties or anticipate difficulty paying, encourage them to contact their creditors and discuss potential solutions. Explain how proactive communication can help avoid negative consequences, such as late fees or credit damage.

Recognizing Signs of Predatory Lending: Educate children about the dangers of predatory lending practices and how to recognize them. Discuss red flags such as high-interest rates, hidden fees, or aggressive sales tactics. Encourage them to seek advice or guidance from trusted adults if they encounter questionable credit offers.

Saving for Major Purchases: Instil the habit of saving money for major purchases instead of relying solely on credit. Teach children to set financial goals and save a portion of their income towards those goals. This practice reduces the need for credit and instils a sense of discipline and delayed gratification.

Regular Financial Check-ins: Encourage children to conduct regular checks to assess their credit and overall financial health. Teach them to review their credit statements, track their spending, and evaluate their financial goals. This habit helps them stay on top of their credit and make necessary adjustments to their financial behaviours.

Checking for Promotions or Benefits: Teach children to be proactive in checking for promotions or benefits related to credit management. Encourage them to explore credit card offers, bank accounts, or financial products that offer rewards, cashback, or other incentives. Explain the importance of comparing different options to find the ones that provide the most value for their financial needs. By teaching them to take advantage of promotions or benefits, they can maximize their savings and make their credit work for them.

By teaching and reinforcing these good credit habits, you can empower children to make wise financial decisions and build a solid foundation for their future financial well-being.

NAVIGATING COMMON DEBT TRAPS: TIPS FOR A DEBT-FREE FUTURE

Managing debt responsibly is an essential skill that everyone should learn. Falling into debt traps can have long-lasting consequences on our financial well-being. To help you avoid these pitfalls, we've compiled a list of common debt traps and practical tips to avoid them. Understanding the risks and implementing intelligent financial practices can pave the way for a debt-free future.

Overspending and Impulse Purchases: One of the most common debt traps is succumbing to the temptation of overspending and impulse purchases. To avoid this, encourage responsible spending habits by teaching children the importance of budgeting, distinguishing between needs and wants, and practicing delayed gratification. They can prevent unnecessary debt accumulation by setting spending limits, making thoughtful purchase decisions, and avoiding impulsive buying.

Payday Loans and Cash Advances: Payday loans and cash advances may seem like quick solutions during financial emergencies, but they often come with exorbitant interest rates and hidden fees. Teach kids to prioritize building an emergency fund instead so they have a financial safety net to rely on during unexpected situations. Emphasize the importance of exploring alternative options, such as borrowing from family or friends, negotiating payment plans, or seeking assistance from reputable financial institutions.

Credit Card Misuse and High-Interest Debt: Credit cards can be powerful financial tools when used responsibly. However, misusing credit cards and accumulating high-interest debt can lead to a never-ending cycle of financial strain. Educate children about the importance of paying credit card bills in full and on time to avoid interest charges. Teach them to keep credit card balances low, utilize credit wisely, and review credit card statements regularly for accuracy and fraudulent charges.

Lack of Financial Planning and Emergency Funds: Not having a financial plan and emergency fund can leave individuals vulnerable to unexpected expenses and debt accumulation. Teach kids the importance of setting financial goals, creating budgets, and saving for the future. Encourage them to establish an emergency fund to cover unexpected costs, such as medical expenses or car repairs. By planning and being prepared, they can avoid the need for excessive borrowing and fall into debt traps.

Student Loans and Education Debt: Higher education can be a valuable investment, but excessive student loans and education debt can burden individuals for years. Teach children about the implications of student loans and the importance of exploring scholarships, grants, and alternative education options. Encourage them to research affordable colleges or universities and consider part-time jobs or work-study programs to help offset the cost of education.

Co-signing Loans: Co-signing a loan for someone else can have significant financial implications. Teach children about the risks of co-signing, which means taking responsibility for someone else's debt. Emphasize the importance of carefully considering the financial situation, trustworthiness, and ability to repay the person seeking a co-signer. Encourage them to fully understand the terms and consequences before agreeing to co-sign any loan.

Medical Debt: Medical expenses can quickly accumulate and lead to substantial debt. Teach kids the importance of maintaining health insurance coverage and seeking preventive care to minimize unexpected medical costs. Encourage them to understand medical bills, review insurance statements for accuracy, and negotiate payment plans or discounts when necessary. Emphasize the significance of early intervention, staying proactive about health, and seeking financial assistance or resources if needed.

Avoiding common debt traps requires a combination of financial literacy, responsible decision-making, and a proactive approach to managing finances. By instilling these principles in children from a young age, they can develop sound financial habits that will serve them well into adulthood. Remember, the key is to prioritize financial well-being, make informed choices, and always consider the long-term impact of financial decisions. With these tips in mind, you can empower your children to navigate the complex world of personal finance and build a secure and debt-free future.

EXPLORING REAL-WORLD FINANCIAL SITUATIONS: LEARNING ABOUT MONEY IN EVERYDAY LIFE

Welcome to real-world financial situations, where kids can learn valuable lessons about money and develop essential skills for their future. In this guide, we will explore common scenarios that children may encounter daily and provide practical tips to help them understand and navigate these situations confidently.

Understanding Allowances: One of the kids' first real-world financial situations is receiving an allowance. Teach them the concept of earning money by completing household chores or tasks. Encourage them to allocate their allowance wisely by dividing it into different categories, such as savings, spending, and giving. This helps them learn about budgeting and setting financial goals early.

Making Smart Purchase Decisions: Kids often desire toys, games, or treats they come across while shopping. Teach them about making informed purchase decisions by discussing the value and cost of the item, comparing prices, and considering alternatives. Encourage them to prioritize their wants and needs, understanding that not every desire requires immediate fulfilment.

Saving for a Goal: Help children develop a savings mindset by introducing the concept of saving for a specific goal. Whether it's a new bicycle, a special toy, or a family outing, encourage them to set a savings target and contribute regularly. Teach them about patience, delayed gratification, and the satisfaction of achieving their goals through disciplined saving.

Sharing and Giving: Teach children about the importance of sharing and giving. Encourage them to set aside some of their money for charitable donations or acts of kindness. Discuss the impact their contributions can make in the lives of others, fostering empathy and a sense of social responsibility.

Planning for Special Events: Birthdays, holidays, and other special occasions often involve financial considerations. Teach children about the value of planning and budgeting for these events. Encourage them to think creatively and find cost-effective ways to celebrate, such as making homemade gifts or organizing shared experiences with family and friends.

Exploring Entrepreneurship: Encourage children with an entrepreneurial spirit to explore small business opportunities, such as setting up a lemonade stand or selling handmade crafts. Help them understand the basics of profit, expenses, and customer service. This experience will introduce them to the world of entrepreneurship and teach valuable lessons about hard work, responsibility, and financial management.

Understanding the Role of Banks: Introduce children to the concept of banks and the importance of savings accounts. Teach them about depositing money, earning interest, and the security banks provide. Help them understand basic banking transactions, such as withdrawing money, checking balances, and monitoring account activity.

Real-world financial situations offer children valuable opportunities to learn about money, develop responsible habits, and make informed decisions. By equipping them with the knowledge and skills to navigate these situations, we empower them to become financially savvy individuals who can confidently manage their finances in the future.

NAVIGATING REAL-WORLD FINANCIAL SITUATIONS: PRACTICAL EXAMPLES FOR KIDS

Introduction: Facing real-world financial situations can sometimes feel overwhelming, but children can confidently approach these challenges with the proper knowledge and skills. This guide will explore practical examples of how kids can tackle various real-world financial situations and make informed decisions that align with their financial goals.

Saving for a Desired Item: Let's say your child has their eyes set on a new video game console. Encourage them to create a savings plan by setting a specific goal and identifying money-saving ways. They can explore options such as allocating a portion of their allowance, finding extra chores to earn money, or setting up a savings jar. By consistently saving towards their goal, they will learn the value of patience, discipline, and delayed gratification.

Comparison Shopping: Imagine your child wants to buy a new toy or a pair of sneakers. Teach them the importance of comparison shopping by exploring different stores or websites to find the best price. Encourage them to read customer reviews and consider the item's quality, durability, and features. By making informed choices, they can get the most value for their money and develop critical thinking skills.

Handling Unexpected Expenses: Sometimes unexpected expenses arise, such as a broken electronic device or a lost library book. Help your child understand the importance of budgeting for unexpected costs and planning for emergencies. Encourage them to set aside a portion of their allowance or earnings as an emergency fund. This way, they will be prepared to handle unexpected expenses without feeling overwhelmed or resorting to borrowing money.

Planning for Family Outings: Family outings or vacations require financial planning. Involve your child by discussing the budget, researching affordable options, and considering different activities or destinations. Encourage them to contribute ideas that align with the family's budget and financial goals. This experience will help them understand the value of planning, prioritizing, and making conscious spending choices.

Earning Extra Money: Children can explore opportunities to earn extra money beyond their regular allowance. Encourage them to be entrepreneurial by offering services like pet sitting, lawn mowing, or helping neighbours with household chores. This teaches them the value of hard work and responsibility and provides practical experience in managing their earnings and tracking expenses.

Giving Back to the Community: Teach your child the importance of giving back by involving them in charitable activities or fundraising events. They can participate in food drives, clothing donation campaigns or volunteer at local organizations. By experiencing the joy of giving; they will develop empathy, gratitude, and a sense of social responsibility.

Exploring Basic Investing: Introduce your child to the concept of investing by discussing the idea of saving money in a bank account that earns interest. Explain how their savings can grow over time through the power of compound interest. This can help them understand the benefits of long-term financial planning and the potential rewards of investing wisely.

Managing Debt: As children grow older, they may encounter situations where borrowing money becomes necessary, such as student loans or mortgages. Teach them the importance of responsible borrowing, understanding interest rates, and making timely payments. Discuss the potential consequences of accumulating excessive debt and the benefits of maintaining a good credit history.

Buying a Home: When your child reaches adulthood, they may consider purchasing a home. Educate them about buying a house, including saving for a down payment, understanding mortgage terms, and budgeting for homeownership expenses like property taxes and maintenance costs. Help them explore different housing options within their budget and emphasize the importance of making informed decisions.

Planning for Retirement: Introduce the concept of retirement planning early on to instil the habit of long-term financial security. Teach your child about retirement savings accounts, such as a 401(k) or an individual retirement account (IRA).

Discuss the benefits of starting to save for retirement early, the power of compound interest over time, and the importance of setting achievable retirement goals.

Navigating real-world financial situations equips children with valuable life skills to serve them well into adulthood. By providing practical examples and guidance, parents can empower their kids to make informed decisions, manage debt responsibly, plan for significant life events like homeownership and retirement, and develop a strong foundation of financial literacy. Remember, the lessons learned at a young age can significantly impact their future financial well-being.

NAVIGATING THE FINANCIAL MAZE OF COLLEGE FINANCING: CRACKING THE CODE

Financing college for a kid can be a significant financial challenge for many families. So here is a strategy to help:

Set College Savings Goals: Determine how much you want to contribute to your child's college education. Consider factors such as tuition, living expenses, and potential scholarships or financial aid. Set realistic savings goals based on your financial capabilities and aspirations for your child's education.

Start a College Savings Account: Open a dedicated college savings account, such as a 529 plan or an Education Savings Account (ESA). These accounts offer tax advantages and are specifically designed to save for education expenses. Research and compare different account options to find one that aligns with your financial goals and risk tolerance.

Create a Budget: Establish a household budget that includes regular contributions to the college savings account. Identify areas where you can reduce expenses and redirect those funds toward college savings. Encourage your child to contribute by allocating some of their earnings from part-time jobs or other sources to their college fund.

Explore Financial Aid Options: Educate yourself about

available financial aid options, such as grants, scholarships, and student loans. Research government programs, private scholarships, and merit-based awards your child may qualify for. Stay informed about application deadlines and requirements to maximize your chances of securing financial assistance.

Encourage Academic Excellence: Motivate your child to excel academically and pursue extracurricular activities that enhance their college application. Many scholarships and grants are based on academic achievement, leadership skills, or specific talents. Emphasize the importance of maintaining good grades and exploring opportunities for academic recognition.

Research College Affordability: Help your child explore colleges and universities that align with their academic interests and financial considerations. Compare tuition costs, financial aid packages, and potential scholarships at different institutions. Consider in-state options or community colleges, which can be more affordable alternatives without compromising educational quality.

Seek Guidance from Financial Aid Offices: Reach out to college financial aid offices for assistance in understanding the financial aid process, available scholarships, and potential grants. They can provide valuable insights into navigating the complex landscape of college financing and help you identify additional funding opportunities.

Explore Work-Study Programs: Encourage your child to consider work-study programs while attending college. These programs allow students to work part-time on campus, earning money to offset educational expenses. Work-study not only provides financial support but also offers valuable work experience and networking opportunities.

Evaluate Loan Options: Research and carefully evaluate student loan options if necessary. Compare interest rates and repayment terms, and consider federal student loans as they often offer more favourable terms and borrower protections.

Help your child understand the long-term implications of borrowing and emphasize responsible borrowing practices.

Refinance Existing Debt: If you or your child already have existing debt, such as high-interest credit card debt or student loans, consider refinancing options. Refinancing involves obtaining a new loan with more favourable terms to replace the existing debt. By refinancing, you may be able to secure a lower interest rate, reduce monthly payments, or extend the repayment period.

Continuously Monitor and Adjust: Review your college savings plan regularly and adjust as needed. Monitor the progress towards your savings goals, reassess your budget, and explore additional opportunities to save or invest. Stay informed about changes in financial aid policies and adapt your strategies accordingly.

Remember, starting early, being proactive, and educating yourself about the various financing options will significantly contribute to your child's college funding success. By implementing these strategies, you can help alleviate the financial burden of college and ensure that your child can pursue higher education without unnecessary financial stress. Remember to consult with financial professionals or advisors if you need personalized guidance on refinancing strategies and how they may impact your financial situation.

ACHIEVING YOUR DREAM OF HOMEOWNERSHIP:
INTELLIGENT STRATEGIES FOR SAVING

Set a Savings Goal: Start by determining the amount you need to save for a down payment on your desired home. Research the housing market in your area to get an idea of the average home prices and the typical down payment percentage required by lenders. Set a realistic savings goal that aligns with your budget and timeline.

Create a Budget: Review your income and expenses to create a comprehensive budget that allows you to save a specific monthly amount towards your down payment goal. Look for areas where you can reduce expenses or cut back on discretionary spending to allocate more funds towards savings.

Automate Savings: Set up automatic transfers from your checking account to a separate savings account specifically dedicated to your down payment. Automating your savings ensures that a portion of your income is consistently allocated towards your goal, making it easier to stay on track.

Cut Costs and Increase Income: Look for opportunities to cut costs daily. This may include reducing dining out, entertainment expenses, or subscription services. Additionally, consider ways to increase your income, such as taking on a side job or freelancing, to accelerate your savings.

Track Progress: Regularly monitor your progress towards your savings goal. Keep track of the amount saved, the remaining balance, and the timeline you've set for yourself. This will help you stay motivated and adjust your saving strategy if needed.

Explore Down Payment Assistance Programs: Research potential down payment assistance programs available in your area. These programs can provide grants, loans, or other financial assistance to help individuals and families achieve homeownership. Look into eligibility criteria and application processes to determine whether you qualify for these programs.

Consider Financial Windfalls: Take advantage of unexpected financial windfalls, such as bonuses, tax refunds, or monetary gifts, to boost your down payment savings. Instead of spending these windfalls, direct them toward your savings account to expedite your progress.

Evaluate Housing Options: During the saving period, continue to evaluate your housing options. Keep an eye on the real estate market and monitor housing prices. Adjust your savings goal and timeline if necessary based on any market changes or your circumstances.

Remember, saving for a down payment requires discipline, consistency, and patience. Staying focused on your goal and maintaining a long-term perspective is essential. Regularly review your savings strategy and adjust as needed to ensure you're on track to achieving homeownership.

ACHIEVING YOUR DREAM OF BUYING A CAR: INTELLIGENT STRATEGIES FOR SAVING

Buying a car is a significant financial decision, and it's essential to approach it with a strategic savings plan. By adopting innovative saving strategies, you can make your dream of owning a car a reality while ensuring financial stability.

Here are some effective strategies to help you save for buying a car:

Set a Specific Goal: Determine the type of car you want to buy and set a specific savings goal. Consider factors such as the car's make, model, and approximate cost. Having a clear goal will give you a target to work towards.

Create a Budget: Evaluate your current income and expenses to create a realistic budget. Identify areas where you can reduce unnecessary expenses and redirect that money toward your car savings. This might include reducing dining out, entertainment expenses, or subscription services.

Automate Savings: Set up automatic transfers from your primary bank account to a separate savings account dedicated to your car fund. Automating savings ensures consistent contributions without relying on willpower alone. Treat your car savings as a priority and commit to regular deposits.

Reduce Debt: Prioritize paying off any existing debt, such as credit cards or student loans. By reducing your debt burden, you'll free up more disposable income for your car savings. A lower debt-to-income ratio will also enhance your eligibility for favourable financing options.

Explore Financing Options: Research financing options,

such as traditional auto loans or lease-to-own programs. Understand each option's terms, interest rates, and down payment requirements. Saving for a larger down payment can help you secure a better loan with lower interest rates and more favourable terms.

Comparison Shopping: Take the time to research and compare prices from different car dealerships or private sellers. Look for sales, discounts, or special promotions that could lower the car cost you want. Be patient, and don't rush into a purchase. Waiting for the right deal can save you a significant amount of money.

Consider Used Cars: Buying a used car instead of a brand-new one can save you considerable money. Research the market for reliable used cars that fit your needs and budget. Ensure you have the vehicle's history checked, get a professional inspection, and purchase from reputable sources.

Avoid Impulse Purchases: Stay focused on your savings goal and resist the temptation of impulse purchases. Delay gratification and remind yourself of the long-term benefits of saving for a quality car that meets your needs. Stick to your budget and financial plan to stay on track.

Negotiate and Shop Smart: When you're ready to buy a car, negotiate the price and terms to ensure you get the best deal possible. Research the fair market value of the car you want and be prepared to negotiate with the seller. Consider getting pre-approved for a loan from your bank or credit union to understand your budget better and strengthen your negotiating position.

Maintain the Car: Once you've purchased your car, take good care of it to protect your investment. Regular maintenance, such as oil changes, tire rotations, and inspections, can extend the life of your vehicle and minimize unexpected repair costs.

By implementing these strategies, you can save efficiently and achieve your goal of buying a car. Remember, balancing your car savings with other financial priorities, such as emergency and retirement savings, is crucial. With disciplined saving habits and careful planning, you'll be well on your way to purchasing the car of your dreams.

PARENTAL RESPONSIBILITY: INSTILLING FINANCIAL KNOWLEDGE AND RESPONSIBILITY IN KIDS

As parents, we are essential in shaping our children's financial knowledge and behaviour. Teaching kids about finance and money is a crucial parental responsibility that equips them with essential life skills and sets them on the path to financial well-being.

Here are some critical aspects of parental responsibility when it comes to teaching kids about finance:

Start Early: It's never too early to introduce children to money. From a young age, parents can teach basic concepts such as identifying different coins and bills, understanding the value of money, and distinguishing between wants and needs. By starting early, children develop a foundation of financial literacy that can be built upon as they grow.

Lead by Example: Children learn best by observing their parents' behaviour. Model good financial habits and responsible money management. Show them how you budget, save, and make thoughtful spending decisions. Let them witness your financial values, such as prioritizing saving for the future and giving to others. By being a positive financial role model, you provide a valuable example for your children to follow.

Open Communication: Establish an open and ongoing dialogue about money with your children. Encourage them to ask questions, share their thoughts, and express their financial goals. Discuss financial topics in age-appropriate ways, explaining budgeting, saving, and earning concepts. Use real-life examples and engage them in discussions about money-related decisions, like making purchases or saving for a family vacation.

Allow Money Management: Children can manage their own money, even from a young age. Consider providing them with a piggy bank or a small savings account to save their allowance or money from chores. Encourage them to set savings goals and choose how they spend their money. Through these experiences, children learn the value of money, the importance of saving, and the consequences of spending decisions.

Teach Wise Spending: Teach children the difference between needs and wants, and help them make wise spending choices. Encourage them to think critically before purchasing, considering quality, value, and long-term satisfaction. Teach them to prioritize their spending based on their goals and values rather than succumbing to impulsive buying habits. This helps develop their decision-making skills and fosters responsible spending behaviour.

Introduce Budgeting: Introduce the concept of budgeting to children as they grow older. Teach them how to create a simple budget by allocating their money to different categories, such as saving, spending, and giving. Encourage them to track their income and expenses, helping them understand the importance of planning and making informed financial choices. Budgeting instils financial discipline and empowers children to take control of their money.

Encourage Saving: Foster a culture of saving by encouraging children to save a portion of their money regularly. Help them set savings goals and establish a savings plan. Consider offering incentives or matching their savings contributions to motivate them further. Teach them about the benefits of saving, such as achieving long-term goals, building an emergency fund, and having financial security.

Introduce Basic Investing Concepts: As children mature, introduce them to basic investing concepts. Teach them about the power of compound interest and how investing can help grow their money over time. Explain investment vehicles such as stocks, bonds, and mutual funds. Encourage them to explore simulated investment platforms or educational resources for young investors.

Discuss Philanthropy and Giving Back: Teach children the importance of giving back to their community and those in need. Discuss philanthropy and engage them in age-appropriate volunteer activities or donation drives. Encourage them to set aside a portion of their money for charitable causes, fostering a sense of empathy, generosity, and social responsibility.

Continual Learning: Recognize that financial education is an ongoing process. Encourage your children to pursue further financial knowledge through books, articles, online resources, and educational programs. Stay updated on personal finance topics yourself so that you can provide accurate and relevant information. Emphasize the importance of lifelong learning and adaptability in the ever-evolving financial landscape.

By fulfilling our parental responsibility to teach our children about finance and money, we empower them to make informed financial decisions, develop healthy money habits, and navigate the complexities of the financial world. By instilling these valuable skills and values, we set them up for a lifetime of financial well-being and independence.

PARENTAL GUIDANCE: NURTURING FINANCIAL SUCCESS IN CHILDREN FOR A SECURE FUTURE

The role of a parent in helping their children succeed financially as they prepare to enter adulthood is critical. As parents, we are responsible for equipping our children with the necessary knowledge, skills, and mindset to navigate the complex world of finance and set them up for a secure financial future. By actively participating in their financial education, we can empower them to make informed decisions, avoid common pitfalls, and build a strong foundation for financial success.

One of the primary ways parents can support their children's financial development is by being role models. Children often learn by observing their parents' behaviours and attitudes toward money. Therefore, it is essential to demonstrate responsible financial practices, such as budgeting, saving, and making wise spending choices. By modelling good financial behaviour, parents can teach valuable lessons about the importance of financial discipline, delayed gratification, and long-term planning.

Additionally, parents can actively engage their children in conversations about money. These discussions can occur in everyday situations, such as during shopping trips, paying bills, or discussing family finances. By involving children in these discussions, parents can demystify money and help children understand budgeting, earning, and the value of money. Using age-appropriate language and examples that resonate with children is crucial to ensure they grasp the concepts effectively.

Furthermore, parents can provide valuable opportunities for their children to practice financial skills. This can include giving them allowances or encouraging them to earn money through chores or part-time jobs. Parents can foster a sense of responsibility and accountability by allowing children to manage their own money, make choices, and experience the consequences of their financial decisions. It is essential to guide and support them through the process, offering advice and discussing the outcomes to help them learn from their experiences.

Parents should also teach their children about goal setting and saving. Encouraging children to set financial goals, whether saving for a special purchase or setting aside money for the future, instils a sense of purpose and discipline. Parents can assist their children in creating a savings plan, setting aside a portion of their income, and tracking progress toward their goals. Parents can cultivate a habit of responsible financial management by helping children understand the importance of saving and delayed gratification.

Lastly, parents should educate their children about financial risks and the importance of managing them. This includes discussing topics such as avoiding excessive debt, understanding interest rates, and the potential consequences of poor financial decisions. Parents can introduce concepts like credit scores, loans, and budgeting for expenses to help children make informed choices and develop strategies for mitigating financial risks.

The role of a parent in preparing children for financial success is crucial. By being positive financial role models, engaging in open conversations, providing valuable opportunities, teaching goal setting and saving, and educating about financial risks, parents can empower their children with the knowledge and skills necessary to make sound financial decisions. Investing in their financial education is an investment in their future, equipping them with the tools to navigate the complex financial landscape and achieve financial well-being.

EMPOWERING FUTURE FINANCIAL SUCCESS

Introducing Children to Money Management and Financial Activities

Financial freedom is available to those who learn about it and work for it.

Robert Kiyosaki

Introducing kids to finance-related activities is fun and engaging to teach them essential life skills such as budgeting and saving, and investing. In addition, these activities provide an early understanding of finance and help foster a positive attitude toward money management, setting them up for future financial success.

HERE ARE SOME FUN AND EDUCATIONAL
FINANCE-RELATED ACTIVITIES FOR KIDS:

Money Math Games: Engage your child in fun math games that involve counting money, making changes, and solving money-related problems. This helps them develop basic math skills while learning about currency and its value.

Budgeting Challenge: Give your child a specific amount of money and help them create a budget for a week or a month. Encourage them to allocate funds for food, entertainment, and saving expenses. This activity teaches them the importance of budgeting and making wise spending choices.

Savings Challenge: Set a savings goal with your child, such as saving for a toy or a special outing. Help them track their progress and celebrate milestones along the way. This activity promotes saving habits and patience while working towards a goal.

Virtual Stock Market Simulation: Use online resources or apps that simulate stock market trading. Help your child create a virtual investment portfolio and guide them through buying and selling stocks. This activity introduces them to the basics of investing and teaches them about risks and rewards.

Entrepreneurial Ventures: Encourage your child to start a small business, such as a lemonade stand, a craft sale, or a yard work service. Guide them through budgeting, pricing, marketing, and tracking profits. This activity helps them understand earning money, managing costs, and the value of entrepreneurship.

Coin Sorting and Counting: Provide your child with a jar of mixed coins and ask them to sort and count them. You can make it more challenging by setting time limits or asking them to identify different coin denominations. This activity improves their coin recognition skills and basic math abilities.

Start a Piggy Bank: Encourage your child to start a piggy bank or a savings jar to develop the habit of saving money. Provide them with a designated container and teach them the importance of saving a portion of their money. They can regularly deposit coins or small bills into their piggy bank and watch their savings grow. This activity teaches them the value of saving, setting goals, and delaying gratification.

Financial Literacy Worksheets: Utilize age-appropriate financial literacy worksheets and activities available online or from educational resources. These worksheets cover budgeting, saving, spending, and basic financial concepts. They provide structured exercises to reinforce learning.

Family Money Talks: Include your child in age-appropriate discussions about family finances. Share information about household expenses, budgeting decisions, and saving for the future. This activity helps them understand the importance of financial responsibility and decision-making.

Money Management Apps: Explore kid-friendly apps that offer interactive features, such as setting savings goals, tracking expenses, and earn virtual rewards. These apps make financial management engaging and accessible for children.

Field Trips to Financial Institutions: Take your child on a field trip to a bank, credit union, or financial institution. Show them how money is deposited, withdrawn, and managed. This real-world experience helps them understand the role of financial institutions and the importance of banking services.

Remember to adapt these activities based on your child's age and interests. The goal is to make learning about finance enjoyable, interactive, and applicable to their daily lives.

MONEY MATH GAMES

"Money Math Games" are interactive and educational activities designed to teach children about basic financial concepts and develop their math skills related to money. These games make learning about money engaging, fun, and practical, allowing children to apply math principles in real-life scenarios.

Money math games often involve simulated or virtual environments where children can practice various financial transactions and calculations. These games typically cover counting money, making changes, budgeting, saving, and investing. By incorporating gameplay elements and challenges, they aim to make learning enjoyable and encourage active participation.

These games give children hands-on opportunities to apply mathematical concepts in managing money. They may involve counting and adding money, calculating discounts and sales prices, budgeting expenses, and making financial decisions. Engaging in these activities teaches children valuable skills such as numeracy, problem-solving, critical thinking, and financial decision-making.

Money math games often feature interactive visuals, colourful graphics, and user-friendly interfaces, making them accessible and appealing to children of different ages. They may be available as online games, mobile apps, or physical board games. Many educational websites, apps, and financial literacy programs provide money math games suitable for different age groups and skill levels.

The benefits of money math games extend beyond mathematical proficiency. By playing these games, children also develop essential life skills such as financial literacy, money management, and responsible decision-making. They learn about earning, spending, saving, and budgeting, which lay the foundation for sound financial habits later in life.

Money math games are interactive and educational activities that combine math learning with real-world financial scenarios. They provide children with engaging opportunities to practice money-related math skills, develop financial literacy, and cultivate responsible money management habits. By making learning about money fun and interactive, these games empower children to become confident and capable of handling their finances.

BUDGETING CHALLENGE

A "Budgeting Challenge" for kids is designed to introduce them to budgeting and help them develop essential money management skills. It presents a scenario where children are given a specific amount of money and a set of expenses or financial goals they need to allocate their funds towards.

In a budgeting challenge, children are tasked with creating a budget that balances their income (allowance, earnings, or a hypothetical amount) with their expenses or savings objectives. They must decide how to allocate their money wisely, considering different categories such as saving, spending, and giving.

The challenge often involves providing children with a list of expenses or financial goals they might encounter daily, such as buying toys, saving for a special event, contributing to charity, or budgeting for school supplies. Children must prioritize and allocate their funds accordingly, making choices based on their needs, wants, and long-term financial goals.

Budgeting challenges for kids can be implemented in various ways. They may be presented as a hands-on activity where children physically allocate play money into different envelopes or jars representing different budget categories. Alternatively, they can be conducted using online budgeting tools or interactive budgeting apps designed specifically for children.

A budgeting challenge aims to teach children the importance of budgeting, making thoughtful spending decisions, and managing their resources effectively. Through this activity, children learn valuable lessons about setting financial goals, distinguishing between needs and wants, making trade-offs, and practicing self-control.

Participating in budgeting challenges helps children develop essential financial skills such as budget planning, tracking expenses, and understanding the concept of limited resources. It promotes critical thinking, problem-solving, and decision-making as children consider the consequences of their financial choices.

By engaging in budgeting challenges from an early age, children develop a practical understanding of money management, which can set them on a path toward financial responsibility and independence as they grow older. It also helps them develop a mindset of intentional spending, saving, and setting financial priorities, enabling them to make informed financial decisions throughout their lives.

SAVINGS CHALLENGE

A "Savings Challenge" for kids is an engaging and interactive activity that encourages children to develop good saving habits and set savings goals. The challenge involves setting a target amount of money for children to save within a specific timeframe, and it encourages them to make regular contributions towards reaching their savings goal.

A savings challenge aims to teach children the value of saving money, delayed gratification, and the importance of setting goals. It helps them develop essential financial skills such as budgeting, planning, and self-discipline.

HERE'S HOW A SAVINGS CHALLENGE FOR KIDS CAN WORK

Set a savings goal: Discuss with your child what they would like to save money for, whether it's a toy, a special outing, or a long-term savings goal. Help them set a realistic savings target that aligns with their goal.

Define the timeframe: Determine a specific period for the savings challenge, such as a month or several weeks. A defined timeframe helps children stay motivated and focused on their savings goals.

Track progress: Give your child a visual representation of their progress towards their savings goal. This could be a savings chart, a piggy bank, or a digital savings tracker. Each time they contribute, they mark their progress and celebrate their achievements.

Encourage regular savings: Encourage your child to save regularly by setting aside a portion of their allowance or earnings. Discuss the importance of consistency and the benefits of incremental savings over time.

Offer incentives: Consider providing small incentives or rewards to motivate your child to reach their savings goal. For example, you could match a portion of their savings or offer a small bonus when they achieve a milestone.

Discuss saving strategies: Use the savings challenge to teach your child about different strategies. Talk about the importance of saving before spending, distinguishing between needs and wants, and making thoughtful spending decisions.

Celebrate milestones: When your child reaches their savings goal or achieves significant milestones, celebrate their success. Acknowledge their efforts and encourage them to set new goals for future savings challenges.

A savings challenge helps children develop financial responsibility, patience, and the habit of saving money. It also fosters a sense of accomplishment and empowerment as children witness their savings grow over time.

By engaging in savings challenges, children gain practical experience managing money, setting goals, and making choices that align with their financial priorities. These valuable lessons lay the foundation for a lifetime of innovative money management and financial well-being.

VIRTUAL STOCK MARKET SIMULATION

A "Virtual Stock Market Simulation" for kids is an educational activity that allows children to experience investing in stocks in a safe and simulated environment. It provides them a hands-on opportunity to learn about the stock market, investment strategies, and the potential risks and rewards associated with investing.

In a virtual stock market simulation, children are provided with virtual money that they can use to buy and sell stocks of various companies. They can create a portfolio, track the performance of their investments, and make decisions based on real-time market data.

Here's how a virtual stock market simulation for kids works:

Choose a virtual stock market platform: Several online platforms and apps are specifically designed for virtual stock market simulations for kids. These platforms often provide a user-friendly interface, educational resources, and real-time stock market data.

Set up an account: Help your child create an account on the chosen platform. They may need to provide basic information and create a username and password.

Allocate virtual money: Once the account is set up, your child will be given a certain amount to invest in stocks. This can vary depending on the platform and the rules of the simulation.

Research and select stocks: Encourage your child to research different companies and learn about their businesses, financial performance, and market trends. They can then use this information to decide which stocks to buy.

Buy and sell stocks: Using the virtual money in their account, your child can start buying stocks from their chosen companies. They can monitor the stock prices, track their portfolio's performance, and decide when to buy or sell stocks based on their investment strategy.

Learn from the experience: As your child engages in the virtual stock market simulation, they will gain first-hand experience in tracking stock prices, analysing market trends, and making investment decisions. Encourage them to reflect on their choices, understand the factors influencing stock prices, and learn from successes and setbacks.

Follow market news and events: Teach your child to stay updated with financial news and market events that can impact stock prices. This will help them understand how external factors influence the stock market and develop a broader perspective on investing.

Virtual stock market simulations provide a risk-free environment for children to explore the world of investing. They can experiment with different investment strategies, learn about diversification, and gain a deeper understanding of the concepts related to stocks and financial markets.

While the virtual stock market simulation does not involve real money, it offers valuable learning opportunities that can translate into practical knowledge and skills for future financial decision-making. It helps children develop critical thinking, analytical skills, and a long-term perspective when it comes to investing.

Note: It's important to emphasize to children that virtual stock market simulations are for educational purposes only and do not guarantee actual investment results.

ENTREPRENEURIAL VENTURES

"Entrepreneurial Ventures" for kids refers to activities or projects that encourage children to explore their creativity, problem-solving skills, and business acumen by starting and running their small businesses. It involves identifying opportunities, developing ideas, and taking the initiative to bring them to life.

Here's an explanation of how entrepreneurial ventures can be introduced to kids:

Idea generation: Encourage children to brainstorm business ideas based on interests, hobbies, or talents. They can think about products or services they can offer, considering factors such as demand, target audience, and uniqueness.

Business planning: Teach kids the importance of planning by guiding them to create a simple business plan. This includes defining the purpose of the business, identifying potential customers, outlining costs and pricing, and determining marketing strategies.

Product or service development: Help children develop their products or services. This could involve creating handmade crafts, offering pet-sitting or lawn-mowing services, organizing bake sales, or any other age-appropriate business venture they are passionate about.

Financial management: Teach children the basics of financial management by helping them set prices for their products or services, track their income and expenses, and calculate profits. Encourage them to allocate a portion of their earnings for savings and reinvestment.

Marketing and promotion: Guide kids on effectively marketing their products or services. This can include creating flyers, setting up a small website or social media page, word-of-mouth advertising, or participating in local community events. Teach them the importance of customer service and building positive customer relationships.

Sales and customer interaction: Encourage children to interact face-to-face with potential customers. This helps them develop communication and negotiation skills, build confidence, and learn the value of providing quality products or services.

Learning from experiences: Children will encounter challenges and successes throughout the entrepreneurial venture. Encourage them to reflect on their experiences, learn from setbacks, and celebrate their achievements. This fosters resilience, adaptability, and a growth mindset.

Entrepreneurial ventures for kids offer numerous benefits. They allow children to develop essential life skills such as critical thinking, problem-solving, decision-making, creativity, and resilience. Kids learn about financial literacy, risk assessment, and the value of hard work and perseverance. Moreover, these ventures foster an entrepreneurial mindset, which can be valuable in any aspect of life. They encourage children to think outside the box, identify opportunities, and take calculated risks. The experience of starting and managing a business at a young age can ignite a passion for entrepreneurship and lay a strong foundation for future endeavours.

Providing guidance and supervision during entrepreneurial ventures is essential to ensure children's safety and appropriate decision-making. Parental involvement, mentorship, and discussions about ethical practices are essential to create a positive and responsible entrepreneurial experience for kids.

COIN SORTING AND COUNTING

"Coin Sorting and Counting" for kids is an activity that involves sorting and organizing different denominations of coins and counting their total value. It is a hands-on and interactive way to introduce children to basic math skills, money recognition, and financial literacy.

Here's an explanation of how coin sorting and counting can be done with kids:

Gathering coins: Collect various denominations, such as pennies, nickels, dimes, and quarters. Ensure they are clean and in good condition for easier sorting and counting.

Sorting by denomination: Begin by showing children how to sort the coins into separate piles based on their denominations. You can use trays, bowls, or sorting mats labelled with different coin values to assist in the sorting process. Encourage them to identify the different coins and become familiar with their names and values.

Counting individual coins: Once the coins are sorted, guide kids in counting the coins in each pile. Start with one denomination at a time, such as counting all the pennies or nickels. Help them practice counting by ones and reinforce the concept of skip counting for larger coin values.

Calculating total value: After counting the individual coins, show children how to determine the total value of each coin pile. Help them assign the correct value to each coin and guide them in adding up the values of the coins in each pile. For instance, if they have 5 pennies and each penny is worth 1 cent, they can learn that the total value of the pile is 5 cents.

Sorting and counting mixed coins: Once children are comfortable sorting and counting individual coin piles, introduce them to the challenge of sorting and counting them. Provide opportunities for them to practice sorting a handful of coins containing multiple denominations and then counting the total value.

Engaging in play-based activities: Make the coin sorting and counting process fun and engaging for kids by incorporating games and activities. For example, you can create a "store" scenario where they use the sorted coins to "purchase" items of different values or engage in a friendly competition to see who can sort and count coins the fastest.

Reinforcing financial concepts: Use the coin sorting and counting activity to reinforce financial concepts such as saving, spending, and making changes. Discuss with kids how different combinations of coins can be used to make specific amounts and how they can apply these skills in real-life situations, such as making purchases or saving money in a piggy bank.

Coin sorting and counting activities help children develop

essential math skills, including counting, sorting, and basic addition. They also foster early financial literacy by introducing children to different coin denominations, their values, and the concept of money. This hands-on experience enables kids to gain a practical understanding of money and its uses tangibly and engagingly.

Remember to provide guidance and supervision during the activity, especially when dealing with small coins, to ensure children's safety. With practice, children will become more confident in their coin sorting and counting abilities, setting a foundation for their future financial understanding and responsibility.

START A PIGGY BANK

"Start a Piggy Bank" is a fun and simple activity that introduces kids to saving money and helps them develop good financial habits early on. It involves creating a dedicated container, often in the shape of a pig, where children can deposit their coins and bills regularly.

Here's an explanation of how to start a piggy bank with kids:

Choose a piggy bank: Let your child pick one that they find appealing. It can be a traditional pig-shaped bank or any other container designed to save money. Encourage them to select one that reflects their style or interests. This will make the activity more enjoyable and meaningful for them.

Explain the purpose: Sit down with your child and explain the purpose of a piggy bank. Help them understand that it is a special place to keep their money safe and to save for things they want in the future. Talk about the benefits of saving, such as being able to afford more significant purchases or achieving long-term goals.

Set savings goals: Encourage your child to set savings goals. These can be small, short-term goals like buying a toy or saving for a special treat or larger, long-term goals like saving for a bike or a future event. Help them understand that saving money regularly will bring them closer to reaching their goals over time.

Start saving: Give your child coins or bills to put in their piggy bank as an initial deposit. Explain that this is the start of their savings journey. Encourage them to regularly add to their piggy bank by saving a portion of any money they receive, such as allowances, gifts, or earnings from small tasks or jobs. Remind them that even small amounts can add up over time.

Track progress: Keep track of your child's savings progress by periodically counting and recording the amount of money in the piggy bank. This can be done together as a fun activity. Create a chart or a savings log where your child can visually see their progress. Celebrate milestones and achievements along the way to keep them motivated and engaged.

Discuss savings choices: As your child's savings grow, engage them in discussions about making choices with their money. Talk about the difference between spending money immediately and saving it for something they truly value or need. Encourage them to consider their goals and priorities before making purchasing decisions.

Reinforce saving habits: Encourage your child to develop a habit of saving regularly. Set a specific day or time each week or month for them to deposit money into their piggy bank. Make it a positive and routine part of their financial habits.

Plan for withdrawals: Discuss with your child the importance of balancing saving and spending. Teach them that it's okay to withdraw money from their piggy bank for planned purchases or when they have reached their savings goals. This helps them understand the concept of delayed gratification and responsible money management.

Starting a piggy bank helps children learn the value of saving, develop patience, and cultivate good financial habits. It gives them a tangible and visual representation of their progress and fosters a sense of ownership and responsibility over their money. As they watch their savings grow, they will gain a sense of accomplishment and empowerment, laying the foundation for future financial success.

Remember to lead by example and demonstrate good saving habits yourself. By involving your child in the process and providing guidance and support, you can help them develop a lifelong habit of saving and instil valuable financial skills that will serve them well into adulthood.

FINANCIAL LITERACY WORKSHEETS

"Financial Literacy Worksheets" are educational tools designed to help kids learn and practice various aspects of personal finance and money management. These worksheets typically include activities, exercises, and questions that engage children in hands-on learning experiences related to financial concepts.

Here's an explanation of how financial literacy worksheets can benefit kids:

Introduction to financial concepts: Financial literacy worksheets introduce children to important financial concepts in an age-appropriate and engaging manner. They cover money recognition, budgeting, saving, spending, investing, and more. These worksheets provide a structured way to introduce and reinforce critical financial concepts to kids.

Hands-on learning: Worksheets offer hands-on learning experiences where children actively participate in activities related to money management. They may involve counting money, budgeting for a specific scenario, identifying needs versus wants, tracking expenses, or making financial decisions. This interactive approach allows kids to apply their knowledge and skills in a practical context.

Skill development: Financial literacy worksheets help children develop essential financial skills. Kids learn to manage money, make informed choices, set goals, budget effectively, and understand fundamental financial terminology through worksheets. By practicing these skills, children become more confident and competent in handling their finances.

Critical thinking and problem-solving: Worksheets often include problem-solving scenarios and critical thinking exercises. These activities encourage children to analyse situations, think critically, and make sound financial decisions. They learn to evaluate options, consider consequences, and make choices that align with their goals and values.

Reinforcement of concepts: Worksheets provide opportunities for reinforcement of financial concepts taught in other educational settings. They serve as a valuable tool for reviewing and consolidating knowledge and skills. By revisiting and practicing these concepts regularly, children reinforce their understanding and build a solid foundation of financial literacy.

Personalized learning: Financial literacy worksheets can be tailored to children's specific needs and abilities. They can be adapted for different age groups and learning levels, ensuring each child's content is appropriate and engaging. This customization allows for a personalized learning experience that meets the child's unique needs.

Parental involvement: Worksheets can be used as a tool for parents to engage their children in discussions about money and finance. Parents can work through the worksheets with their kids, providing guidance, explanations, and answering questions. This involvement creates an opportunity for meaningful conversations about financial topics and strengthens the parent-child relationship.

Financial literacy worksheets are valuable for teaching kids about money management, financial decision-making, and developing essential life skills. They provide a structured and interactive approach to learning, allowing children to practice and practically apply their knowledge. By incorporating these worksheets into their education, kids can develop a strong foundation in financial literacy and gain the necessary skills to make informed financial choices throughout their lives.

FAMILY MONEY TALKS

"Family Money Talks" refers to open and regular discussions within the family about financial matters and money management. These conversations involve parents and children coming together to discuss various aspects of money, including budgeting, saving, spending, financial goals, and more. Here's an explanation of how family money talks can benefit kids:

Financial awareness: Family money talks help children understand financial matters from an early age. By discussing topics like income, expenses, and financial decision-making, kids gain awareness of the value of money, how it is earned, and how it is used to meet needs and wants. These conversations provide a foundation for financial literacy and equip kids with essential knowledge about money management.

Learning from real-life examples: Family money talks allow kids to learn from real-life examples within the family. Parents can share their experiences, successes, and challenges related to money management, which helps children grasp the practical aspects of handling finances. This first-hand knowledge allows kids to see the direct impact of financial decisions and understand the consequences of different choices.

Financial responsibility: Engaging in family money talks helps children develop a sense of financial responsibility. They learn that money is a shared resource within the family and everyone has a role to manage it wisely. Kids can participate in discussions about setting financial goals, making spending decisions, and saving for future needs. Through these conversations, they develop a sense of ownership and responsibility towards money.

Decision-making skills: Family money talks allow children to practice decision-making skills. When families discuss financial choices, kids learn to consider different options, weigh pros and cons, and make informed decisions. They understand the importance of prioritizing needs over wants, setting goals, and making thoughtful spending choices. These decision-making skills are transferable to other areas of life and contribute to developing critical thinking abilities.

Goal setting and planning: Within family money talks, parents and children can collaborate on setting financial goals and creating plans to achieve them. Kids learn the value of saving, budgeting, and making choices aligned with their goals. They understand the importance of planning for both short-term and long-term financial objectives. By actively participating in these discussions, children develop skills in goal setting, planning, and working towards financial milestones.

Open communication and trust: Family money talks foster open communication and trust between parents and children. When financial matters are openly discussed, it creates an environment where kids feel comfortable asking questions, expressing concerns, and seeking guidance. This open dialogue strengthens the parent-child relationship and builds trust. It also establishes a foundation for ongoing conversations about money, enabling children to navigate future financial challenges with support from their parents.

Financial values and habits: Family money talks provide an opportunity to discuss financial values and instil positive money habits in children. Parents can share their values regarding money, such as the importance of saving, giving back, and making wise financial choices. These discussions help shape children's attitudes toward money and influence the development of responsible money habits. By regularly engaging in family money talks, parents can impart valuable financial values that will guide their children's financial decisions in the future.

Family money talks are crucial in shaping children's understanding of money, financial responsibility, and decision-making skills. These discussions provide a platform for learning, sharing experiences, setting goals, and developing healthy financial habits. Parents empower children with the knowledge and skills necessary to make informed financial choices and achieve financial well-being throughout their lives by involving children in financial conversations from an early age.

MONEY MANAGEMENT APPS

"Money Management Apps" for kids refers to mobile applications designed to help children learn about money management, budgeting, saving, and financial literacy. These apps provide a fun and interactive platform for kids to explore various aspects of personal finance. Here's an explanation of how money management apps can benefit kids:

Hands-on learning: Money management apps offer a hands-on learning experience for kids. These apps typically feature interactive games, simulations, and activities that teach children about budgeting, saving, and making financial decisions. Through engaging visuals and user-friendly interfaces, kids can actively participate in managing virtual money and understand the consequences of their financial choices.

Financial literacy: Money management apps contribute to the development of financial literacy skills in children. They introduce critical financial concepts, such as income, expenses, budgeting, saving, and goal-setting, in an age-appropriate manner. Kids can learn about different financial terms and practices through interactive lessons, quizzes, and challenges within the app. This exposure helps them build a solid foundation of financial knowledge.

Budgeting and saving: Money management apps teach kids about budgeting and saving money. They often include features that allow children to allocate virtual funds to different categories, set savings goals, and track their progress. By engaging with these tools, kids learn the importance of budgeting their resources, distinguishing between needs and wants, and prioritizing spending. They can practice saving for specific goals and witness the rewards of delayed gratification.

Goal setting and tracking: Money management apps enable kids to set financial goals and track their progress toward achieving them. Whether it's saving for a toy, a new gadget, or a charitable donation, these apps provide a platform for kids to define their goals and work toward them. Children develop a sense of accomplishment by monitoring their savings, making adjustments, celebrating milestones, and learning the value of setting and achieving financial objectives.

Financial responsibility: Using money management apps encourages children to take responsibility for their finances. They learn the importance of making informed financial decisions, staying within their budget, and managing resources effectively. These apps can simulate real-life scenarios, such as earning an allowance, making purchases, or dealing with unexpected expenses, helping kids understand the consequences of their choices and the impact on their overall financial well-being.

Parental involvement and oversight: Money management apps often have features that allow parents to monitor their child's progress and provide guidance. Parents can set up accounts for their kids, establish spending limits, and track their child's financial activities within the app. This level of parental involvement promotes discussions about money, provides opportunities for guidance, and ensures that kids are using the app responsibly and in line with family values.

Technological fluency: Money management apps help kids develop technological fluency and adaptability. Children become familiar with mobile technology, navigation, and digital interfaces by using these apps. They learn to operate within a digital financial environment, which is increasingly essential in today's technology-driven world. Developing these skills prepares kids for the future and enhances their digital literacy.

Money management apps offer kids a fun and interactive way to learn about money, budgeting, saving, and financial decision-making. Children gain practical experience, develop financial literacy skills, and cultivate responsible money habits by engaging with these apps. Parents can supplement their child's financial education by exploring reputable money management apps that align with their values and provide a safe and educational environment for their kids to learn and grow financially.

FIELD TRIPS TO FINANCIAL INSTITUTIONS

"Field Trips to Financial Institutions" for kids involve visits to financial institutions such as banks, credit unions, or investment firms to provide children with a first-hand experience of how these institutions operate and learn about financial concepts in a practical setting. Here's an explanation of how field trips to financial institutions can benefit kids:

Experiential learning: Field trips allow children to engage in experiential learning, where they can see and experience the workings of financial institutions first-hand. They get a chance to observe the different departments, interact with professionals in the industry, and learn about the services these institutions provide. This hands-on experience allows kids to grasp financial concepts more concretely and meaningfully.

Understanding financial services: Field trips to financial institutions help kids understand the various financial services available and how they can benefit individuals and businesses. They can see how banks accept deposits, process transactions, offer loans, and provide other services. Kids can also learn about saving, budgeting, and making informed financial decisions. Exploring different types of accounts, investment options, and financial products can broaden their knowledge of the financial landscape.

Building financial literacy: Children can enhance their financial literacy skills by visiting financial institutions. In a real-world context, they can learn about basic financial terms, such as savings accounts, interest rates, credit, and loans. Professionals at these institutions can explain complex financial concepts in a simplified manner, making it easier for kids to grasp and apply their knowledge. This exposure helps build a foundation for financial literacy, which is crucial for their future financial well-being.

Career exploration: Field trips to financial institutions can inspire children to consider careers in the financial industry. They can interact with professionals in various roles, such as bankers, financial advisors, or investment analysts. Kids can learn about the qualifications, skills, and responsibilities associated with these roles, opening their eyes to potential career paths in finance. This early exposure can spark their interest and motivation to pursue finance-related studies or careers in the future.

Money management skills: Field trips can reinforce the importance of money management skills. Children can observe how financial institutions help individuals and businesses manage their money, make financial plans, and achieve their goals. They can learn about budgeting, saving, and responsible borrowing practices. These principles can make the concepts more relatable and encourage kids to adopt healthy money management habits.

Building confidence and independence: Field trips to financial institutions allow children to practice independence and build confidence. They can navigate the setting, ask questions, and converse with professionals. This interaction helps children develop their communication skills, critical thinking abilities, and confidence in dealing with financial matters. It empowers them to take an active role in financial decision-making as they grow older.

Community engagement: Field trips to financial institutions promote community engagement and understanding. Children can learn about the role of financial institutions in supporting economic growth, providing banking services to individuals and businesses, and contributing to the local community. They can develop an appreciation for the importance of financial institutions in society and understand how their own financial choices can impact the larger community.

Field trips to financial institutions offer valuable learning experiences for kids, allowing them to witness financial concepts in action and develop a deeper understanding of the financial world. These trips bridge theoretical knowledge and practical application, helping children build essential financial skills, cultivate responsible financial habits, and explore potential career paths. Children can gain confidence, knowledge, and a solid foundation for their financial journeys by immersing themselves in real-world financial settings.

HERE ARE SOME FINANCE-RELATED GAMES THAT CAN BE BOTH EDUCATIONAL AND ENJOYABLE FOR KIDS

Monopoly: Monopoly is a classic board game that teaches kids about money management, investing, and property ownership. It involves buying, selling, trading properties, collecting rent, and making financial decisions.

Cashflow for Kids: Cashflow for Kids is a board game specifically designed to teach children about financial concepts. It simulates real-life financial scenarios and helps kids learn about earning income, managing expenses, and making investments.

The Game of Life: The Game of Life is a popular board game that allows kids to experience different life stages and make financial decisions. It introduces budgeting, career choices, investing, and managing unexpected expenses.

Financial Football: Financial Football is an interactive online game developed by Visa that teaches kids about money management and personal finance through a football-themed quiz. It covers saving, budgeting, and making smart financial choices.

Money Metropolis: Money Metropolis is an online game created by Practical Money Skills that allows kids to explore a virtual city while completing financial tasks and challenges. It helps them understand earning, saving, spending, and making wise financial decisions.

Payday: Payday is a board game that teaches kids about budgeting, managing expenses, and dealing with unexpected financial situations. Players navigate through a month, facing various financial challenges and opportunities.

ThriveTime for Teens: ThriveTime for Teens is a financial literacy board game that teaches teenagers about money management, investing, and entrepreneurship. It aims to help them develop the skills needed to succeed financially.

Lemonade Stand: Lemonade Stand is a simple online game where kids can run their virtual lemonade stand. They make decisions about pricing, purchasing supplies, and managing costs to maximize profits. It teaches them about entrepreneurship and basic financial concepts.

Stock Market Game: The Stock Market Game is an online simulation that introduces kids to the basics of investing in the stock market. It allows them to create a virtual portfolio, buy and sell stocks, and track their performance. This game provides hands-on experience with investing.

Financial Soccer: Financial Soccer is an interactive game developed by Visa that combines soccer trivia with financial education. Players answer financial questions and earn points for correct answers. It helps kids engagingly learn about money management.

Play "Store": Set up a pretend store at home where kids can take on the roles of both customers and store owners. Use play money or create your currency. Kids can practice making purchases, calculating change, and even negotiating prices.

This activity helps them understand the value of money, practice basic math skills, and learn about buying and selling.

Price Scavenger Hunt: Organize a scavenger hunt where kids have to find specific items in a store or around the house. Assign each item a price tag and provide a budget for the hunt. Kids can compare prices, make choices based on their budget, and practice calculating the total cost of their finds. This activity enhances their understanding of prices, budgeting, and making decisions within financial constraints.

These finance-related games provide kids with an interactive and enjoyable way to learn about money, budgeting, investing, and other critical financial concepts. They combine fun gameplay with valuable lessons, allowing children to develop financial skills while having a great time.

MONOPOLY

Monopoly is a classic board game that can be enjoyed by kids and adults alike. It is a game of strategy, negotiation, and financial decision-making. Here's an explanation of how Monopoly works and what kids can learn from playing it:

Objective: The objective of a Monopoly is to become the wealthiest player by buying, renting, and trading properties while strategically managing money and investments.

Gameplay: Each player starts with a set amount of money and moves around the board, buying properties they land on or auctioning them if they choose not to purchase. Properties are grouped into colour sets, and owning all the properties in a set allows players to build houses and hotels, increasing the rent they can charge.

Rent and Income: When other players land on a property you own, they pay you rent. This income can be used to buy more properties or invest in houses and hotels to generate even higher rents. Players must also manage expenses such as property taxes, mortgage payments, and other unexpected costs that may arise during the game.

Negotiation and Trading: Monopoly encourages negotiation and trading between players. You can make deals to exchange properties, cash, or other resources to strengthen your position and weaken your opponents'. This game aspect teaches kids the value of negotiation, compromise, and strategic decision-making.

Financial Decision-Making: Monopoly requires players to make financial decisions throughout the game. They must determine whether to buy a property, invest in houses or hotels, or save money for future opportunities. Players must also consider the risks and rewards associated with their decisions, such as the potential return on investment from upgrading properties versus the costs and potential losses involved.

Risk Management: Monopoly also involves risk management. Players must assess the risks associated with various properties and investments, considering property values, rental potential, and the likelihood of other players landing on their properties. Making calculated decisions and weighing the risks and rewards are essential skills to develop in the game.

Strategic Thinking: Monopoly requires strategic thinking and planning. Players must analyse the board, predict opponents' moves, and make decisions that align with their overall strategy. They must balance short-term gains with long-term goals and adjust their plans as the game progresses. Strategic thinking is crucial for success in the game and can be applied to real-life financial decision-making.

Financial Literacy: Monopoly introduces kids to financial concepts such as income, expenses, investments, risk, and negotiation. It helps them understand the basics of property ownership, managing money, and making financial decisions. Playing Monopoly can spark conversations about financial literacy topics and provide practical examples that children can relate to.

Social Skills: Monopoly is a social game that encourages interaction, communication, and teamwork. Players engage in discussions, negotiations, and friendly competition. They learn to take turns, express their thoughts, and resolve conflicts. Playing the game can help kids develop social skills and improve their ability to work with others towards common goals.

Monopoly is an engaging and educational game that teaches kids about money management, strategic thinking, negotiation, and risk assessment. It provides an enjoyable way for children to learn financial concepts and develop essential life skills that can be applied in real-world situations.

CASHFLOW FOR KIDS

Cashflow for Kids is a board game designed to teach children about financial literacy and the basics of money management. It is a simplified version of the popular adult game called Cashflow 101. Here's an explanation of how Cashflow for Kids works and what kids can learn from playing it:

Objective: Cashflow for Kids aims to learn how to make money work for you and develop financial intelligence. The game simulates real-life financial scenarios and encourages players to make wise financial decisions to build wealth.

Income and Expenses: Each player starts with a professional card that determines their income. They receive a monthly pay check and have various expenses, such as buying toys, paying for candy, or saving for big-ticket items. The game emphasizes managing income and expenses to achieve financial goals.

Assets and Liabilities: Cashflow for Kids introduces the concept of assets and liabilities. Players can invest their money in real estate, stocks, or businesses. These assets generate passive income and can help players increase their cash flow. On the other hand, liabilities, such as credit card debt or unnecessary expenses, can hinder financial progress.

Financial Decisions: Players are faced with financial decisions throughout the game. They must decide whether to save, invest, or spend their money. They also learn about the consequences of different choices, such as the potential investment returns or the risks of taking on too much debt. The game encourages critical thinking and strategic decision-making.

Dealing with Unexpected Events: Cashflow for Kids includes random event cards representing unexpected financial situations. These events can be positive, such as receiving a gift or earning extra money, or negative, such as unexpected expenses or setbacks. Players learn to adapt to these events and adjust their financial plans.

Investing and Passive Income: The game teaches kids about the power of investing and generating passive income. Players can purchase assets such as rental properties or businesses that generate cash flow. They learn about the benefits of investing early, diversifying their portfolio, and leveraging their money to create wealth over time.

Teamwork and Cooperation: Cashflow for Kids can be played individually or in teams. In team play, players learn the importance of cooperation and collaboration. They must collaborate to make financial decisions, share resources, and achieve common goals. The game promotes teamwork and communication skills.

Financial Vocabulary: Cashflow for Kids introduces financial vocabulary and terms, such as income, expenses, assets, liabilities, cash flow, and passive income. Players become familiar with these terms and understand their meaning in personal finance.

Financial Mindset: By playing Cashflow for Kids, children develop a financial mindset and start thinking about money differently. They learn that money can be a tool to build wealth and achieve financial freedom. The game helps them understand financial concepts and instils positive financial habits from a young age.

Cashflow for Kids is an interactive and educational game that teaches children about financial literacy, money management, and investing. It provides an engaging platform for kids to learn about real-world financial scenarios in a fun and interactive way. Through playing the game, kids can gain valuable financial knowledge and skills that can benefit them throughout their lives.

THE GAME OF LIFE

The Game of Life is a classic board game that simulates different life stages and teaches kids about making choices, managing money, and navigating life's ups and downs. Here's an explanation of how The Game of Life works and what kids can learn from playing it:

Objective: The objective of The Game of Life is to make choices and navigate through various life stages, from college to retirement, while accumulating wealth and achieving personal goals.

Choosing a Career and Salary: At the start of the game, players choose a career and receive a salary card. Different careers offer different salaries, and this decision sets the foundation for the financial journey throughout the game. Kids learn about the connection between education, career choices, and earning potential.

Income and Expenses: Throughout the game, players receive income based on their career choice and other factors. They also encounter various expenses, such as paying for education, buying a house, getting married, or having children. Kids learn about managing their money, budgeting, and making decisions based on their financial resources.

Making Life Choices: The Game of Life presents players with choices at various points in the game. They may choose to go to college, start a career immediately, get married, have children, or pursue other life events. Each choice has consequences and can impact their finances and overall game progress. Kids learn about decision-making, weighing options, and considering the financial implications of their choices.

Investments and Risks: As players progress through the game, they have opportunities to invest their money in stocks or real estate. These investments can generate additional income or potentially incur losses. Kids learn about investing, assessing risks, and understanding that financial decisions come with opportunities and risks.

Dealing with Life Events: The Game of Life incorporates various life events that players must navigate, such as paying for unexpected expenses, receiving bonuses, or encountering setbacks. Kids learn about adapting to unexpected circumstances and adjusting financially to stay on track.

Insurance and Protection: In the game, players can purchase insurance to protect themselves from certain risks and financial challenges. This introduces kids to the concept of risk management and the importance of protecting their assets and financial well-being.

Retirement Planning: Towards the end of the game, players reach their retirement phase. They receive money based on their accumulated wealth and make final decisions about allocating their funds. This teaches kids about the importance of long-term planning, retirement savings, and financial preparations for the future.

Financial Literacy: The Game of Life incorporates financial concepts and vocabulary, such as income, expenses, savings, investments, and insurance. Kids become familiar with these terms and develop a basic understanding of personal finance concepts.

Social Skills and Interaction: The Game of Life can be played with multiple players, encouraging social interaction, communication, and negotiation skills. Kids learn about taking turns, playing fair, and engaging with others in a cooperative and friendly manner.

The Game of Life provides an entertaining and educational experience for kids to learn about money management, decision-making, and the challenges and opportunities they may encounter. It introduces them to significant financial concepts and helps develop their critical thinking, problem-solving, and social skills.

FINANCIAL FOOTBALL

Financial Football is an educational game developed by Visa and the National Football League (NFL) to teach kids about personal finance through the exciting world of football. Here's an explanation of how Financial Football works and what kids can learn from playing it:

Objective: The objective of Financial Football is to answer financial questions correctly to advance down the football field and score touchdowns. The game combines football trivia with personal finance knowledge, making it engaging and educational.

Gameplay: Financial Football is typically played on a computer, smartphone, or tablet. Players choose their favourite NFL team and select the difficulty level. The game presents a series of financial questions, and players must select the correct answer from multiple choices. Each correct answer allows the player's team to move closer to the opponent's end zone.

Financial Topics: The questions in Financial Football cover various personal finance topics, including budgeting, saving, investing, credit, banking, and more. The game provides a fun way for kids to learn about these essential financial concepts while enjoying the excitement of football.

Different Levels: Financial Football offers different difficulty levels, allowing players to choose the appropriate level of challenge based on their knowledge and skills. This makes the game accessible to various age groups and financial literacy levels.

Interactive Gameplay: The game features interactive elements like animated football players and stadiums to create an engaging and immersive experience. Players feel involved in the game as they make financial decisions and progress toward scoring touchdowns.

Team Play: Financial Football can be played individually or in teams, promoting collaboration and friendly competition among players. Kids can play against their friends or family members, adding a social and interactive element to the learning experience.

Real-Life Scenarios: The financial questions in Financial Football often present real-life scenarios that kids may encounter when managing their money. Players learn how to make informed decisions and understand the potential consequences of their choices.

Instant Feedback: Players receive immediate feedback on whether their choice was correct after selecting an answer. If they answer incorrectly, the game explains the correct answer, helping kids understand its reasoning.

Educational Resources: Financial Football is often accompanied by additional educational resources, such as lesson plans and discussion guides, which parents or educators can use to facilitate further learning and discussions about personal finance.

Benefits: Playing Financial Football helps kids develop essential financial skills, such as decision-making, critical thinking, problem-solving, and financial literacy. It also enhances their knowledge of football trivia and promotes teamwork and collaboration.

Financial Football combines the excitement of football with the educational aspects of personal finance, creating an engaging and interactive learning experience for kids. It teaches them essential money management skills, helps them make informed financial decisions, and prepares them for a financially responsible future.

MONEY METROPOLIS

Money Metropolis is an online game developed by Practical

Money Skills, a financial literacy program created by Visa. The game is designed to teach kids about money management and financial responsibility in a fun and interactive way. Here's an explanation of how Money Metropolis works and what kids can learn from playing it:

Objective: The objective of Money Metropolis is to navigate through a virtual city and complete various money-related missions. Players are tasked with earning, saving, spending, and managing their money wisely to achieve their financial goals.

Gameplay: Money Metropolis is typically played on a computer, smartphone, or tablet. Players start by creating their characters and selecting a gender and avatar. They are then introduced to the virtual city with different locations and activities.

Financial Activities: In Money Metropolis, players engage in a range of financial activities. They can work part-time jobs, such as delivering newspapers or working at a café, to earn money. They can also visit the bank to deposit or withdraw funds, set savings goals, and track their progress.

Budgeting and Spending: Players can spend their money on various items and experiences within the city. They must make thoughtful decisions about their spending, considering their budget and financial goals. They learn the importance of prioritizing needs over wants and making informed choices.

Goal Achievement: Money Metropolis encourages players to set financial goals and work towards achieving them. They can save for more significant purchases, such as a bicycle or a pet, and learn about the patience and discipline required to reach their goals.

Financial Challenges: Players face financial challenges and unexpected events throughout the game, such as emergencies or tempting sales. These challenges test their ability to make sound financial decisions and manage their money effectively.

Money Management Skills: Money Metropolis helps kids develop critical money management skills. They learn about budgeting, saving, spending wisely, setting financial goals, and making trade-offs. The game emphasizes the value of making informed choices and the consequences of impulsive or irresponsible spending.

Interactive Features: The game includes interactive features that make the experience engaging and immersive. Players can interact with characters in the city, explore different locations, and complete missions to earn rewards and progress in the game.

Educational Resources: Money Metropolis is often accompanied by additional educational resources, such as lesson plans and activities, which parents or educators can use to extend the learning beyond the game. These resources provide valuable insights and discussion points about money management.

Benefits: Playing Money Metropolis helps kids develop practical financial skills, encourages critical thinking and problem-solving, and fosters responsible money habits. It promotes financial literacy, empowers kids to make smart financial choices, and prepares them for real-world money management.

Money Metropolis provides an interactive and entertaining platform for kids to learn about money management. By navigating through the virtual city and engaging in various financial activities, kids gain valuable financial knowledge and skills playfully and enjoyably.

PAYDAY

Payday is a classic board game that simulates the ups and downs of personal finance. It's designed to teach kids about money management, budgeting, and decision-making. Here's an explanation of how Payday works and what kids can learn from playing it:

Objective: The objective of Payday is to manage your finances over the course of a month and accumulate the most money by the end of the game. Players must decide about earning, spending, and saving money while navigating unexpected financial events and opportunities.

Gameplay: Payday is typically played with 2-4 players. The game board represents a calendar month divided into days, and players move their tokens along the board as they progress through the month.

Income and Expenses: Each player starts the game with a set amount. They encounter spaces representing different financial events as they move along the board. These events include earning a pay check, receiving unexpected bills, paying groceries, shopping, or investing.

Budgeting and Decision-Making: Players must choose how to allocate their money throughout the game. They can choose to save, spend, or invest their earnings. They also have to manage unexpected expenses and balance their budgets to ensure they have enough money for necessities while saving for the future.

Financial Events: Payday includes various financial events that can impact players' finances. These events reflect real-life situations, such as receiving a bonus, vacationing, or experiencing a flat tire. Players must navigate these events and make decisions that align with their financial goals.

Loans and Investments: Players can take out loans or make investments during the game. Loans provide immediate funds but come with interest that must be paid back. Investments can yield returns but also carry risks. Players must weigh the potential benefits and drawbacks of these financial choices.

End of the Month: The game concludes at the end of the month, and players calculate their total wealth based on their cash on hand, savings, and assets. The player with the highest net worth is declared the winner.

Educational Benefits: Payday helps kids learn valuable financial skills and concepts. They develop budgeting skills by managing income and expenses, practice decision-making by weighing different financial options, and understand the consequences of their financial choices. The game also introduces concepts like loans, investments, and unexpected expenses, fostering financial literacy and critical thinking.

Family Interaction: Payday encourages family interaction and discussion about money management. Players can share their strategies, discuss financial events, and learn from each other's experiences. The game allows parents or guardians to teach financial concepts and have meaningful conversations about money with their children.

Payday is an engaging and educational game that teaches kids about money management in a fun and interactive way. By playing the game, kids can develop financial skills, learn about budgeting and decision-making, and better understand personal finance concepts that can be applied to real-life situations.

THRIVETIME FOR TEENS

ThriveTime for Teens is a board game designed to teach teenagers about personal finance, entrepreneurship, and life skills. It provides an engaging and interactive experience that simulates real-world financial situations and challenges. Here's an explanation of how ThriveTime for Teens works and what kids can learn from playing it:

Objective: ThriveTime for Teens aims to become financially successful by making wise financial decisions, managing resources effectively, and building entrepreneurial skills. Players aim to accumulate wealth, invest in businesses, and navigate life events while learning valuable lessons about money management.

Gameplay: ThriveTime for Teens is typically played with 2-6 players. Each player assumes the role of a teenager facing various financial and life situations. They move their tokens along the board, making choices and taking actions that affect their financial well-being.

Financial Decision-Making: Throughout the game, players encounter different scenarios and challenges related to money, such as starting a business, managing expenses, saving for goals, and dealing with unexpected events. They must make decisions that align with their financial goals and values.

Entrepreneurship: ThriveTime for Teens places a strong emphasis on entrepreneurship. Players have opportunities to start and run their businesses, learn about marketing and sales, manage costs and profits, and understand the risks and rewards of entrepreneurship. This aspect of the game promotes creativity, problem-solving, and strategic thinking.

Financial Skills and Knowledge: The game covers various financial topics, including budgeting, investing, saving, banking, credit, and consumer choices. Players learn about financial terms, concepts, and strategies as they progress through the game. They gain practical knowledge that can help them make informed financial decisions in real life.

Life Skills: Besides financial literacy, ThriveTime for Teens incorporates life skills into the gameplay. Players learn about time management, goal setting, communication, teamwork, and decision-making. These skills are essential for success in the financial realm and various aspects of life.

Goal-Oriented: The game encourages players to set personal financial goals and work towards achieving them. Whether saving a certain amount of money, starting a successful business, or investing in real estate, players learn the importance of setting goals, creating action plans, and staying focused.

Collaboration and Competition: ThriveTime for Teens allows players to collaborate and compete. While they strive for personal financial success, they can also form partnerships, negotiate deals, and learn from each other's experiences. This aspect of the game promotes teamwork, negotiation skills, and cooperation.

Real-World Application: The scenarios and challenges presented in ThriveTime for Teens reflect real-world financial situations that teenagers may encounter. By playing the game, kids can develop the skills and knowledge necessary to make wise financial decisions in their own lives. The game serves as a bridge between theoretical concepts and practical applications.

ThriveTime for Teens provides a dynamic and educational gaming experience that empowers teenagers to become financially savvy and develop essential life skills. Through the game, kids can learn about entrepreneurship, money management, decision-making, and goal-setting engagingly and interactively. It serves as a valuable tool for preparing teenagers for the financial challenges and opportunities they may encounter as they transition into adulthood.

LEMONADE STAND

Lemonade Stand is a classic educational game that simulates the experience of running a lemonade stand business. It is designed to teach kids about basic business principles, financial management, and decision-making. Here's an explanation of how the Lemonade Stand game works and what kids can learn from playing it:

Objective: Lemonade Stand aims to run a successful lemonade stand business by making intelligent decisions about pricing, inventory, and marketing. Players aim to maximize their profits over a series of virtual days.

Gameplay: In Lemonade Stand, players assume the role of a business owner responsible for managing all aspects of their lemonade stand. They make daily decisions regarding pricing, recipe choices, inventory levels, and advertising strategies. Each virtual day represents a business day, and players must analyse the weather forecast and adjust their decisions accordingly.

Supply and Demand: The game introduces players to supply and demand. They learn that the demand for lemonade can vary based on factors like the weather and the price they set. Players must analyse these factors and decide how much lemonade to produce and what price to charge to maximize their sales and profits.

Financial Management: Lemonade Stand teaches kids about financial management skills. Players must consider the costs of ingredients, supplies, and advertising when making pricing decisions. They also learn about revenue, expenses, and calculating profits. The game encourages players to consider cost control, revenue generation, and profitability.

Risk and Uncertainty: Lemonade Stand introduces kids to risk and uncertainty in business. Players must consider unpredictable factors like the weather, which can impact customer demand and sales. They learn to assess risks and make decisions based on the available information and their understanding of business dynamics.

Marketing and Advertising: The game emphasizes the importance of marketing and advertising in attracting customers. Players can allocate a budget to advertise their lemonade stand through various channels, such as flyers, signs, or radio ads. They learn about the impact of marketing efforts on customer awareness and sales.

Trial and Error: Lemonade Stand encourages kids to experiment and learn from their mistakes. Players can adjust their pricing, recipe, and advertising strategies based on each day's sales outcomes. Through trial and error, they gain insights into the factors influencing business success and learn to make better decisions over time.

Critical Thinking and Decision-Making: Lemonade Stand promotes critical thinking and decision-making skills. Players must analyse data, consider various factors, and make strategic choices to optimize their lemonade stand's performance. They learn to think analytically, weigh pros and cons, and make informed decisions to achieve their business goals.

Time Management: The game teaches kids about time management as they need to plan their actions within a limited number of virtual days. They must allocate time for buying supplies, preparing the lemonade, setting prices, and monitoring sales. This aspect of the game helps children understand the importance of managing time effectively in a business setting.

Lemonade Stand provides a hands-on and interactive experience that allows kids to learn about basic business principles while having fun. Kids can develop their financial literacy, critical thinking, and decision-making skills by playing the game. They gain a practical understanding of business concepts and learn valuable entrepreneurship, marketing, and financial management lessons. Lemonade Stand is an engaging introduction to the business world and can inspire kids to explore their entrepreneurial ideas.

STOCK MARKET GAME

The Stock Market Game is an educational game that simulates the experience of investing in the stock market. It is designed to teach kids about the basics of investing, the stock market, and the principles of risk and reward. Here's an explanation of how the Stock Market Game works and what kids can learn from playing it:

Objective: The Stock Market Game aims to make intelligent investment decisions and achieve the highest returns on invested capital. Players aim to grow their virtual portfolio by buying and selling stocks based on market trends and their analysis of various companies.

Gameplay: In the Stock Market Game, players start with a virtual budget or a set amount of virtual money. They can use this money to purchase stocks from various companies listed on a simulated stock market. The prices of stocks fluctuate based on market conditions and news events, mimicking the real-world stock market.

Research and Analysis: The game encourages players to research and analyse different companies before making investment decisions. Players can study company profiles, financial statements, and news articles to gain insights into a company's performance and potential for growth. They learn to evaluate stocks based on company fundamentals, industry trends, and market conditions.

Buying and Selling Stocks: Players can use their virtual funds to buy shares of stocks they believe will perform well in the stock market. They can track the performance of their portfolio and make decisions to buy or sell stocks based on their analysis and market trends. The game introduces concepts such as bid and asks prices, order types, and the impact of supply and demand on stock prices.

Risk and Reward: The Stock Market Game teaches kids about risk and reward in investing. Players learn that investing in stocks involves potential gains as well as losses. They experience the thrill of making profitable trades and the consequences of poor investment decisions. The game encourages players to understand and manage risk by diversifying their portfolios and making informed choices.

Market Dynamics: Kids understand market dynamics through the Stock Market Game and how various factors can impact stock prices. They learn about the influence of economic news, company announcements, and market sentiment on stock performance. Players become familiar with market volatility and the need to monitor market trends.

Portfolio Management: The game promotes portfolio management skills, as players must monitor their holdings, track performance, and adjust their portfolios over time. They learn about the importance of diversification, asset allocation, and the long-term view of managing investment portfolios. Players can evaluate the performance of their portfolio compared to benchmark indices and other players' portfolios.

Financial Literacy: The Stock Market Game enhances financial literacy by introducing kids to investment concepts, stock market terminology, and the importance of long-term financial planning. Players learn about the potential benefits of investing, such as wealth accumulation and building passive income. They also gain awareness of the role of the stock market in the economy.

Critical Thinking and Decision-Making: The Stock Market Game encourages critical thinking and decision-making skills. Players must analyse information, assess risks and rewards, and make strategic investment choices. When making investment decisions, they learn to consider company performance, industry trends, and market conditions.

The Stock Market Game provides a practical and interactive way for kids to learn about investing and the stock market. Kids can develop their financial knowledge, analytical skills, and decision-making abilities by participating in the game. They gain insights into finance and investing, helping them make informed financial decisions in the future. The game fosters an understanding of the potential rewards and risks associated with investing and promotes a long-term wealth-building perspective.

FINANCIAL SOCCER

Financial Soccer is an educational game that combines the excitement of soccer with financial literacy lessons. It is designed to teach kids about personal finance topics while engaging them in a fun and interactive soccer-themed game. Here's an explanation of how Financial Soccer works and what kids can learn from playing it:

Objective: The objective of Financial Soccer is to answer financial literacy questions correctly and advance the soccer ball toward the opponent's goal. Players aim to score goals by correctly answering questions and outsmarting their opponents.

Gameplay: In Financial Soccer, players form teams and compete against each other in a virtual soccer match. The game presents a series of financial literacy questions in different categories, such as budgeting, saving, investing, and credit. Players must choose the correct answers to move their soccer player and ball closer to the opponent's goal. Each correct answer earns them a chance to score a goal.

Financial Topics: The game covers a wide range of relevant financial topics for kids. It introduces concepts such as budgeting, goal setting, earning income, spending wisely, saving, investing, and managing credit. The questions test players' knowledge and understanding of these topics, helping them learn and reinforce critical financial concepts.

Difficulty Levels: Financial Soccer offers different difficulty levels, allowing players to choose a level that matches their financial knowledge and skills. As players progress through the game and answer questions correctly, the difficulty level may increase, providing a challenge and encouraging further learning.

Competition and Collaboration: Financial Soccer can be played in a team format, promoting competition and collaboration. Players can form teams and compete against each other, answering questions to score goals. The game also encourages collaboration as players can discuss and strategize to select the best answers and score more goals.

Real-Time Feedback: The game provides real-time feedback on players' answers. If players select the correct answer, they receive positive feedback and can advance their soccer player. If players select the wrong answer, they receive feedback explaining the correct answer, helping them better understand the financial concept.

Educational Resources: Financial Soccer often provides additional educational resources alongside the game. These resources can include explanations of financial concepts, tips for managing money, and suggestions for further learning. Players can access these resources to deepen their understanding of personal finance topics beyond the game.

Benefits: Financial Soccer offers several benefits to kids. It helps improve their financial literacy skills by teaching essential money management concepts engagingly and interactively. The game promotes critical thinking as players must analyse and choose the correct answers. It also fosters teamwork and collaboration as players work together to score goals and win the game.

Financial Soccer combines the excitement of soccer with financial literacy education, making it an enjoyable and effective tool for teaching kids about personal finance. By playing the game, kids can enhance their financial knowledge, develop critical money management skills, and gain confidence in making sound financial decisions.

PLAY "STORE"

"Play Store" is an interactive game that allows kids to experience the role of both the shopkeeper and the customer. It simulates a real-life store environment where children learn about money, basic math skills, and buying and selling goods. Here's an explanation of how the game works and what kids can learn from playing it:

Setup: To play "Store," kids can set up a pretend store using items from their toy collection or by creating their own play money and merchandise. They can designate a specific area as the store and arrange items on shelves or display tables.

Roles: The game involves two leading roles: the shopkeeper and the customer. Kids can take turns playing each role, allowing them to experience both sides of the buying and selling.

Shopkeeper's Role: When playing as the shopkeeper, kids are responsible for managing the store and selling products. They can set prices for each item, arrange them in an organized manner, and handle customer interactions. This role helps children understand the concept of pricing, managing inventory, and providing customer service.

Customer's Role: Kids can select items they want to purchase from the store when playing as the customer. They can explore the store, choose products, and bring them to the shopkeeper for purchase. This role helps children learn about making choices, budgeting, and counting money.

Money Transactions: The game involves using play money or creating a currency system using tokens or paper notes. As customers select items, they must pay the shopkeeper the appropriate amount. This interaction helps kids practice basic math skills, including counting, addition, and subtraction.

Price Negotiation: Kids can also engage in price negotiation during the game. They can haggle or bargain with the shopkeeper to reach a mutually agreed-upon price. This activity teaches children about negotiation, compromise, and understanding the value of goods.

Change Calculation: When customers pay for items, they may need to receive the change back from the shopkeeper. This game aspect allows kids to practice calculating and giving the correct amount of change.

Social Skills: "Play Store" encourages social interaction and role-playing. Kids can practice communication skills, manners, and politeness while playing the shopkeeper or customer. They can learn to greet customers, assist, and engage in friendly interactions.

Benefits: "Play Store" offers several benefits for kids. It promotes basic math skills, such as counting, addition, subtraction, and money recognition. The game helps children understand the concept of buying and selling, the value of money, and the importance of making choices within a given budget. Additionally, it fosters creativity, imagination, and social skills as kids engage in pretend play and interact with others.

"Play Store" provides an interactive and educational experience for kids to learn about money, math, decision-making, and social skills in a fun and playful setting. It offers a hands-on approach to teaching financial concepts and encourages children to explore the world of commerce and transactions.

PRICE SCAVENGER HUNT

The game "Price Scavenger Hunt" is an exciting and educational activity that encourages kids to explore and compare prices of items in various locations. Here's an explanation of how the game works and what children can learn from playing it:

Setup: To play the "Price Scavenger Hunt," you'll need a list of items and their corresponding prices. This can be created beforehand or obtained from real-store advertisements or online listings. You can also assign different point values to each item based on price.

Gameplay: Divide the kids into teams or have them play individually. Provide each team or player with the list of items and their assigned point values. Set a specific time limit for the scavenger hunt.

Objective: The game's objective is for players to find and record the prices of the listed items in various locations, such as grocery stores, department stores, or online retailers. They can physically visit these places or search for the items and prices online.

Scoring: Players earn points based on the accuracy of the prices they find. If the actual price matches the recorded price, they receive the assigned point value for that item. The team or player with the highest total score at the end of the game wins.

Learning Opportunities: The "Price Scavenger Hunt" offers several learning opportunities for kids:

Price Comparison: Children learn to compare prices for the same items by searching for prices in different locations. They can understand how prices may vary and develop the ability to make informed purchasing decisions based on the best available options.

Budgeting Skills: The game promotes budgeting skills as players must decide which items to search for and record within a limited time. They learn to prioritize and make strategic choices based on their assigned point values.

Math and Calculation: The game involves recording and

comparing prices, which enhances math skills such as addition, subtraction, and mental calculations. Kids practice arithmetic skills as they calculate the total value of items and keep track of their scores.

Research and Technology: Kids develop research skills and learn to navigate e-commerce websites or marketplaces if the game involves searching for prices online. They also gain familiarity with technology and digital resources.

Critical Thinking: Players must critically analyse prices to determine their accuracy. They may need to consider discounts, promotions, or other factors that affect the final price.

Benefits: The "Price Scavenger Hunt" encourages active learning, problem-solving, and critical thinking skills. It helps children become savvy consumers by teaching them the importance of price comparison and making informed purchasing decisions. Additionally, the game fosters teamwork, collaboration, and friendly competition among players.

"Price Scavenger Hunt" provides an engaging way for kids to develop financial literacy skills, enhance math abilities, and understand the value of money. It promotes the real-world application of price analysis and encourages children to become savvy shoppers.

CREATE A BUDGET TOGETHER: TEACHING KIDS THE VALUE OF FINANCIAL PLANNING

Teaching children about budgeting is essential in preparing them for a financially responsible future. Parents can instil crucial money management skills and help their children develop a healthy relationship with money by involving them in the budgeting process. Creating a budget together as a family is educational and an opportunity to foster open discussions about finances and values. Through this collaborative process, children can learn the value of financial planning, responsible spending, and making informed choices.

Set Financial Goals: Begin by discussing the importance of setting financial goals. Talk about short-term goals, like saving for a specific toy or outing, and long-term goals, such as saving for college or a family vacation. Help children understand the concept of saving for something they genuinely want or need and how budgeting plays a vital role in achieving those goals.

Identify Income and Expenses: Guide your child in understanding different sources of income, such as allowances or money earned from chores. Discuss expenses, including fixed (e.g., bills, groceries) and variable (e.g., entertainment, outings). This exercise will help children recognize that money needs to be allocated wisely, ensuring that essential needs are met while leaving room for savings and discretionary spending.

Track and Prioritize Expenses: Encourage children to track their expenses by keeping a record of what they spend their money on. This could be as simple as using a notebook or a budgeting app. Guide them in categorizing expenses and identifying areas where they can save money or make more mindful spending choices. Teach them the importance of prioritizing needs over wants and making informed financial decisions.

Allocate Income and Set Spending Limits: Work together to allocate income into different categories, such as savings, necessities, and discretionary spending. Help your child determine appropriate spending limits for each category based on their financial goals and values. Emphasize the significance of saving a portion of their income to build a safety net and achieve their long-term goals.

Review and Adjust the Budget: Regularly review the budget with your child to assess their progress, discuss any challenges, and make necessary adjustments. This ongoing dialogue will reinforce the importance of financial planning and the flexibility required to adapt to changing circumstances. Celebrate milestones and achievements together, providing positive reinforcement for their efforts.

Creating a budget with your child effectively teaches them valuable financial skills and instils responsible money habits. By involving them in budgeting, you empower them to make informed financial decisions, prioritize their spending, and work towards their financial goals. This collaborative approach imparts practical skills, strengthens the parent-child bond, and sets the foundation for a lifetime of financial well-being.

SET FINANCIAL GOALS

Setting financial goals is essential to creating a budget together as a family. Here's an explanation of what it means to set financial goals and how it can be incorporated into the process of creating a budget as a parent and kids:

Definition of Financial Goals: Financial goals are specific targets you set for your money. These goals can be things you want to save for, such as a new toy, a family vacation, or even long-term goals like saving for college or buying a house. Financial goals help you prioritize your spending and saving habits and give you something to work towards.

Discussing Goals as a Family: As a parent, involve your kids in discussing financial goals. Ask them what they want to save money for and encourage them to consider short-term and long-term goals. Listen to their ideas and help them understand the importance of setting goals and planning to achieve them.

Making Goals Specific and Measurable: To effectively work towards financial goals, it's essential to make them specific and measurable. For example, instead of saying "saving money," set a specific amount or percentage of their allowance or earnings that they want to save. This helps them track their progress and see the results of their efforts.

Prioritizing Goals: Help your kids prioritize their financial goals. Discuss which goals are most important to them and why. Encourage them to think about what they value and want to achieve with their money. This can help them make informed decisions about how to allocate their funds.

Break Goals into Actionable Steps: Break down the financial goals into smaller, actionable steps. Help your kids identify what they need to do to reach their goals. For example, if they want to save a certain amount for a new video game, you can help them create a plan to save a portion of their allowance each week or find ways to earn extra money through chores or small jobs.

Incorporating Goals into the Budget: Show your kids how to incorporate their financial goals into a budget. Help them understand that a budget is a tool that helps them manage their money effectively. Allocate funds towards each goal, ensuring they save a portion of their income specifically for their goals.

Regularly Review and Adjust Goals: It's essential to review and adjust financial goals as circumstances change regularly. Encourage your kids to reassess their goals periodically and make any necessary adjustments. This teaches them the importance of flexibility and adaptability in managing their finances.

By involving your kids in setting financial goals and creating a budget, you teach them valuable skills such as goal-setting, budgeting, and decision-making. They learn the importance of planning, saving, and making wise choices with their money. It also promotes communication and teamwork within the family as you work towards shared financial goals.

IDENTIFY INCOME AND EXPENSES

Identifying income and expenses is crucial in creating a budget together as a family. Here's an explanation of what it means to identify income and expenses and how it can be incorporated into the process of creating a budget as a parent and kids:

Understanding Income: Income refers to the money that comes into the family, including allowances, earnings from part-time jobs, or any other sources of income. Kids must understand where their money comes from and how much they can allocate toward different categories.

Listing Sources of Income: As a parent, help your kids list all their sources of income. This could include their weekly or monthly allowance, money earned from chores or odd jobs, or any other sources of income they may have. Make sure to include both regular and irregular income sources.

Discussing Expenses: Expenses are the money spent on various items or activities. This includes everything from necessities like food and clothing to discretionary spendings like entertainment or hobbies. Help your kids understand the difference between needs and wants and guide them in categorizing their expenses accordingly.

Listing and Categorizing Expenses: Encourage your kids to list their expenses by category. Some common expense categories include food, transportation, clothing, entertainment, savings, and charity. This exercise helps them see where their money is going and facilitates discussions about priorities and potential areas for savings.

Tracking and Estimating Expenses: Help your kids track their expenses over a while, such as a month. They can record their spending in a notebook or use budgeting apps designed for kids. If certain expenses occur irregularly, guide them in estimating the average amount they typically spend in those categories.

Differentiating Fixed and Variable Expenses: Teach your kids about fixed and variable expenses. Fixed expenses are regular, recurring costs that remain relatively constant, such as monthly subscriptions or utility bills. Variable expenses, on the other hand, fluctuate from month to month, such as dining out or buying new toys. Understanding these distinctions helps with planning and budgeting.

Analysing Income and Expenses: Once all income and expenses are identified, help your kids analyse the numbers. Discuss whether their income covers all their expenses or if adjustments must be made. This allows them to understand the importance of living within their means and making informed decisions about spending and saving.

Making Adjustments: If their expenses exceed their income, guide your kids in adjusting their spending habits. Encourage them to prioritize their needs and consider ways to reduce discretionary expenses. This helps them develop financial discipline and make conscious choices about their spending.

Encouraging Savings: Emphasize the importance of saving by allocating a portion of their income towards savings. Help them understand the benefits of saving for short-term goals like buying a new toy and long-term goals like college or future expenses. Encourage them to set aside a specific amount or percentage of their income for savings.

By involving your kids in identifying income and expenses, you are helping them develop a deeper understanding of money management. They learn to recognize their income sources, differentiate between needs and wants, and make informed decisions about their spending. This exercise also promotes transparency and open communication about financial matters within the family.

TRACK AND PRIORITIZE EXPENSES

Tracking and prioritizing expenses is essential in creating a budget together as a family. Here's an explanation of what it means to track and prioritize expenses and how it can be incorporated into the process of creating a budget as a parent and kids:

Tracking Expenses: Tracking expenses involves recording all the money spent during a specific period. It helps you and your kids understand where money is going, identify spending patterns, and make informed budgeting decisions. Encourage your kids to keep track of their expenses using a notebook, a budgeting app, or a spreadsheet.

Recording Expenses: Teach your kids to record their expenses accurately and consistently. They should note each expense's date, description, and amount spent. This includes both cash purchases and transactions made using digital payment methods. By recording expenses, they better understand their spending habits and can identify areas where they can cut back or make adjustments.

Categorizing Expenses: Guide your kids in categorizing their expenses based on different budget categories, such as food, transportation, clothing, entertainment, education, and savings. Categorizing expenses helps them visualize their spending patterns and enables discussions on where they can adjust to align with their financial goals.

Analysing Expenses: Review the recorded data to help your kids analyse their expenses. Discuss which categories account for most of their spending and whether those expenses align with their priorities and financial goals. This analysis allows them to identify areas where they may need to cut back or find alternative, more cost-effective options.

Prioritizing Expenses: Encourage your kids to prioritize their expenses based on their needs and values. Teach them the importance of distinguishing between essential expenses and discretionary expenses. Essential expenses are necessary for their well-being and basic needs, such as food, housing, and education. Discretionary expenses are non-essential and can be adjusted or reduced as needed.

Identifying Potential Savings: Through tracking and analysing expenses, your kids can identify potential areas where they can save money. Discuss with them the possibility of reducing discretionary expenses or finding more cost-effective alternatives for certain purchases. Encourage them to set goals for saving money in specific categories or purposes.

Regular Reviews: Make it a habit to review the expenses with your kids regularly. This allows you to monitor their progress, provide guidance, and address any concerns or questions they may have. It also reinforces the importance of tracking and prioritizing expenses consistently as part of their ongoing money management routine.

Adjustments and Flexibility: Emphasize to your kids that budgeting is a dynamic process that may require adjustments over time. Encourage them to be flexible and adapt their spending habits as circumstances change or new financial goals arise. Help them understand that budgeting is not about restriction but about making intentional choices with their money.

By tracking and prioritizing expenses, your kids better understand where their money goes and learn to align their spending with their financial goals and priorities. This process encourages them to be mindful of their expenses, make conscious decisions, and develop good money management habits. It also promotes open communication and collaboration within the family, as everyone works together to create a budget that reflects their shared values and aspirations.

ALLOCATE INCOME AND SET SPENDING LIMITS

Allocating income and setting spending limits are essential in creating a budget together as a family. Here's an explanation of what it means to allocate the income and set spending limits and how it can be incorporated into the process of creating a budget as a parent and kids:

Determine Available Income: Begin by identifying the total income available to the family. This includes income from parents, allowances, and any other sources of income for the kids. Discuss the family's overall financial situation and the income that can be allocated towards various expenses and savings.

Prioritize Essential Expenses: Start by allocating income towards essential expenses necessary for the family's well-being and basic needs. This may include housing, utilities, groceries, transportation, healthcare, and education. Prioritize these expenses to ensure they are covered first.

Set Spending Limits: Encourage your kids to actively participate in setting spending limits for different categories of expenses. Discuss what is realistic and reasonable based on the available income and the family's financial goals. This helps kids develop a sense of financial responsibility and understand living within their means.

Identify Fixed and Variable Expenses: Differentiate between fixed expenses (rent/mortgage, insurance premiums, or subscription services) and variable expenses (such as groceries, entertainment, or discretionary purchases). Allocate a portion of the income towards fixed expenses and then determine spending limits for variable expenses based on the remaining income.

Allocate for Savings and Financial Goals: Teach your kids the importance of saving money and setting financial goals. Allocate a portion of the income towards savings, such as an emergency fund or long-term savings for future goals like education or purchasing a car. Encourage your kids to set their savings goals and contribute a portion of their income.

Consider Financial Trade-offs: Help your kids understand that budgeting requires making choices and sometimes prioritizing certain expenses over others. Discuss the trade-offs in spending decisions and how they impact overall financial well-being. Encourage them to evaluate their spending choices in light of their financial goals.

Review and Adjust Regularly: Review the budget with your kids to track progress and adjust as needed. Encourage open dialogue about any challenges or changes in circumstances that may require modifying spending limits or reallocation of income. This helps foster a sense of financial awareness and adaptability.

Encourage Responsibility and Accountability: Teach your kids the importance of being responsible with money and sticking to the agreed-upon spending limits. Help them track their expenses and monitor their progress. Encourage them to reflect on their spending habits and make conscious choices that align with their financial goals.

By allocating income and setting spending limits, your kids learn to prioritize expenses, make thoughtful spending decisions, and develop a sense of financial discipline. They also better understand the value of money and the trade-offs involved in financial choices. Through active participation in the budgeting process, they become more responsible with their finances and develop essential money management skills that will serve them well.

REVIEW AND ADJUST THE BUDGET

Reviewing and adjusting the budget is crucial in creating a budget together as a family. Here's an explanation of what it means to review and adjust the budget and how parents and kids can engage in this practice:

Regular Review: Set a designated time to regularly review the budget as a family. This could be monthly, quarterly, or as needed, depending on your family's preference and financial situation. Gather everyone together to assess the budget's effectiveness and discuss any changes or updates that may be necessary.

Track Actual Expenses: Compare the budgeted amounts with the expenses incurred during the review period. Encourage your kids to participate by tracking their expenses and actively sharing information. This helps create awareness of spending patterns and allows a more accurate assessment of the budget's effectiveness.

Identify Variances: Identify discrepancies or variances between the budgeted amounts and the actual expenses. This includes both overspending and underspending in different categories. Discuss the reasons behind these variances and explore potential adjustments that can be made to align the budget more closely with the family's financial goals.

Analyse Financial Goals: Revisit the family's financial goals and assess the progress made towards achieving them. Discuss whether the budget adequately supports those goals or if modifications are required. This may involve reprioritizing expenses, increasing savings contributions, or adjusting spending limits in specific categories.

Address Changing Circumstances: Life circumstances can change, and it's essential to adapt the budget accordingly. If there are income, expenses, or family priorities changes, discuss how those changes impact the budget and identify any necessary adjustments. Encourage your kids to share their insights and perspectives on how the budget can be modified to accommodate these changes.

Seek Input and Feedback: Make the budget review process inclusive by seeking input and feedback from all family members, including your kids. Encourage them to share their thoughts, observations, and ideas for improving the budget. This helps foster a sense of ownership and responsibility, making it a collective effort to effectively manage the family's finances.

Make Adjustments: Based on the review and discussions, make necessary adjustments to the budget. This may involve reallocating funds, revising spending limits, or modifying savings goals. Emphasize the importance of flexibility and adaptability in budgeting, as it is a dynamic process that evolves with changing needs and circumstances.

Set New Goals: Use the budget review to set new financial goals or revise existing ones. Encourage your kids to identify their financial aspirations and incorporate them into the budget. This helps them develop a forward-thinking mindset and stay motivated to manage their money effectively.

Regularly reviewing and adjusting the budget allows your family to stay on track with financial goals, address changing needs, and ensure that the budget remains a relevant and effective tool for managing your finances. It promotes financial awareness, encourages open communication, and reinforces the importance of ongoing financial responsibility and accountability for everyone involved.

EXPLORING INVESTMENT OPTIONS: EMPOWERING CHILDREN TO MAKE INFORMED FINANCIAL DECISIONS

Teaching children about investment options is valuable in their financial education journey. Parents can equip their children with the knowledge and skills to make informed financial decisions by discussing various investment opportunities. Exploring investment options together promotes critical thinking and financial literacy and encourages children to consider long-term financial planning and wealth-building strategies.

Define Investments: Begin by explaining what investments are and why people choose to invest their money. Discuss investing money to earn potential returns over time and the difference between saving and investing. Emphasize that investments come with varying levels of risk and potential rewards, highlighting the importance of making informed decisions based on individual financial goals and risk tolerance.

Explore Different Investment Vehicles: Introduce your child to different investment options, such as stocks, bonds, mutual funds, and real estate. Explain the essential characteristics of each investment vehicle, including how they work, potential risks and rewards, and their role in building wealth. Use age-appropriate language and examples to help children grasp and relate the concepts to real-life scenarios.

Discuss Risk and Reward: Teach children about the relationship between risk and reward in investments. Explain that higher potential returns often come with higher risk, while lower-risk investments may offer more stability but lower returns. Encourage them to consider their risk tolerance and time horizon when making investment decisions. Help them understand the importance of diversification and not putting all their eggs in one basket.

Highlight Long-Term Thinking: Emphasize the value of long-term thinking regarding investments. Discuss the power of compounding and how investing early can potentially lead to more significant wealth accumulation over time. Help children understand that investments are not get-rich-quick schemes but vehicles for long-term financial growth and stability. Encourage patience and discipline when it comes to investing decisions.

Encourage Research and Learning: Foster a sense of curiosity and encourage your child to research and learn more about different investment options. Introduce them to reputable resources, books, and educational websites that provide information about investments and personal finance. Discuss investment strategies, market trends, and staying informed about financial markets.

Discussing investment options with children is an essential step in their financial education. By exploring different investment vehicles, understanding risk and reward, and emphasizing long-term thinking, parents can empower their children to make informed financial decisions. These conversations foster critical thinking, promote financial literacy, and set the stage for responsible wealth-building practices in the future. By instilling a mindset of investing and a willingness to learn, parents can help their children navigate the world of investments and set them on a path toward financial success.

DEFINE INVESTMENTS

Defining investments is an essential step when exploring investment options with your kids. Here's an explanation of what it means to define investments and how you can introduce this concept to them:

Understanding Investments: Start by explaining to your kids that investments refer to putting money or resources into something with the expectation of generating a return or profit over time. Emphasize that investments are not just about saving money but also about making intelligent choices to grow wealth.

Different Types of Investments: Introduce your kids to various investment options, such as stocks, bonds, mutual funds, real estate, and savings accounts. Explain that each investment type has its characteristics, risks, and potential returns. Simplify the explanations based on your child's age and understanding, ensuring the information is accessible and relatable.

Risk and Return: Help your kids understand the risk and return associated with investments. Explain that investments with higher potential returns often come with higher risk, while investments with lower risk may offer more modest returns. Use simple examples and analogies to illustrate this concept, such as comparing it to a game or a chance to earn rewards.

Investment Goals: Discuss the importance of setting investment goals. Explain that goals can be short-term (e.g., saving for a specific purchase) or long-term (e.g., saving for college or retirement). Encourage your kids to think about their financial goals and aspirations and how investments can help them achieve them.

Research and Learning: Teach your kids the value of research and learning regarding investments. Explain that informed decision-making is crucial, and they should gather information, study market trends, and understand the companies or assets they're investing in. Encourage them to seek reliable sources of information and ask questions to deepen their understanding.

Diversification: Introduce the concept of diversification, which means spreading investments across different assets or types. Explain that diversification helps reduce risk by not putting all their eggs in one basket. Use relatable examples, such as having a mix of different toys or games rather than just one, to illustrate the idea of diversification.

Start Small: Emphasize that investing doesn't always require much money. Encourage your kids to start small by setting aside a portion of their savings for investments. Explain that even small amounts can grow over time and the habit of investing that matters.

Long-Term Perspective: Help your kids understand that investments are typically intended for the long term. Explain that the value of investments can fluctuate in the short term but has the potential to grow over a more extended period. Teach them patience and the importance of staying committed to their investment goals.

By defining investments and introducing these concepts to your kids, you lay the foundation for their understanding of how money can grow through intelligent investment choices. Encourage curiosity, answer questions, and provide age-appropriate resources or books to enhance their knowledge further. This early exposure to investments can help them develop a positive mindset towards saving and investing, setting them on a path toward financial independence and success in the future.

EXPLORE DIFFERENT INVESTMENT VEHICLES

Exploring different investment vehicles is essential when discussing investment options with your kids. Here's an explanation of what it means to explore different investment vehicles and how you can introduce this concept to them:

Investment Vehicles: Explain to your kids that investment vehicles are the different ways or methods through which individuals can invest their money to earn a return potentially. These vehicles can include stocks, bonds, mutual funds, real estate, certificates of deposit (CDs), and more. Each investment vehicle has its characteristics, risks, and potential returns.

Stocks: Introduce the concept of stocks, which represent ownership in a company. Explain that by investing in stocks, individuals become shareholders and can benefit from the company's growth and profits. Discuss how stocks can be bought and sold on stock exchanges and the importance of researching companies before investing.

Bonds: Help your kids understand that bonds are loans made to governments or corporations. Explain that when someone invests in bonds, they are lending money to the issuer in exchange for regular interest payments and the return on the initial investment at maturity. Emphasize that bonds are generally considered lower risk compared to stocks.

Mutual Funds: Introduce the idea of mutual funds, which are investment vehicles that pool money from multiple investors to invest in a diversified portfolio of stocks, bonds, or other assets. Explain that mutual funds are managed by professionals who make investment decisions on behalf of the investors. Discuss the benefits of diversification and how mutual funds offer an easy way to access a diversified investment portfolio.

Real Estate: Discuss the concept of real estate as an investment. Explain that investing in real estate involves purchasing properties, such as houses, apartments, or commercial buildings, expecting to generate income through rent or appreciation in value over time. Help your kids understand the potential benefits and risks of real estate investments.

Savings Accounts: Explain that savings accounts are a basic form of investment where individuals deposit their money in a bank or credit union. Discuss how savings accounts offer a safe place to store money and earn interest, although the returns are typically lower than other investment options.

Age-Appropriate Investments: Tailor the discussion to your child's age and understanding. For younger children, you can focus on more straightforward concepts like saving money in a piggy bank or opening a savings account. As they grow older, they introduce more complex investment vehicles and strategies that align with their ability to comprehend.

Learning Opportunities: Encourage your kids to explore and learn about different investment vehicles. Suggest age-appropriate books, websites, or videos that provide information about investments. Consider taking them to investment seminars or workshops designed for young investors, if available.

Risk and Return: Discuss the concept of risk and return about different investment vehicles. Help your kids understand that investments with potentially higher returns often have more significant risks. Teach them the importance of balancing risk and return based on their investment goals and comfort levels.

Financial Advisor: Consider involving a financial advisor, if feasible, to provide guidance and help explain investment options in more detail. A financial advisor can provide personalized advice and recommendations based on your family's financial situation and goals.

Exploring different investment vehicles exposes your kids to various options for growing their money. Encourage them to ask questions, discuss investment choices, and reinforce the importance of making informed decisions. This early exposure to investment vehicles can lay the groundwork for their financial literacy and help them develop the skills needed for long-term financial success.

DISCUSS RISK AND REWARD

Discussing risk and reward is crucial when exploring investment options with your kids. Here's an explanation of what it means to discuss risk and reward and how you can approach this topic with them:

Risk and Reward: Explain to your kids that all investments involve risk and reward. Risk refers to the possibility of losing some or all of the invested money, while reward relates to the potential for earning a return or profit.

Risk Tolerance: Help your kids understand the concept of risk tolerance, which refers to their comfort level with taking on investment risks. Explain that everyone has a different risk tolerance, and finding a balance between taking risks and preserving capital is essential.

Diversification: Emphasize the importance of diversification in managing risk. Discuss how diversification involves spreading investments across different assets, such as stocks, bonds, and real estate, to reduce the impact of a single investment's performance on the overall portfolio. Use relatable examples to illustrate how diversification can help mitigate risk.

Time Horizon: Discuss the concept of a time horizon, which refers to the time an investor plans to hold onto their investments. Explain that longer time horizons generally allow for a higher tolerance for risk, as there is more time to recover from market fluctuations and potentially benefit from long-term growth.

Investment Goals: Encourage your kids to think about their investment goals and what they hope to achieve by investing. Discuss short-term goals, such as saving for a specific purchase, and long-term goals, like funding education or retirement. Help them understand that different investment options align with goals and time horizons.

Risk Assessment: Engage your kids in conversations about the risks of different investment options. Talk about the factors that can affect investment performance, such as market volatility, economic conditions, and company-specific risks. Encourage them to consider the potential risks before making investment decisions.

Research and Due Diligence: Teach your kids the importance of conducting research and due diligence before investing. Discuss the significance of understanding the fundamentals of an investment, such as analysing a company's financial health, evaluating market trends, and seeking professional advice when needed.

Reward Potential: Explain that higher-risk investments often come with the potential for higher rewards, while lower-risk investments typically offer more modest returns. Help them understand that different investments carry varying levels of potential reward based on market conditions, performance history, and other factors.

Investment Simulations: Consider using investment simulations or virtual trading platforms that allow kids to experience the ups and downs of investing in a risk-free environment. This can help them understand how different investment decisions can lead to varying outcomes and develop a better grasp of risk and reward.

Learning from Mistakes: Discuss the importance of learning from investment mistakes and failures. Encourage your kids to view setbacks as learning opportunities and to approach investing with a long-term mindset. Help them understand that mistakes can happen, but with proper knowledge and experience, they can make more informed investment decisions in the future.

By discussing risk and reward with your kids, you empower them to make informed investment choices and develop a realistic understanding of the potential outcomes. Encourage open dialogue, answer their questions, and guide them toward making prudent investment decisions that align with their risk tolerance and goals.

HIGHLIGHT LONG-TERM THINKING

Highlighting long-term thinking is essential when exploring investment options with your kids. Here's an explanation of what it means to highlight long-term thinking and how you can incorporate it into your discussions:

Time Horizon: Explain to your kids that investments are typically considered for the long term. Help them understand that the value of investments can fluctuate in the short term, but historically, they have the potential to grow and provide returns over an extended period.

Compound Interest: Teach your kids about the power of compound interest. Explain that when they invest their money, it has the potential to earn interest or returns, which can then be reinvested to generate even more earnings over time. Illustrate the concept using relatable examples to help them understand the benefits of starting early and allowing their investments to grow.

Goal Planning: Encourage your kids to consider their long-term goals and aspirations. Discuss how investing can help them achieve those goals, such as saving for college, buying a house, or funding their retirement. Emphasize the importance of aligning their investment decisions with their long-term goals.

Patience and Discipline: Instil the values of patience and discipline when investing. Help your kids understand that successful investing requires sticking to a long-term plan and resisting the urge to make impulsive decisions based on short-term market fluctuations. Highlight the benefits of staying invested and avoiding reactionary behaviour.

Historical Performance: Share historical data and examples to illustrate how long-term investing has succeeded. Show them how various investment options, such as stocks or mutual funds, have grown in value despite short-term market volatility. This can help them develop confidence in the potential of long-term investments.

Investment Education: Provide educational resources to help your kids learn more about investing and its long-term benefits. Books, articles, videos, and online courses tailored for kids and young adults can be valuable tools to expand their knowledge and understanding of long-term investment strategies.

Investment Horizons: Discuss different investment horizons and how they align with specific goals. Explain that certain investment options, like stocks or real estate, may be more suitable for long-term growth, while others, like bonds or savings accounts, may offer more stability for short-term needs.

Regular Contributions: Encourage your kids to make regular contributions to their investments. Discuss the concept of dollar-cost averaging, which involves investing a fixed amount of money at regular intervals regardless of market conditions. This approach can help mitigate the impact of short-term market volatility and take advantage of potential opportunities over the long run.

Monitoring Progress: Teach your kids the importance of monitoring their investments' progress over time. Help them understand how to track their investments' performance and make adjustments if necessary. Show them how periodically reviewing and rebalancing their portfolios can help maintain alignment with their long-term goals.

Emphasize Long-Term Benefits: Reinforce the idea that long-term investing is a way to build wealth and achieve financial goals over time. Help your kids understand that investing is not a get-rich-quick scheme but a means to secure their financial future. By highlighting the potential rewards of long-term thinking, you motivate them to adopt a patient and goal-oriented approach to investing.

By highlighting long-term thinking, you help your kids develop a mindset focused on the future and the benefits of patient investing. Encourage them to think beyond short-term gains and consider their investment decisions' long-term potential. This perspective can empower them to make informed choices and set themselves up for financial success in the future.

ENCOURAGE RESEARCH AND LEARNING

Encouraging research and learning is a crucial aspect when exploring investment options with your kids. Here's an explanation of what it means to encourage research and learning and how you can incorporate it into your discussions:

Understanding Investment Basics: Start by explaining the fundamental concepts of investing to your kids. Teach them about investment options such as stocks, bonds, mutual funds, and real estate. Help them understand the risks, potential returns, and how these investments work.

Online Resources and Books: Introduce your kids to age-appropriate online resources and books to help them learn more about investing. Numerous educational websites, articles, and books are available that simplify financial concepts for young learners. Encourage them to explore these resources and expand their knowledge.

News and Market Updates: Share relevant news articles or market updates with your kids to help them understand how current events and trends can impact investments. Discuss the importance of staying informed about economic factors, company news, and global events that can influence investment decisions.

Virtual Trading Simulators: Consider using virtual trading simulators or investment apps specifically designed for educational purposes. These platforms allow kids to experience investing in a simulated environment without risking real money. It helps them understand the dynamics of buying and selling investments and the impact of their decisions.

Investment Case Studies: Explore real-life investment case studies with your kids. Discuss success stories and examples of investments that didn't perform well. Help them analyse the factors contributing to these outcomes and identify valuable lessons from each case study.

Company Research: Teach your kids the importance of researching companies before making investment decisions. Encourage them to explore a company's financial statements, business model, products or services, competitive landscape, and growth potential. This exercise helps them develop critical thinking skills and make informed investment choices.

Diversification: Explain the concept of diversification and its role in managing investment risk. Help your kids understand the benefits of spreading their investments across different asset classes and industries. Discuss how diversification can potentially lower the impact of a single investment's performance on its overall portfolio.

Investment Goals and Risk Tolerance: Guide your kids in setting investment goals and understanding their risk tolerance. Help them define their financial objectives, such as saving for a specific purchase or long-term wealth accumulation. Discuss the relationship between risk and potential returns, ensuring they are comfortable with the level of risk associated with their investments.

Financial News Discussions: Regularly discuss financial news and investment-related topics. Encourage your kids to ask questions and express their opinions. This promotes critical thinking, helps them develop a deeper understanding of the financial world, and strengthens their ability to make informed decisions.

Mentorship and Expert Guidance: Consider seeking expert guidance or mentorship to give your kids additional insights into investment options. This can be through a financial advisor, investment workshops, or connecting with professionals in the financial industry who can share their expertise and experiences.

By encouraging research and learning, you empower your kids to participate in their financial journey actively. Instil a curiosity for understanding investments and provide them with the necessary tools and resources to expand their knowledge. This approach fosters a sense of independence, critical thinking, and confidence when exploring and making investment decisions.

BEYOND THE BASICS

Exploring Additional Financial Concepts and Strategies

The best investment you can make is in yourself.' By understanding key financial concepts and implementing effective strategies, you can shape a prosperous future and achieve your financial goals.

Warren Buffett

Some primary and non-discussed topics related to personal finance that many people may not be aware of or may not discuss as much include

Tax: Many people don't understand the various taxes they have to pay or how to plan for them effectively. This can lead to paying more taxes than necessary or missing out on tax deductions and credits.

Entrepreneurship: Entrepreneurship is designing, launching, and running a new business venture or enterprise to make a profit. It involves taking calculated risks and creating value through innovation and creativity.

Inflation: Inflation is the increase in the prices of goods and services over time. It can erode the value of savings and investments, but many people may not fully understand how inflation works or how to protect their wealth from its effects.

Compound Interest: Compound interest is interest earned not only on the principal amount but also on any interest earned on that amount. It can be a powerful tool for building wealth over time, but many people may not fully understand how it works or how to take advantage of it.

Estate Planning: Estate planning involves preparing to transfer one's assets after one passes away. It can include creating a will, setting up trusts, and naming beneficiaries. Many people may not think about estate planning until later in life, but it's essential to start planning early to ensure that one's assets are distributed according to their wishes.

Royalties: Royalties can be an essential source of income for those who work in creative fields. However, many people may not understand how royalties work, how they are calculated, and how to negotiate.

Depreciation: As we mentioned earlier, depreciation is the decrease in the value of an asset over time. It is an important concept to understand when it comes to buying and selling assets, but it is not discussed as much as other personal finance topics.

Money Works for Us: "Money Works for Us" means that instead of working for Money, we make it work for us by investing it in various assets, such as stocks, real estate, or mutual funds. Doing so allows us to earn passive income and build wealth over time without working harder or longer hours.

Behavioural Finance: Behavioural finance is the study of how people make financial decisions and how their behaviour can affect their finances. It can include cognitive biases, emotional decision-making, and financial literacy. Many people may not know behaviour's role in financial decisions, but understanding it can help them make better financial choices.

Paying Ourselves First: 'Paying Ourselves First' means setting aside a portion of our income for saving and investing before we use it for any other expenses. It is a financial strategy emphasizing the importance of prioritizing saving and investing for long-term financial goals rather than spending all our income on immediate wants and needs. By paying ourselves first, we make saving and investing a habit and ensure we consistently build wealth for our future.

These topics are important because they can significantly impact an individual's financial well-being. By understanding taxation, royalties, depreciation, compounding, and other related concepts, individuals can make informed decisions about their finances and potentially save or earn more Money in the long run. Additionally, knowledge of these concepts can help individuals navigate the financial world more effectively and confidently.

TAX

Tax is mandatory financial charge governments impose on individuals, businesses, and other entities to fund public services and government activities. Taxes can take many forms, including income, sales, property, and corporate taxes. The tax is usually calculated based on a percentage of the individual or entity's income, assets, or transactions. The rates and rules vary depending on the jurisdiction and the type of tax.

Taxation is a crucial aspect of government finance. It provides a significant portion of the revenue needed to fund public goods and services, such as education, healthcare, infrastructure, and social welfare programs.

Many different types of taxes are implemented worldwide, including.

Income Tax: This is a tax on the income earned by individuals, businesses, and other entities. The tax paid is usually calculated as a percentage of the income earned.

Sales Tax: A sales tax is on consumer goods and services. The tax is usually calculated as a percentage of the sale price.

Property Tax: This tax on real estate, including land, buildings, and other structures. The tax is usually calculated as a percentage of the property's assessed value.

Value-added tax (VAT): This type of sales tax is based on the value added to a product or service at each production stage.

Corporate tax: This is a tax on the profits earned by corporations.

Estate tax: Estate tax is a tax on the value of an individual's estate after death.

GST, or Goods and Services Tax: This value-added tax is similar to a sales tax. It is a tax on the supply of goods and services in many countries worldwide, including India, Canada, Australia, and New Zealand. GST is usually levied at the final point of sale to the consumer, but it is also collected and remitted by businesses throughout the supply chain. The rate of GST varies depending on the jurisdiction, but it is typically a percentage of the sale price or value added.

These are just a few examples of the many different types of taxes worldwide. The rates and rules governing each type of tax vary depending on the jurisdiction and the purpose of the tax.

Here are some tips on teaching kids about the importance of knowing various taxations connected with Money:

Start by explaining what taxes are: Kids need to understand what taxes are and how they work before they can appreciate their importance. Explain that taxes are the fees that individuals and businesses pay to the government to support public goods and services, such as roads, schools, and hospitals.

Use real-life examples: Show your kids how taxes work in real life. Point out the sales tax on a receipt or explain how property taxes fund their school.

Explain the different types of taxes: Introduce your kids to the different types of taxes, such as income tax, sales tax, property tax, and value-added tax. Explain how each tax works and what it is used for.

Teach them about tax brackets: Show your kids how different tax brackets work and how they affect the amount of taxes paid. Explain that the more money someone earns, the higher their tax rate.

Discuss the importance of paying taxes: Talk to your kids about the importance of paying taxes to support public goods and services. Explain that taxes help create a better society for everyone, and everyone is responsible for paying their fair share.

Discuss the consequences of not paying taxes: Explain to your kids the consequences of not paying taxes, such as fines, penalties, and even legal consequences like imprisonment.

Encourage them to ask questions: Encourage your kids to ask questions about taxes and Money. Answer their questions honestly and in a way that they can understand. This will help them better understand how taxes and money work and the importance of staying informed about financial matters.

CONVERSATIONS BETWEEN PARENTS AND CHILDREN:
(IMPORTANCE OF UNDERSTANDING TAX)

EXAMPLE -1:

Parent: Hey, do you know what taxes are?

Child: Taxes? I've heard that word before but am unsure what it means.

Parent: Well, taxes are Money we must pay the government. They help pay for things like schools, roads, hospitals, and other things we use.

Child: Oh, I see. Why do we have to pay taxes?

Parent: That's a great question. We pay taxes because we are all responsible for contributing to what makes our community a great place to live. So, when we pay our taxes, we are doing our part to help make sure that we have good schools, safe roads, and good healthcare.

Child: So, everyone has to pay taxes?

Parent: Yes, that's right. Everyone who earns Money has to pay taxes. And there are different kinds of taxes that people have to pay depending on how much they earn and what they do for a living.

Child: Wow, that's a lot to understand.

Parent: It can seem a bit overwhelming at first, but it's essential to know about taxes because they affect all of us. As you grow up and earn Money, you'll need to know about taxes to ensure you're paying the right amount and taking advantage of any deductions or credits you're eligible for.

Child: Okay, I'll try to remember that. Thanks for explaining it to me.

EXAMPLE -2:

Parent: Hey, Buddy/Princess, do you know the taxes?

Child: No, what are taxes?

Parent: Well, taxes are a certain amount of money people must pay to the government. The government uses this Money for essential things like schools, hospitals, and roads.

Child: Oh, okay. So why is it important to understand taxes?

Parent: It's essential because taxes are a part of how the world works and affect everyone. Even kids like you can start learning about taxes and how they work. One day, you'll have to pay taxes, too, so it's good to understand how they work and what they're used for.

Child: Oh, I see. How do I learn more about taxes?

Parent: We can start by looking up some information online or talking to an expert like an accountant or financial advisor. It's never too early to start learning about taxes and how they affect our lives.

EXAMPLE -3:

Parent: Hey, do you know what taxes are?

Child: Umm, not really.

Parent: Well, taxes are a percentage of your income or the Money you spend on the government. It pays for schools, hospitals, roads, and other public services.

Child: Oh, okay. So, why is it essential for me to know about taxes?

Parent: Understanding taxes is essential because it helps you know how much you'll need to pay for things you buy, like toys or video games. And as you grow older and start earning your own Money, you'll need to pay taxes on your income too.

Child: That sounds like a lot of Money. How do I know how much I have to pay?

Parent: Well, that's where it can get a little complicated. Countries and states have different tax rates, and your pay depends on how much you earn and spend. But the good news is that you don't have to figure it out alone. Some people can help, like accountants or tax professionals.

Child: I see. So, taxes help pay for things like schools and hospitals, and I have to pay them when I start working. Is there anything else I should know?

Parent: Yes, there's something called "tax returns," which you file each year to tell the government how much you earned and how much tax you paid. If you paid too much tax, you might get a refund, which means the government owes you Money back. And if you didn't pay enough tax, you might owe money to the government.

Child: Wow, I never knew taxes were so important. Thanks for explaining it to me, Mom/Dad.

Parent: You're welcome, Buddy/Princess. It's never too early to learn about Money and its workings.

ENTREPRENEURSHIP

Entrepreneurship is designing, launching, and running a new business venture or enterprise to make a profit. It involves taking calculated risks and creating value through innovation and creativity.

An entrepreneur starts, operates, and grows a business by identifying a need in the market and finding ways to fill that need profitably. They are willing to invest their time, Money, and energy into creating something new and unique that has the potential to make a significant impact on the economy and society.

There are several types of entrepreneurship, including

Small Business Entrepreneurship: The most common type, where an individual or a group of individuals start a small business venture to fulfil a local demand. These types of businesses are typically self-funded or funded by friends and family.

Scalable Start-up Entrepreneurship involves starting a business venture to increase and achieve a significant market share. Venture capitalists or angel investors typically fund these types of businesses.

Social Entrepreneurship: This type involves starting a business venture with a social or environmental mission and generating profits. These types of businesses are often structured as non-profit organizations or social enterprises.

Corporate Entrepreneurship: This involves innovating within an existing company or organization to create new products, services, or business units within an existing company or organization.

Digital Entrepreneurship: This type of Entrepreneurship tool leverages technology and the internet to start a business venture or create a digital product.

Lifestyle Entrepreneurship: This type involves starting a business venture that aligns with an individual's lifestyle and values. These types of businesses are devised and self-funded, and the primary goal is to create a sustainable become stream while maintaining a desired work-life balance.

Each type of entrepreneurship requires different skills, strategies, and approaches to be successful.

You are explaining entrepreneurship to a kid in a simple and easy-to-understand way. Here's an example:

Entrepreneurship is valuable for your business or developing new ideas and ways to make Money. It's like being the boss of your own company! Entrepreneurship benefits them by taking risks and working hard to make their ideas a reality. They think of creative solutions to problems and always look for ways to improve. They must also be good at managing Money, time, and resources to make their business successful.

You can give examples of successful entrepreneurs such as Bill Gates, Steve Jobs, and Mark Zuckerberg to help them understand the concept. You can also encourage them to think of ideas for a business or a product they could create.

CONVERSATIONS BETWEEN PARENTS AND
CHILDREN: (ENTREPRENEURSHIP)

EXAMPLE -1:

Parent: Have you ever heard the word entrepreneurship, dear?

Child: No, mom/dad. What is that?

Parent: Well, entrepreneurship is all about taking the initiative, being creative, and being willing to take risks to

create something new that will benefit others.
Child: That sounds cool! How do you become an entrepreneur?
Parent: Anyone can become an entrepreneur, but it takes a lot of hard work and dedication. You need to identify a need in the market or a problem that people are facing and devise a solution to address it. It could be a new product or service you create or a way to improve an existing one.
Child: I see. Why is it important to learn about entrepreneurship?
Parent: Understanding entrepreneurship is important because it can help you develop problem-solving, decision-making, and creativity skills. These skills are valuable not only for business but also in other areas of life.
Additionally, entrepreneurship can lead to innovation and economic growth, which benefits everyone.
Child: That makes sense. Can you give me an example of an entrepreneur?
Parent: Sure. Let's take Steve Jobs, the co-founder of Apple, as an example. He identified the need for personal computers and mobile devices that are user-friendly and aesthetically pleasing. He came up with the idea of creating the Macintosh computer and later the iPhone and iPad, which revolutionized the tech industry and changed how we communicate and work.
Child: Wow, that's amazing. I want to be an entrepreneur too!
Parent: I'm glad to hear that, dear. Being an entrepreneur is not easy, but you can achieve great things if you have the passion, determination, and willingness to learn.

EXAMPLE -2:
Parent: Have you ever heard of the word "entrepreneurship"?
Child: No, what is it?
Parent: Well, it's when someone starts their own business and takes on financial risks to make a profit. It's about being creative and developing new ideas for products or services that people need or want.

Child: Oh, I see. Why is it important to know about entrepreneurship?

Parent: Understanding entrepreneurship can be helpful because it can teach you about creating opportunities and self-sufficiency. Instead of just working for someone else, you can create your job and become your boss. It can also help you learn about the value of hard work, taking risks, and learning from failure.

Child: That sounds interesting. Can anyone be an entrepreneur?

Parent: Yes, anyone can become an entrepreneur if they have the right mindset and are willing to put in the time and effort. It's not always easy, but with perseverance and dedication, anyone can start their own business and succeed.

Child: Wow, I never thought about being an entrepreneur before. It sounds exciting!

Parent: Yes, it can be exciting, but it's important to remember that it also takes a lot of hard work and determination. But if you're passionate about your actions and believe in yourself, you can accomplish great things.

EXAMPLE -3:

Parent: Hey, Buddy/Princess, have you ever heard of entrepreneurship?

Child: No, what is that?

Parent: Entrepreneurship is when someone creates and starts their own business. They turn an idea into a way to make money for themselves and help others simultaneously.

Child: Oh, that sounds cool. Why is it important to know about it?

Parent: Great question! Knowing about entrepreneurship can help you think creatively and develop new ideas to solve problems. It can also give you the tools to start your own business one day and be your boss. Plus, entrepreneurs often create products or services that help make our lives easier or better in some way.

Child: Wow, I never thought about it like that. So, how can I learn more about entrepreneurship?

Parent: Well, there are lots of books, articles, and videos out there that can help you learn more about entrepreneurship. You can also talk to people who have started their businesses and ask about their experiences. And who knows, maybe one day you'll be an entrepreneur and positively impact the world!

INFLATION

Inflation is a general increase in prices of goods and services over time, which causes the purchasing power of a currency to decline. It is usually measured as a percentage increase in the price level of a basket of goods and services in an economy over some time, such as a year.

Inflation occurs when the demand for goods and services exceeds the supply, causing prices to rise. This can happen due to an increase in money supply, a decrease in productivity, and external factors like changes in global commodity prices. Inflation affects the economy, including businesses, households, and the government, and can have positive and negative effects depending on the level of inflation.

Several factors can cause inflation, including.

Demand-Pull Inflation: This type of inflation occurs when demand for goods and services outstrips supply, increasing prices.

Cost-Push Inflation: This type of inflation occurs when the costs of production increase, leading to an increase in prices.

Currency Inflation: This type of inflation occurs when there is an increase in the supply of Money in the economy, leading to a decrease in the value of Money and an increase in prices.

Structural Inflation: This type of inflation occurs due to long-term changes in an economy's structure, such as changes in technology, demographics, or regulations.

Inflation is generally measured by the Consumer Price Index

(CPI), which tracks the price changes of a basket of goods and services over time. High inflation can be a problem as it erodes the value of Money, leads to increased costs for businesses and consumers, and can harm economic growth.

To teach a kid about inflation, try the following approach:
Start with the basics: Explain to the child what Money is and what it's used for. You can use everyday examples like buying toys, candy, or other things they may be interested in.
Define inflation: Once the child understands Money, you can introduce the concept of inflation. Explain to the child that inflation is when the prices of things they buy increase over time. Several factors, such as supply and demand changes or the economy, can cause this.
Use real-life examples: Show the child how inflation works in real life using examples they can relate to. For instance, you can tell them how the candy bar cost has increased or how their favourite toy now costs more than it did a few years ago.
Explain the impact of inflation: Help the child understand how inflation affects their purchasing power. Explain that if they don't keep up with inflation, they won't be able to buy as much with their money as they could before. You can use examples like how they might need more money to buy the same amount of candy or toys they used to.
Encourage savings: Finally, encourage the child to save their money to help combat the effects of inflation. Explain that by saving their Money, they can earn interest to help their money grow faster than inflation. You can also talk about the importance of investing in stocks or other assets that can help their money grow even faster.

CONVERSATIONS BETWEEN PARENTS
AND CHILDREN: (INFLATION)

EXAMPLE -1:
Parent: Hey, Buddy/Princess, do you know what inflation is?
Child: No, what is it?

Parent: Well, inflation is when prices of goods and services increase over time. For example, a loaf of bread costs $2 today, but next year it might cost $2.10 or even $2.50. This is because Money's value decreases over time for various reasons.

Child: Oh, I see. Why is it essential for me to know about inflation?

Parent: It's essential because inflation can affect the buying power of your Money. If you save Money in a bank account, you may need more than e interest rate you earn to keep up with the inflation rate. That means the Money you save might be worth less in the future than it is now.

Child: What can I do to protect my Money from inflation?

Parent: Good question! One way is to invest your money in assets that have the potential to earn more than the inflation rate. Another way is to budget your money wisely and save for future goals. It's also important to monitor inflation and adjust your financial strategies accordingly.

Child: Okay, I understand now.

Thank you for explaining it to me, Mom/Dad!

EXAMPLE -2:

Parent: Do you remember when we bought that toy for you last year for $10?

Child: Yes, I remember.

Parent: Well, do you think that same toy would cost $10 now?

Child: Hmm, I'm still determining.

Parent: because of inflation, the cost of things increases over time. That same toy might cost $11 or $12 now. That's why it's important to understand inflation to plan for the future and ensure we can afford what we need and want.

Child: Oh, I get it. So we must ensure we have enough money to buy things when they cost more later.

Parent: Yes, exactly! And there are ways we can do that, like saving Money, investing, and making intelligent financial decisions.

EXAMPLE -3:
Parent: Have you ever heard of the term inflation?
Child: No, what is it?
Parent: Inflation is when prices of things go up over time. For example, if a candy bar used to cost $1 but now costs $1.50, that's inflation.
Child: Oh, I see. Why does that happen?
Parent: There are different reasons for inflation, but one reason is that when there is too much Money in the economy, it can lead to higher prices because there is more demand for goods and services than supply.
Child: So, what does that mean for us?
Parent: Our Money may not be worth as much because prices will likely increase. That's why learning about inflation and considering ways to protect our Money from losing value over time is essential.

COMPOUND INTEREST

Compound interest refers to the interest earned on the principal amount and the interest accumulated over time. As interest accrues, it is added to the principal amount, and the subsequent interest calculation is based on this new, higher balance.

Compound interest is a powerful tool for growing wealth over time, as the interest earned on interest can snowball into significant earnings over a long period. It is often used in investments like savings accounts, bonds, and stocks.

Here's an example of how compound interest works:
Let's say you deposit $1,000 into a savings account that earns 5% annual interest, compounded annually. After the first year, your account will have earned $50 in interest, bringing your total balance to $1,050. In the second year, your account will earn interest not only on the original $1,000 but also on the $50 in interest you earned in the first year, resulting in $52.50

in interest for the second year. At the end of the second year, your account balance will be $1,102.50.

Over time, the power of compounding can add up. If you left your Money in the account for ten years, your balance would grow to $1,628.89 – $628.89 in earned interest! This is because the interest earned each year is added to the principal amount, resulting in a more extensive base for future interest calculations.

Here are some tips on teaching a kid how compound interest works:

Start with the basics: Before diving into compound interest, ensure your child understands simple interest. Explain that simple interest is calculated based on the initial Money invested and the interest rate.

Use real-life examples: Give your child real-life examples of compound interest, such as a savings account, investment account, or loan. Explain how compound interest affects the growth of their money over time.

Show the math: Use a calculator or spreadsheet to demonstrate how compound interest is calculated. Start with a simple example and gradually increase the complexity as your child becomes more comfortable with the math.

Use visual aids: Draw graphs or charts to show the effects of compound interest over time. Seeing the growth of their Money can help your child understand the power of compound interest.

Practice with scenarios: Give your child scenarios to practice calculating compound interest, such as calculating the interest earned on a savings account over some time.

Keep it fun: Make the learning experience fun by incorporating games or challenges involving compound interest. For example, you could challenge your child to find the best interest rate on a savings account.

Reinforce the concept: Reinforce the concept of compound interest by using it in everyday conversations about Money.

Help your child see how understanding compound interest can help them make smart financial decisions in the future.

CONVERSATIONS BETWEEN PARENTS AND
CHILDREN: (COMPOUND INTEREST)

EXAMPLE -1:

Parent: Hey, Buddy/Princess, do you know what compound interest is?

Child: No, I don't think so.

Parent: Well, it's an excellent concept in finance. It's like interest that keeps building on itself over time. Let me give you an example. Suppose you put $100 in a savings account with 5% annual interest. After one year, you'd have $105.

Child: Yeah, I get it.

Parent: But with compound interest, that $105 would earn another 5% the following year. So after two years, you'd have more than $110. And the following year, you'd earn interest on that amount plus the interest from the previous years. It just keeps adding up and growing bigger and bigger.

Child: Wow, that's cool! So it's like free Money?

Parent: Well, not exactly. You must still save and invest your money wisely to earn compound interest. But it's a powerful tool to help you grow your wealth over time.

Child: Okay, I want to learn more about it!

Parent: Great! We can explore more examples and discuss how to use compound interest in your savings and investment goals. It's important to understand, especially when planning for your future.

EXAMPLE -2:

Parent: Hey, Buddy/Princess, do you know what compound interest is?

Child: No, what is it?

Parent: Well, it's like magic. When you save Money in a bank account, the bank pays you extra on top of what you saved. That's called interest. But with compound interest, the bank pays you interest on your original savings and the interest you earned.

Child: Wow, that sounds cool. But why is it essential to understand compound interest?

Parent: Because over time, that extra interest can add up. If you save $100 and earn 5% interest each year, you'll have $105 after one year. But with compound interest, the bank will pay you interest on that $105 next year, so you'll have even more Money. And the longer you save, the more your money will grow.

Child: So if I save money now, I'll have even more money when I'm older?

Parent: Exactly! That's why it's essential to start saving early and take advantage of compound interest. The more money you save now, the more you'll have later.

EXAMPLE -3:

Parent: Have you heard of compound interest before?

Child: No, what is that?

Parent: It's an excellent concept to help you grow your Money. Let me give you an example. Say you have $100 and put it in a bank account that earns 5% interest each year. After the first year, you'll have $105.

Child: Yes.

Parent: Instead of taking that $5 out, leave it in the account and earn interest on $105 the following year. That means you'll earn $5.25 in interest the second year for $110.25. And it keeps going like that, where you earn interest on the original amount plus the interest you've already earned.

Child: Oh, so you earn more and more money as time goes on?

Parent: Exactly! That's why it's called compound interest. And it's important to understand because it can help you save for big purchases or invest for your future.

ESTATE PLANNING

Estate planning is arranging for managing and distributing

a person's assets after death. It involves creating a will, establishing trusts, designating beneficiaries, and making other legal arrangements to ensure that the person's wishes are carried out, and their assets are distributed in the most effective and tax-efficient manner possible. Estate planning can also include deciding on healthcare and end-of-life decisions and managing assets if someone becomes incapacitated.

Estate planning examples include:
Drafting a will or trust ensures that your assets are distributed according to your wishes after your death.
Establish a power of attorney to authorize someone to make legal or financial decisions if you become incapacitated.
Creating a health care directive or living will to communicate your end-of-life wishes and authorize someone to make medical decisions if you cannot do so.
You are setting up a life insurance policy or a trust to provide for your family's financial needs after your death and making gifts to family members or charitable organizations to reduce your estate tax liability, and transferring assets to a trust or LLC to protect them from creditors or lawsuits and to review and to update your estate plan regularly to reflect your current wishes and circumstances.

Teaching kids about estate planning can be done in simple terms that are easy to understand. Here are some steps to follow:
Start by explaining what estate planning is: It is the process of preparing for what will happen to a person's property, assets, and belongings after they pass away.
Use relatable examples: You can use relatable examples like discussing how a person can pass on their favourite toy or game to someone else when they are done playing with it. This helps to illustrate the concept of passing on assets.
Introduce the concept of wills and trusts: Explain the

difference between a will and a trust and how they work. You can use examples such as well-being, like instructions for who gets what, and trust is like a particular container to keep things safe until it is time to give them away.

Discuss the importance of estate planning: Explain that it is essential because it helps ensure that a person's wishes are carried out after they pass away and that their loved ones are cared for.

Keep it age-appropriate: The information provided should be age-appropriate depending on the child's age. Younger children may need more straightforward explanations, while older children may be able to understand more complex concepts.

Encourage children to ask questions and clarify any confusion they may have. This helps to reinforce their understanding and makes them more comfortable discussing the topic.

CONVERSATIONS BETWEEN PARENTS AND CHILDREN: (ESTATE PLANNING)

EXAMPLE -1:

Parent: Hey, Buddy/Princess, I wanted to talk to you about something important. Do you know what Estate planning is?

Child: No, I don't. What is it?

Parent: Well, Estate planning ensures that your assets and property are distributed according to your wishes after you pass away. It involves making important decisions about who should inherit your property, who should take care of your children, and how children should manage your assets.

Child: Oh, I see. But why is this important?

Parent: It's essential to ensure your loved ones are cared for even after you're gone. By having an Estate plan in place, you can ensure that your assets are distributed how you want them to be and that your loved ones don't have to worry about legal issues or financial problems after you pass away.

Child: That makes sense. How do you make an Estate plan?

Parent: Well, it can be a complex process, and working with a lawyer specializing in Estate planning is essential. But you might need to consider writing a will, choosing a guardian for your children, setting up a trust, and ensuring that all your important documents are organized and easily accessible.

Child: Okay, I understand. It sounds like a lot to think about, but I can see why it's essential.

Parent: It is a lot to think about, but it's never too early to start planning for the future. And by learning about estate planning now, you'll be better prepared to make crucial decisions when the time comes.

EXAMPLE -2:

Parent: Hey, Buddy/Princess, have you heard of estate planning?

Child: No, what is that?

Parent: Estate planning is the process of preparing for the transfer of your assets to your beneficiaries after you die. Planning for this is essential because it ensures your loved ones receive your assets and properties without legal complications.

Child: Oh, I see.

Why is this important for me to know?

Parent: You'll also have assets and properties one day, like a house or car. When that time comes, you'll want to make sure you have a plan for what will happen to those things when you're no longer around. It's also essential to consider your medical care and how someone else will manage your finances if you cannot do so yourself.

Child: That makes sense. So what can we do to plan?

Parent: We can start by talking to a lawyer or financial advisor who can help us create a plan tailored to our specific needs and circumstances. It may seem daunting, but taking care of these things is essential to have peace of mind knowing that we've planned for the future.

EXAMPLE -3:

Parent: Hey, Buddy/Princess, do you know what estate planning is?

Child: No, what is it?

Parent: Well, it's a way to make sure that when we pass away, our belongings and assets go to the people we want them to go to. It's like planning what happens to our things after we're gone.

Child: Oh, okay. Why is that important?

Parent: Well, let's say we didn't make a plan and just left everything up to chance. It could create confusion and even arguments among our loved ones when we're no longer here to explain our wishes. By having an estate plan, we can make sure everyone knows exactly what we want to happen to our things, making things easier for everyone.

Child: I see, that makes sense. So it's like ensuring our family knows what to do with our stuff after we're gone?

Parent: Yes, exactly! And it's not just about our physical belongings - an estate plan can also help ensure our Money and investments go to the right people and are used how we want them.

Child: Okay, I think I get it. So it's like ensuring we control what happens to our things even when we're not around anymore.

Parent: Yes, that's a great way to put it. And it's never too early to start thinking about estate planning, even if we have many years ahead. It's always better to be prepared and have a plan in place.

ROYALTIES

Royalties are payments made to the property or asset owner in exchange for using that property or asset. Royalties, such as patents, trademarks, copyrights, and even music or books, are often paid for using intellectual property. These payments are typically made regularly and are often based on a percentage of the revenue generated from using the property or asset.

Royalties refer to Money paid to an individual or entity in exchange for using their property or assets. This can include intellectual property such as patents, trademarks, copyrights, and physical property such as land, minerals, or natural resources. The royalty payment is typically a percentage of the revenue generated using the property or asset. Royalties are commonly paid in music, publishing, and oil and gas extraction industries, where intellectual property or natural resources are essential for business operations.

HERE ARE SOME EXAMPLES OF ROYALTIES:

Music royalties: Musicians and songwriters earn royalties when their music is played on the radio, streamed online, or used in movies, TV shows, and commercials.

Book royalties: Authors earn royalties when their books are sold. The royalty amount is usually a percentage of the book's retail price.

Patent royalties: Companies that hold patents earn royalties when other companies use their patented technology. The royalty amount is usually a percentage of the revenue generated by the technology.

Mineral royalties: Landowners can earn royalties when companies extract minerals such as oil, gas, coal, or metals from their property.

Franchise royalties: Franchise owners pay the franchisor a percentage of their revenue as a royalty fee for using the brand name, trademark, and business model.

Film and television royalties: Actors, writers, and directors earn royalties when their work is used in movies, TV shows, and other media.

Video game royalties: Game developers and publishers earn royalties when their games are sold or downloaded. The royalty amount is usually a percentage of the revenue generated by the game.

Teaching kids about royalties can be a bit complex, but here are some steps to be followed:

Introduce the concept: Start by explaining royalties to your child. Tell them that it's a type of payment someone receives for allowing someone else to use their work or property.

Use examples: Give examples of how royalties work. For instance, if a child loves music, you can explain that a musician can earn royalties every time their song is played on the radio, on streaming platforms, or purchased by someone. Similarly, if a child is into writing or illustration, you can use examples of authors and artists who earn royalties every time someone purchases their book or uses their artwork.

Simplify the math: Royalties are usually calculated as a percentage of the total sales, so you can use simple math to explain how it works. For instance, if an author earns a 10% royalty on each book sold and costs $20, they earn $2 for each book sold.

Discuss the importance: Finally, discuss why royalties are essential. Explain that they are a way for creators to earn money for their hard work and creativity and that royalties can continue to provide income for years after we created the work.

The key is to make it relatable and easy to understand for the child. Using examples relevant to their interests and breaking down the math can make the concept of royalties more accessible.

CONVERSATIONS BETWEEN PARENTS
AND CHILDREN: (ROYALTY)

EXAMPLE -1:

Parent: Hey, Buddy/Princess, do you know what royalties are?

Child: No, I don't know. What are they?

Parent: Royalties are a payment someone gets when their creative work is used or sold. For example, when authors write a book, they get paid a percentage of the book sales as royalties. The same goes for musicians when their songs are played on the radio or streamed online.

Child: Oh, I see. But why is it important to know about royalties?

Parent: It's essential to know about royalties because if you create something valuable and it gets used by others, you have the right to earn money from it. Understanding royalties can help you protect your creative work and get paid for your creative work. It's also important to know about royalties if you want to use someone else's work. You must ensure you have permission and pay them royalties if necessary.

Child: I understand now. If I create something like a story or song, can I earn Money from it?

Parent: Yes! That's why it's important to keep creating and exploring your talents. You always need to find out where it might take you.

EXAMPLE -2:

Parent: Hey, Buddy/Princess, do you know what royalties are?

Child: No, I don't. What are they?

Parent: Royalties are a type of payment someone gets when they allow someone else to use or reproduce something they created. So, for example, if you wrote a book, and someone wanted to make a movie out of it, you could charge them a royalty fee for the right to use your book.

Child: Oh, I see. Why is it important to know about royalties?

Parent: Knowing about royalties can help you understand how artists, writers, and other creative people make money from their work. It's important to respect their rights to work and ensure they get paid fairly for it. Plus, if you ever become a writer or an artist, you'll want to know how to protect your creations and ensure you get paid for them too.

Child: That makes sense. Thanks for explaining it to me, Mom/Dad!

EXAMPLE -3:

Parent: Hey, Buddy/Princess, have you heard of royalties?

Child: No, what is it?
Parent: Royalties are a payment someone receives to use their creative work. For example, if someone writes a book, they can earn royalties when people buy and read it.
Child: Oh, I see. Why is it important to know about royalties?
Parent: It's essential to know about royalties because it can be a way for people to earn money from their creative ideas and hard work. If you have a talent for writing, music, or art, you can earn royalties for the rest of your life. It's a great way to make a living doing what you love.
Child: Wow, that's cool! How do people get royalties?
Parent: To earn royalties, you must create something original and protect it with copyright. This means you own the rights to your work and can control how it's used and who can use it. When someone wants to use your work, like a company that wants to use your song in a commercial, they have to pay you a royalty fee for the right to use it.
Child: I see, so if I create something great, I can earn money from it for a long time.
Parent: That's right! So it's essential always to be creative and think outside the box because you never know what unique ideas you might have.

DEPRECIATION

Depreciation refers to the decrease in the value of an asset over time due to wear and tear, obsolescence, or other factors that cause the asset to become less useful or valuable. It is a measure of the decrease in the value of an asset over its useful life.

Depreciation is commonly used in accounting to allocate the cost of an asset over its useful life to match better the cost of the asset with the revenue it generates.

Depreciation is the gradual decrease in the value of an asset over time due to factors such as wear and tear, age, obsolescence, or changes in market conditions. It is a way of allocating the cost of an asset over its useful life, reflecting the fact that the asset becomes less valuable or useful over time.

For example, if a company buys a new delivery van for $50,000, it may estimate that the van will be helpful for five years before it needs to be replaced. In this case, the company would depreciate the van's value over five years, meaning that it would be written down in value by $10,000 per year. At the end of 5 years, the book value of the van would be zero, reflecting the fact that it has fully depreciated.

Depreciation is essential for accounting and tax purposes, as it allows companies to spread the cost of an asset over its useful life rather than taking the entire cost as an expense in the year of purchase. This helps to match expenses with revenues more accurately and can provide a more accurate picture of the company's financial position over time. Depreciation can also impact the resale value of an asset, as buyers may be willing to pay less for a used asset that has been fully depreciated.

Teaching kids about depreciation can be done through various methods, such as:

Using real-life examples: You can use examples of items that depreciate over time, such as cars, computers, or video games. Show them how the value of these items decreases over time due to wear and tear or advancements in technology.

Explaining the concept of useful life: Help kids understand that everything has a useful life, meaning it will eventually wear out or become obsolete. Explain that depreciation is a way of reflecting this fact by gradually reducing the value of an asset over time.

Visual aids: You can use visual aids like graphs or charts to illustrate the concept of depreciation over time. You can draw a chart showing the value of a car decreasing over time or use online resources to create charts or graphs demonstrating the concept.

Engage them in decision-making: Involve your child in financial decisions, such as buying a new computer or car.

Discuss with them the potential costs of purchasing a new item and how its value might depreciate over time.

Make it relatable: Try to relate the concept of depreciation to something your child is interested in, such as a favourite toy or video game. Explain how the value of that item might decrease over time and what factors could contribute to its depreciation.

Using these methods, you can help your child understand the concept of depreciation and how it applies to their daily lives. It can also help them to make more informed decisions about future purchases and investments.

CONVERSATIONS BETWEEN PARENTS AND CHILDREN: (DEPRECIATION)

EXAMPLE -1:

Parent: Remember when we bought your favourite toy car?

Child: Yes, I love that car!

Parent: That's great. Do you know that the car's value decreases over time?

Child: What do you mean by that?

Parent: The car's value will decrease as it ages and wears out. This is called depreciation.

Child: Why does the value decrease?

Parent: It's because of wear and tear. As you play with the car, it gets scratched, the paint might fade, or the wheels might break, making it less valuable over time.

Child: I see.

Parent: This concept applies to many things, not just toys. For example, cars, computers, and other electronics can lose value over time. That's why taking good care of our belongings is essential to make them last longer.

Child: Okay.

Parent: Understanding depreciation is essential because it can help you make better decisions when you want to buy something. You need to think about how long you'll use it, how much it will cost, and how much it will be worth when you want to sell it. Does that make sense?

Child: Yes, I think I understand. Thanks, Mom/Dad!

EXAMPLE -2:

Parent: Hey, have you noticed our car's price has decreased over the years?

Child: Really? Why is that?

Parent: It's because of depreciation. The car's value decreases over time due to wear and tear, age, and other factors.

Child: Oh, I see.

Parent: Depreciation is essential to understand because it affects many things we buy, not just cars. For example, buying a new phone will lose value over time as new models come out, and if we sell it later, we might not get as much money for it as we paid.

Child: So we must be careful about what we buy and when?

Parent: Exactly! It's important to consider how much we'll use something, how much it will cost, and how much it will be worth later. That way, we can make intelligent choices and save Money in the long run.

Child: I get it. Thanks for explaining it to me, Mom/Dad!

EXAMPLE -3:

Parent: Remember when we bought our family TV?

Child: Yes, I remember.

Parent: Did you know that the TV's value has decreased since we bought it?

Child: Really? Why?

Parent: It's because of depreciation. Like anything else we buy, the TV loses its value over time. It can be due to normal wear and tear or just because newer and better models come out.

Child: That's interesting. But why is it important to know about depreciation?

Parent: Understanding depreciation can help us make better decisions when we want to sell something or when we want to buy something new. For example, we can sell the TV for a lower price than we paid or wait until it's not working well and replace it with a new one.

Child: I see. So it's essential to take good care of our things so that they retain their value quickly.

Parent: Absolutely! Taking care of our things can make them last longer and save Money in the long run. That's why it's essential to understand the concept of depreciation and how it affects what we buy.

MONEY WORKING FOR US

"Money working for us" refers to using our Money to generate more over time through investing and other financial strategies. It means we put our money to work for us instead of simply letting it sit idle or using it for short-term spending.

When we invest our Money in stocks, real estate, mutual funds, or other vehicles, we can earn returns that grow over time. We can compound our gains and earn even more by reinvesting those returns. This is how Money can work for us to build long-term wealth.

The key to making money work for us is to have a long-term perspective and a well-planned financial strategy. It also requires knowledge and education about investment options, risks, and potential returns.

Here are a few examples of the concept of "Money Working for Us":

Investing in stocks: By investing in stocks, we can earn returns on our Money through dividends and capital gains. This means our Money works for us, even while we sleep!

Owning rental property: If we own rental property, we can earn passive income through rent payments. This means our Money works for us, even if we're not actively managing the property.

Saving in a high-yield savings account: We can earn interest by saving our Money in a high-yield savings account. This means our Money works for us, even if we're not actively investing it.

Starting a small business: By starting a small business, we can earn income from our business activities. This means our Money works for us, even if we're not actively working for someone else.

Investing in real estate: By investing in real estate, we can earn income through rental payments or by selling properties at a profit. This means our Money works for us, even if we're not actively managing the properties.

These are just a few examples of how "Money Working for Us" can be applied in real life.

Teaching kids about the concept of "Money Working for Us" can be a great way to help them understand the importance of saving and investing. Here are some tips on how to do it:

Start with the basics: Explain to your child what saving and investing means. Tell them how saving Money can help them achieve their financial goals and how investing can grow their money over time.

Use real-life examples: Use examples your child can relate to, such as saving for a new toy or investing in a college fund. You can also use stories about successful investors or entrepreneurs to help them understand how Money can work for them.

Encourage saving and investing: Encourage your child to save money and consider investing a portion. You can set up a savings or investment account for them, explaining how interest or dividends can add up over time.

Make it fun: Try to make learning about Money and investing fun using games or activities. You can play games that teach about budgeting, investing, or saving Money, or use a pretend store to teach about spending and saving.

Lead by example: Finally, be your child's role model. Show them how you save and invest your Money and talk to them about your financial goals and strategies.

Teaching kids about "Money Working for Us" is a great way to help them develop good financial habits that can last a lifetime. By starting early and making it fun, you can help your child understand the importance of saving and investing and set them up for a financially secure future.

CONVERSATIONS BETWEEN PARENTS AND CHILDREN: ("MONEY WORKING FOR US.")

EXAMPLE -1:

Parent: Hey, Buddy/Princess. Do you remember how we talked about earning Money through different sources like selling lemonades, doing chores, and other things?

Child: Yes, I remember.

Parent: Now, imagine that you have saved up some money from all of your earnings, and instead of spending it all, you decide to invest it in a piggy bank that will grow your money over time. This is where the concept of 'Money Working for Us' comes in.

Child: Hmm, how does it work?

Parent: When we put our money into an investment or savings account, it earns interest, which means our Money grows. For instance, saving $10 in a savings account might grow to $11 or $12 after a year, depending on the interest rate. This is how 'Money Works for Us' as we let it sit and grow without doing any extra work.

Child: Oh, I get it now. But why is it important?

Parent: It's important because when we have more Money, we can use it for essential things, like buying a new toy or saving for something we want. And the more we save and invest, the more our Money grows, and we can achieve our financial goals faster.

Child: That's cool! So, we don't always have to work hard to earn more Money.

Parent: Exactly! By investing our money wisely, we can make

our money work hard for us, so we don't have to work as hard. And that's why it's essential to understand this concept early.

EXAMPLE -2:
Parent: Hey Buddy/Princess, do you know what it means when we say "money working for us"?
Child: Not really; what does that mean?
Parent: Well, it's the idea that we can use our Money to make more without doing much work ourselves. Let's say we put some of our Money into a savings account that earns interest. Over time, our Money will earn even more through interest, like our Money working for us.
Child: Oh, I get it now. So we can use our Money to make even more money without doing anything?
Parent: Yes, exactly! Many ways to do Money work, like investing in stocks or real estate. And the more we can make our money work for us, the easier it is to achieve our financial goals and have the things we want.
Child: Wow, that sounds pretty cool. How do we get started with making our Money work for us?
Parent: Well, it takes some planning and effort, but we can start by setting aside some money to invest and learning more about how to make our money work for us. We can also talk to a financial advisor who can help us create a plan and make intelligent decisions with our Money.

EXAMPLE -3:
Parent: Do you know what it means when we say "money working for us"?
Child: Um, not really.
Parent: Well, it's like having a team of little workers who always make Money for us, even while doing other things. For example, when we put our Money in a savings account, it earns interest over time. So even if we're not actively doing anything, our Money works for us by earning more.
Child: Oh, okay. So we can use that money to buy things we

want later, right?

Parent: Exactly! And the more we save and invest, the more our Money can grow and work for us. It's like planting and watching a seed grow into a big tree. It takes time and patience, but it's ultimately worth it.

Child: That sounds cool. Can we start doing that too?

Parent: Definitely! Let's start by setting up a savings account for you so you can see how it works. And we can also talk about other ways to invest and make our money work harder for us.

BEHAVIORAL FINANCE

Behavioural finance is a field of study that combines principles of psychology and economics to understand how people make financial decisions. It examines how cognitive biases, emotions, and social influences affect financial behaviour and decision-making processes.

Here's an explanation of what behavioural finance entails:

Psychology and Financial Decision-Making: Behavioural finance recognizes that individuals are not always rational and objective when making financial decisions. It considers the psychological factors influencing our choices, such as cognitive biases, emotions, and heuristics (mental shortcuts).

Cognitive Biases: Cognitive biases are systematic patterns of deviation from rationality that can affect our judgment and decision-making. Examples include confirmation bias (favouring information that confirms our existing beliefs), loss aversion (feeling the pain of losses more than the pleasure of gains), and overconfidence bias (overestimating our abilities). Behavioural finance studies these biases to understand how they impact financial decision-making.

Emotions and Investor Behaviour: Emotions play a significant role in financial decision-making. Behavioural finance recognizes that fear, greed, and other emotional responses can influence investment choices and contribute to market volatility. It explores how emotions can lead to irrational behaviour, such as panic selling during market downturns or chasing investment fads during market booms.

Prospect Theory: Prospect theory is a cornerstone of behavioural finance, developed by psychologists Daniel Kahneman and Amos Tversky. It suggests that individuals value gains and losses differently and are more sensitive to potential losses than equivalent gains. This theory helps explain why people may take excessive risks to avoid losses or prefer specific investment strategies based on their perception of potential gains and losses.

Herd Mentality and Social Influence: Behavioural finance also considers the impact of social influence on financial decision-making. People often look to others for guidance and reassurance, leading to a herd mentality in investment markets. This can result in market bubbles or panics as individuals follow the crowd rather than making independent decisions. Behavioural finance studies how social factors affect investment behaviour and market dynamics.

Overcoming Biases and Making Better Decisions: Understanding behavioural finance can help individuals recognize and mitigate the biases that impact their financial decisions. It encourages self-awareness and promotes strategies to make more rational choices. By incorporating behavioural insights into financial planning and investment strategies, individuals can aim to overcome biases and improve decision-making.

Practical Applications: Behavioural finance has practical applications in various areas, such as personal finance, investment management, and policymaking. It informs the design of financial products and services that account for behavioural biases and helps financial advisors tailor their advice to clients' behavioural tendencies. It also provides insights for policymakers promoting financial well-being and consumer protection.

Behavioural finance explores how psychological factors and

biases influence our financial decisions. By understanding these influences, individuals can become more aware of their biases and make more informed and rational financial choices. It offers valuable insights into the complexities of human behaviour in the financial realm and helps shape strategies to improve financial decision-making.

CONVERSATIONS BETWEEN PARENTS AND CHILDREN: (BEHAVIOURAL FINANCE)

EXAMPLE -1:

Parent: Hey, kiddo! I wanted to talk to you about something called behavioural finance today. It's all about how our behaviour and emotions affect how we handle Money.

Child: Really? How does that work, Mom/Dad?

Parent: Well, sometimes our feelings and thoughts can influence the choices we make with our Money. For example, have you ever wanted to buy something because your friends have it?

Child: Yeah! It's hard to resist when everyone else has something extraordinary.

Parent: That's a great example! It's called "keeping up with the Joneses." Sometimes we need to buy things just to fit in, even if it's not the best decision for our financial situation. Understanding behavioural finance helps us recognize these influences and make more intelligent choices.

Child: So, what can we do to make better decisions?

Parent: One crucial thing is to be aware of our emotions regarding Money. We should consider why we want to make a purchase and whether it aligns with our long-term goals. We can ask ourselves, "Do I need this?" or "Will buying this bring me lasting happiness?"

Child: That's a good point. It's easy to get caught up in the moment and forget about the bigger picture.

Parent: Absolutely! Another helpful tip is to set financial goals. When we have clear goals, making choices that support those goals becomes more accessible. It's like having a roadmap for our Money. Plus, involving you in budgeting decisions and teaching you about saving and investing will help you develop good habits early on.

Child: I like the idea of having goals and a plan. It feels more organized.

Parent: I'm glad you think so! Another thing to remember is that it's okay to make mistakes sometimes. We can learn from them and make better choices in the future. It's all part of the learning process.

Child: That's reassuring to know. I don't have to be perfect with my money decisions.

Parent: Exactly! Learning about behavioural finance also helps us understand why others might make confident financial choices. It gives us empathy and helps us support and encourage each other in making intelligent decisions.

Child: Can we learn more about behavioural finance together?

Parent: Absolutely! We can explore books and articles or watch videos explaining it more. We can also have regular conversations about Money and decision-making. The more we learn, the better equipped we'll be to make informed choices.

Child: Sounds like a plan! I'm excited to learn more about behavioural finance and make better decisions with my Money.

Parent: I'm glad to hear that! Remember, I'm here to support you every step of the way. Learning about Money is an important life skill, and I'm proud of you for showing interest in it.

Child: Thanks, Mom/Dad! I appreciate your guidance. Let's dive into the world of behavioural finance together and make smarter choices with our Money.

Parent: Absolutely, my dear! Let's embark on this journey together and empower ourselves with the knowledge to make wise financial decisions. I'm excited to see how we grow and learn through this process!

EXAMPLE -2:

Parent: Hey, sweetheart, I wanted to chat with you about behavioural finance. It's an exciting topic that can help us understand how our behaviour affects our money decisions.

Child: Oh, that sounds cool! What does behavioural finance mean?

Parent: Behavioural finance is all about understanding how our emotions, biases, and cognitive processes can influence how we handle Money. It helps us recognize our tendencies and make more informed choices.

Child: So, does that mean we sometimes make mistakes with Money because of our emotions?

Parent: Exactly! Sometimes our emotions can lead us to make impulsive decisions or overlook important details. For example, have you ever bought something on a whim and later regretted it?

Child: I remember buying that toy I wanted but then hardly played with it.

Parent: That's a great example! We often make decisions based on our immediate desires rather than considering the long-term consequences. Behavioural finance helps us recognize these tendencies and make more intelligent choices.

Child: How can we make better decisions then?

Parent: One strategy is to step back and think before purchasing. We can ask ourselves, "Do I need this?" or "Will this purchase bring me lasting happiness?" It's about being mindful and considering the bigger picture.

Child: That makes sense. It's like thinking about whether something is genuinely worth it.

Parent: Exactly! Another helpful tip is to create a budget. By setting limits on our spending and tracking our expenses, we can make sure our Money is going towards things that truly matter to us. It helps us prioritize and make intentional choices.

Child: Can we make a budget together?

Parent: Of course! I think that's a beautiful idea. We can sit down and plan how we want to allocate our Money, both for the things we need and the things we want. It's a great way to learn about financial responsibility and work towards our goals.

Child: I'm excited to try it out! It sounds like a practical way to ensure we're using our Money wisely.

Parent: I'm glad you're enthusiastic about it! Remember, learning about behavioural finance is not about being perfect but about being aware of our tendencies and improving. It's a journey, and we can learn together as a family.

Child: That sounds great, Mom/Dad! We can explore this topic together and make smarter money decisions.

Parent: I'm proud of you for showing interest in this, my dear. It's an important life skill, and I'm here to support you every step of the way. Together, we'll navigate the world of behavioural finance and build a strong foundation for making wise financial choices.

Child: Thank you, Mom/Dad! I appreciate your guidance. Let's dive into this topic and learn how our behaviour affects our money decisions.

Parent: Absolutely, sweetheart! Let's embark on this exciting journey together and discover new ways to make our money work. I'm excited to see how we grow and become even smarter with our finances.

EXAMPLE -3:

Parent: Hey, buddy, I wanted to talk to you about something called behavioural finance. It's a fascinating concept that can help us understand how our behaviour influences financial decisions.

Child: Oh? What does that mean?

Parent: Well, behavioural finance is all about how our thoughts, feelings, and actions impact how we manage our Money. It's about understanding why we sometimes make confident choices, even when they may not be the best for our long-term financial goals.

Child: So, it's about understanding why we do things with Money, right?

Parent: Exactly! It helps us recognize our natural tendencies and biases to make more informed decisions. For example, have you ever noticed that sometimes we spend money on things we don't need?

Child: Yeah, like buying toys or snacks impulsively.

Parent: That's a great example! Sometimes our emotions and desires can get the best of us, and we make purchases without considering whether we truly need them. Behavioural finance helps us become more aware of these tendencies so we can make more intelligent choices.

Child: How can we make wiser choices then?

Parent: One way is by setting goals and making a plan. By deciding what we want to save for or what we want to achieve with our Money, we can make decisions that align with those goals. It helps us prioritize and avoid impulsive purchases.

Child: So, it's like having a plan for our Money?

Parent: Exactly! It's like a road map guiding us toward our financial goals. Another thing we can do is to pause and think before making a purchase. We can ask ourselves, "Do I need this?" or "Will this item bring me long-term value?"

Child: That sounds like a good idea. I'll try to think more before spending my Money.

Parent: That's wonderful to hear! It's important to make mindful choices rather than letting our impulses guide us. By being more aware of our behaviour, we can make decisions that align with our goals and values.

Child: Can we make a plan together?

Parent: Absolutely! I think that's a fantastic idea. We can sit down and discuss what we want to save for, how we can budget our Money, and how we can make wise financial choices. It's an excellent opportunity for us to learn and grow together.

Child: I'm excited to work on this with you! It sounds like a fun and essential way to handle our Money.

Parent: I'm thrilled to hear that, my dear. Remember, learning about behavioural finance is a lifelong journey. We may make mistakes along the way, but the important thing is to keep learning and improving our financial habits.

Child: Thanks, Mom/Dad! I'm glad we can talk about these things. I feel more confident in managing my Money now.

Parent: You're welcome, sweetheart! I'm here to guide and support you in your financial journey. Together, we'll navigate the world of behavioural finance and make choices that will set you up for a successful future.

Child: I appreciate that, Mom/Dad. Let's maximize this opportunity and become more competent with our Money!

Parent: Absolutely, buddy! Let's dive into this exciting world of behavioural finance and enjoy the journey of becoming financially savvy. I'm proud of you for taking an interest in this topic, and I know we'll make significant progress together.

PAYING OURSELVES FIRST

Paying Ourselves First is a financial concept that involves prioritizing saving and investing a portion of our income before spending it on other expenses. The idea is to set aside a certain percentage of our income for our future financial goals and needs and then live off the remaining amount.

By paying ourselves first, we ensure that we build wealth and secure our financial future rather than spending all our money on current wants and needs. It also helps us to avoid living pay check to pay check and accumulating debt.

Paying ourselves first is a powerful financial habit that can help us achieve our long-term financial goals, such as buying a house, retiring comfortably, or building wealth for future generations.

Here are some examples of "Paying Ourselves First":
Saving a fixed amount or percentage of your monthly income before paying any bills or expenses and investing in retirement

funds with automatic deductions, such as a 401(k) or IRA.

Building an emergency fund by setting aside a certain monthly amount for unexpected expenses.

Paying off high-interest debts first before spending on discretionary items.

Setting aside a budget for personal development or education.

Allocating a percentage of your income towards long-term goals, such as buying a house or starting a business, and investing in yourself through health and wellness activities, such as gym memberships or therapy sessions.

"Paying Ourselves First" prioritizes saving and investing for our financial well-being before spending on other things.

Teaching kids about "Paying Ourselves First" can be done in several ways. One way is to start by explaining that saving Money for the future is essential, just like putting money in a piggy bank. You can explain that paying ourselves first means saving Money before spending it on other things like toys or treats.

Here are some other tips for teaching kids about paying themselves first:

Set an example: Lead by example and show your child you are saving money for the future. This will help them see the importance of the concept and encourage them to start saving as well.

Start small: Encourage your child to start small by saving a portion of their allowance or any money they receive as gifts. Help them set a goal for how much they want to save each week or month and track their progress.

Visual aids: Use visual aids like a piggy bank or savings jar to show your child how their savings are growing over time. This will help them see the benefits of paying themselves first and the importance of saving for the future.

Explain the benefits: Help your child understand that paying themselves first means that they will have Money saved up for things they want or need in the future, like a new toy or college tuition. This can also help them develop good financial habits and reduce the risk of financial stress later in life.

Keep it fun: Encourage your child to set goals for their savings and reward them when they reach those goals. This can help keep them motivated and make paying themselves first more enjoyable.

CONVERSATIONS BETWEEN PARENTS AND
CHILDREN: ("PAYING OURSELVES FIRST.")

EXAMPLE -1:

Parent: Hey, Buddy/Princess, do you know what it means to pay ourselves first?

Child: No, what is it?

Parent: It's a concept that teaches us to save money from our income before paying our bills or spending on other things. It's like setting aside some money for ourselves first and then using the rest for other things.

Child: Why is that important?

Parent: When we pay ourselves first, we ensure we're putting Money towards our goals and dreams. We can save for a vacation, a new toy, or college.

Child: Oh, I get it. So it's like putting Money in our piggy bank before we spend it on other things.

Parent: Exactly! And it's important because it helps us build good saving habits early on in life. Plus, it ensures that we care for our needs and goals before spending on other things.

Child: That's cool! I want to start doing that too.

Parent: Great! Let's start by setting a savings goal for ourselves and putting some money towards it every time we get our allowance or Money as a gift.

Child: Okay, let's do it!

EXAMPLE -2:

Parent: Do you remember discussing the importance of saving Money?

Child: We discussed saving some of our Money instead of

spending it all.

Parent: That's right. But another critical concept goes hand in hand with saving Money. It's called "paying ourselves first."

Child: Paying ourselves first? What does that mean?

Parent: It means we set aside a portion for our savings before spending Money. This is like paying ourselves first before we pay for anything else.

Child: Oh, I see. We ensure we save some money first and then can spend the rest.

Parent: Exactly. Doing this ensures we prioritize our future financial needs first rather than spending everything immediately. It's like making sure our future self is taken care of.

Child: That sounds like a good idea. How much should we save?

Parent: It's a good idea to save at least 10% of our income. So, if we get $10, we save $1, and then we can spend the remaining $9 on what we need or want.

Child: Okay, I understand. It's like ensuring we have Money for later rather than spending everything immediately.

Parent: That's right. And by doing this consistently, we can build up our savings and have more financial security in the future.

EXAMPLE -3:

Parent: Do you know what it means to pay ourselves first, John?

Child: No, I don't.

Parent: Well, it means that whenever we get Money, we save some for our future goals before spending it on other things.

Child: Oh, I see. We should save some money first, and then we can spend the rest.

Parent: That's right. Planning for our Money is essential, and paying ourselves first is an excellent way to ensure we're saving enough for our future needs.

Child: What kinds of things should we save Money for?

Parent: Well, it depends on our goals. We can save for a new bike, college, or retirement. Whatever it is, we should put some money aside every time we get paid.

Child: Okay, I think I understand. So we must plan for our Money and save some of it before spending it all.

Parent: Exactly. And remember, the more we save, the more we'll have to do the things we want to do in the future.

UNLOCK FINANCIAL SUCCESS

Must-Read Books for a Strong Financial Foundation for Kids

The more that you read, the more things you will know. The more that you learn, the more places you'll go.

Dr. Seuss.

Building a solid financial foundation is crucial for children as they grow and navigate the world of money. One effective way to instil financial literacy in kids is through books that teach valuable lessons about money management, budgeting, saving, and investing. Parents and educators can empower children with the knowledge and skills necessary for a lifetime of financial success by introducing children to these must-read books.

Let's explore some of the best books that can unlock financial success for kids.

"The Berenstain Bears' Trouble with Money" by Stan and Jan Berenstain: In this classic children's book, the lovable Berenstain Bears encounter various money-related situations and learn important lessons about the value of money, budgeting, and making wise spending choices. With relatable characters and engaging illustrations, this book teaches children the fundamentals of money management in a fun and accessible way.

"A Smart Girl's Guide: Money" by Nancy Holyoke: This empowering book is specifically geared toward young girls and covers various money-related topics. It explores earning an allowance, budgeting, saving for goals, making smart purchasing decisions, and giving back. Through relatable stories, quizzes, and activities, it encourages girls to take control of their finances and make informed choices.

"Lemonade in Winter: A Book About Two Kids Counting Money" by Emily Jenkins: This engaging picture book introduces children to basic financial concepts like counting and managing money. The story follows siblings Pauline and John-John as they decide to set up a lemonade stand in the winter. Through their entrepreneurial adventure, they learn about earning, spending, and the ups and downs of running a small business. This book is an excellent introduction to financial literacy and teaches children the value of hard work and determination.

"The Kids' Money Book" by Jamie Kyle McGillian: This comprehensive guide covers a wide range of financial topics in a kid-friendly manner. It explores earning money through chores and part-time jobs, saving money for short-term and long-term goals, understanding the concept of investing, and the importance of giving back through charitable donations. The book also includes interactive exercises and quizzes to reinforce learning.

"If You Made a Million" by David M. Schwartz: This book takes children on an imaginative journey of what they could do with a million dollars. It explores earning, saving, spending, and even investing concepts. Children learn about financial concepts creatively and entertainingly through playful illustrations and engaging scenarios.

"Growing Money: A Complete Investing Guide for Kids" by Gail Karlitz and Debbie Honig: This informative guide introduces children to investing and explains concepts such as stocks, bonds, mutual funds, etc. It teaches kids about the potential benefits and risks of investing and provides practical tips for building a diversified investment portfolio. The book includes real-life examples and interactive activities to reinforce learning.

"The Everything Kids' Money Book" by Brette McWhorter Sember: This comprehensive guide is packed with practical advice and fun activities to help kids understand money management. It covers earning, saving, spending, budgeting, and even starting a small business. The book provides real-life examples, quizzes, and puzzles to engage children and encourage active learning.

Introducing children to these must-read books on financial literacy lays the foundation for their long-term financial success. These stories teach valuable money management skills and instil important values such as patience, responsibility, and the joy of giving. By engaging kids with these educational and entertaining books, parents and educators can empower them to make informed financial decisions, setting them toward a solid financial future. The Berenstain Bears

THE BERENSTAIN BEARS' TROUBLE WITH MONEY" BY STAN AND JAN BERENSTAIN

"The Berenstain Bears' Trouble with Money" by Stan and Jan Berenstain is a beloved children's book that tackles the topic of money management in a relatable and entertaining way. The book follows the adventures of the Berenstain Bear family as they encounter various money-related situations and learn valuable lessons along the way.

The story begins when Brother and Sister Bear receive their allowances from Mama and Papa Bear. Excited about having their own money, they quickly become caught up in the allure of spending. They visit the local store and find themselves tempted by all the shiny toys and treats on display. However, they soon realize that their money doesn't stretch very far and are left disappointed.

Realizing that they need to learn about the value of money and make intelligent choices, Mama and Papa Bear step in to teach them a valuable lesson. They explain the importance of budgeting and making decisions based on needs rather than wants. They introduce saving money for more significant and meaningful purchases rather than spending impulsively on short-lived pleasures.

The book teaches children the basic principles of money management through relatable examples and charming illustrations. It introduces them to the concepts of earning, spending, and saving and the idea of delayed gratification. It emphasizes the importance of making wise choices and understanding the consequences of impulsive spending.

"The Berenstain Bears' Trouble with Money" teaches kids about financial literacy and promotes essential values such as responsibility, patience, and setting priorities. It encourages children to think critically about their spending habits and consider the long-term benefits of saving for things that truly matter to them.

The book provides an excellent starting point for discussing money and financial decision-making between parents and children. It offers practical lessons that kids can apply in their lives, such as creating a savings plan, distinguishing between needs and wants, and understanding the value of money.

"The Berenstain Bears' Trouble with Money" is a delightful and educational book that helps children develop a healthy relationship with money. It empowers them with essential financial knowledge and skills while entertaining them with engaging storytelling. Parents can lay the groundwork for a lifetime of responsible money management and financial success by reading this book with their children.

A SMART GIRL'S GUIDE: MONEY" BY NANCY HOLYOKE:

"A Smart Girl's Guide: Money" by Nancy Holyoke is a comprehensive and empowering book that aims to teach young girls about money management, financial independence, and intelligent financial decision-making. With its engaging and relatable content, this book equips girls with the knowledge and skills they need to confidently navigate the world of money.

The book covers a wide range of topics, starting with the basics of money, including earning, saving, and spending. It introduces girls to the concept of budgeting and provides practical tips on how to set financial goals and create a personal budget. Through real-life examples and scenarios, girls learn how to make informed choices about their spending and develop a sense of financial responsibility.

One of the standout features of "A Smart Girl's Guide: Money" is its focus on entrepreneurship and encouraging girls to explore their money-making ventures. The book offers guidance on brainstorming business ideas, marketing products or services, and managing profits. It inspires girls to think creatively, take risks, and seize opportunities to generate income.

In addition to earning and spending, the book emphasizes the importance of saving and investing. It explains the concept of compound interest and introduces girls to different saving and investment options. It encourages girls to think long-term and set aside money for future goals like college, travel, or starting their own businesses.

Moreover, the book addresses the psychological aspects of money, such as understanding wants versus needs, managing peer pressure and cultivating a healthy relationship with money. It promotes self-confidence and empowers girls to make independent financial decisions that align with their values and aspirations.

Throughout the book, the author incorporates interactive elements, including quizzes, worksheets, and real-life stories, to actively engage readers and reinforce their learning. Girls are encouraged to reflect on their financial habits, set personal goals, and track their progress.

"A Smart Girl's Guide: Money" is a valuable resource for girls seeking to develop financial literacy and independence. It equips them with practical tools, knowledge, and strategies to make smart financial choices, build financial resilience, and achieve their dreams. By reading this book, girls can gain a solid foundation in money management and develop the confidence and skills necessary to navigate their financial futures successfully.

LEMONADE IN WINTER: A BOOK ABOUT TWO KIDS COUNTING MONEY" BY EMILY JENKINS

"Lemonade in Winter: A Book About Two Kids Counting

Money" by Emily Jenkins is a delightful children's book that combines a heart-warming story with an introduction to the concept of money and essential math skills. It follows the adventures of siblings Pauline and John-John as they embark on a winter day with a simple yet ambitious goal: to sell lemonade.

The story begins with Pauline and John-John planning their lemonade stand, despite the cold weather. They gather all the necessary supplies and set up their stand, eager to make money. However, they soon realize that selling lemonade in winter is quite different from doing so in the summertime.

As the siblings encounter various challenges throughout their day, such as freezing temperatures and limited customer traffic, they learn important lessons about entrepreneurship, perseverance, and the value of money. Along the way, they explore the fundamental concepts of counting money, making changes, and tracking their earnings.

"Lemonade in Winter" beautifully combines engaging storytelling with colourful illustrations that capture the curiosity and determination of Pauline and John-John. The book teaches children about money and basic arithmetic and valuable life lessons about problem-solving, adaptability, and the rewards of hard work.

Through the journey of Pauline and John-John, young readers are introduced to the concepts of earning, spending, and saving money in a relatable and enjoyable way. The book provides opportunities for children to practice counting and essential addition and subtraction skills. It is an excellent resource for early readers and those beginning to explore the world of money.

"Lemonade in Winter: A Book About Two Kids Counting Money" is an engaging and educational read that introduces children to financial literacy in a fun and accessible manner, encouraging them to develop essential math skills while fostering an entrepreneurial spirit.

THE KIDS' MONEY BOOK" BY JAMIE KYLE MCGILLIAN:

"The Kids' Money Book" by Jamie Kyle McGillian is a comprehensive and interactive guide designed to empower children with essential financial knowledge and skills. This book provides a wealth of information, tips, and activities to help children understand the value of money, learn how to manage it responsibly, and make intelligent financial decisions.

The book is divided into sections covering various money and personal finance topics. It begins by introducing basic concepts such as what money is, where it comes from, and how to earn it. It then explores essential topics like budgeting, saving, spending wisely, and giving back through philanthropy. The author uses friendly and accessible language, making it easy for young readers to grasp and apply the concepts discussed.

One of the highlights of "The Kids' Money Book" is its interactive nature. It features engaging exercises, quizzes, and real-life examples, encouraging children to actively participate in their financial learning journey. Through hands-on activities, such as creating a budget, setting savings goals, and exploring different ways to earn money, children can develop practical money management skills and gain confidence in making financial decisions.

The book also addresses important topics like consumerism, advertising, and the impact of choices on the environment. It teaches children to discern consumers and make responsible choices that align with their values and long-term goals.

Moreover, "The Kids' Money Book" emphasizes the importance of critical thinking and financial independence. It encourages children to ask questions, seek information, and make informed choices. The author also includes valuable tips for parents and caregivers on supporting and guiding children in their financial journey.

"The Kids' Money Book" is an invaluable resource for children, parents, and educators. It equips young readers with the knowledge and skills to navigate the complex world of personal finance confidently. By instilling a solid foundation of financial literacy, this book sets children on a path toward a lifetime of financial success and responsible money management.

IF YOU MADE A MILLION" BY DAVID M. SCHWARTZ

"If You Made a Million" by David M. Schwartz is an engaging and educational book that introduces children to the fascinating world of money and teaches them valuable lessons about earning, saving, and spending wisely. Through captivating illustrations and relatable examples, the author takes young readers on a journey of discovery, exploring the concept of wealth and the possibilities that come with it.

The book follows the story of a young boy named Marvelosissimo, the Mathematical Magician who guides readers through the various aspects of earning and managing money. Marvelosissimo presents different scenarios and poses thought-provoking questions to encourage children to think critically about money and its uses.

Through colourful illustrations and simple explanations, "If You Made a Million" introduces children to essential concepts such as earning an income, work value, and compound interest. It explores various professions and business ventures, highlighting that money can be earned through different means and that hard work and entrepreneurship can lead to financial success.

One of the book's key messages is saving and making wise financial decisions. It introduces children to the concept of a budget and explores the idea of prioritizing needs over wants. It also touches on the importance of giving back and the joy of helping others through charitable acts.

The book incorporates mathematical concepts in a fun and

accessible way. It includes examples of simple calculations, such as counting and essential addition and subtraction, to demonstrate the practical application of math in financial situations. This helps children understand the connection between math skills and managing money effectively.

"If You Made a Million" is an excellent resource for teaching children about money, entrepreneurship, and financial responsibility. It sparks their curiosity, stimulates their imagination, and encourages them to think critically about the role of money in their lives. By presenting financial concepts as engaging and relatable, the book empowers children to develop a positive and responsible attitude toward money from an early age.

GROWING MONEY: A COMPLETE INVESTING GUIDE FOR KIDS" BY GAIL KARLITZ AND DEBBIE HONIG

"Growing Money: A Complete Investing Guide for Kids" by Gail Karlitz and Debbie Honig is a comprehensive and accessible book introducing children to investing and empowering them to make intelligent financial decisions. With its engaging writing style and informative content, this book is an excellent resource for teaching kids about the importance of investing and its potential benefits.

The book is divided into clear and concise chapters that cover a wide range of investment topics. It explains the basic concepts of money, saving, and earning, providing a solid foundation for young readers. It then progresses to more advanced topics, such as stocks, bonds, mutual funds, and real estate investment. The authors use simple language and relatable examples to explain these complex concepts in a way that is easy for children to understand.

One of the standout features of "Growing Money" is its interactive approach. The book includes practical exercises, quizzes, and case studies encouraging children to apply their knowledge and think critically about investment decisions. It provides step-by-step guidance on researching and evaluating investment opportunities, helping kids develop essential skills in financial analysis and decision-making.

The authors also emphasize the importance of setting financial goals and developing a long-term investment strategy. They discuss the concept of risk and reward, teaching children how to assess and manage risks when investing. Additionally, the book highlights the value of patience and the benefits of compounding, instilling in young readers the understanding that investing is a long-term commitment.

"Growing Money" promotes a responsible and ethical approach to investing. It emphasizes the significance of investing in companies and causes that align with one's values and encourages children to consider their investment choices' social and environmental impact. This aspect of the book helps foster a sense of social responsibility. It empowers kids to make investment decisions that yield financial returns and contribute to a better world.

"Growing Money: A Complete Investing Guide for Kids" is a valuable resource for introducing children to investing. It equips them with the knowledge, skills, and mindset to navigate the financial landscape confidently. By teaching kids about investing early on, the book sets them on a path toward financial literacy and empowers them to take control of their financial future.

THE EVERYTHING KIDS' MONEY BOOK" BY BRETTE MCWHORTER SEMBER

"The Everything Kids' Money Book" by Brette McWhorter Sember is a comprehensive and interactive guide designed to teach kids the fundamentals of money management in a fun and engaging way. Packed with valuable information, practical tips, and entertaining activities, this book is a fantastic resource for children to develop a strong understanding of money and how to make intelligent financial decisions.

The book covers many money-related topics, including earning, saving, spending, budgeting, and investing. Each chapter has age-appropriate explanations and examples that resonate with children, making complex concepts easy to grasp. Whether it's explaining the concept of income, teaching kids how to set financial goals, or discussing the importance of giving back, the book presents information clearly and relatable.

One of the standout features of "The Everything Kids' Money Book" is its interactive nature. The book has quizzes, puzzles, and activities that allow children to apply what they've learned and reinforce their understanding. These hands-on exercises make learning enjoyable and encourage critical thinking and problem-solving skills.

The author understands the importance of practical money skills, and as such, the book includes real-life scenarios and practical tips for kids to apply in their daily lives. Whether it's learning how to compare shops, understanding the dollar's value, or making smart choices with their allowance, children are provided with practical strategies to navigate the world of money.

"The Everything Kids' Money Book" also emphasizes the importance of responsible money management. It teaches children the importance of budgeting, distinguishing needs and wants, and making informed spending choices. The book encourages kids to develop good financial habits early on, leading them toward financial independence and success.

Furthermore, the book highlights the value of saving and investing. It introduces children to compound interest and explains how saving money can grow over time. It also discusses basic investment principles in a kid-friendly manner, sparking curiosity and encouraging kids to think about their financial future.

"The Everything Kids' Money Book" is a valuable resource for teaching children about money and financial literacy. It equips them with practical knowledge, skills, and tools to make sound financial decisions early on. By combining informative content with interactive activities, the book ensures that learning about money is enjoyable and impactful for children. It empowers them to develop healthy money habits, make informed choices and lay the foundation for a lifetime of financial well-being.

PLAY YOUR WAY TO FINANCIAL LITERACY

Fun and Educational Finance-Related Games for Kids

Play is the highest form of research.

Albert Einstein

Teaching kids about money and financial literacy can sometimes be challenging, but incorporating fun and interactive games into their learning experience can make it engaging and enjoyable. Finance-related games for kids offer a hands-on approach to learning essential money management skills, decision-making, and critical thinking. These games provide kids with a safe and exciting environment to explore financial concepts, develop money habits, and enhance their financial literacy.

Let's dive into some of the best finance-related games to help kids play their way to financial literacy.

Monopoly: Monopoly is a classic board game that teaches kids valuable lessons about money management, investing, and negotiation. Players buy and trade properties, collect rent, and make strategic decisions to accumulate wealth. Through gameplay, kids learn about budgeting, handling transactions, understanding property values, and the concept of passive income.

Cashflow for Kids: Cashflow for Kids, created by renowned investor Robert Kiyosaki, is an interactive board game designed to teach children about financial independence and wealth creation. Kids learn about different income streams, managing assets and liabilities, and making informed investment decisions. The Game encourages critical thinking and problem-solving and helps kids develop a mindset for financial success.

The Game of Life: The Game of Life is a classic board game that simulates real-life scenarios, guiding players through various life stages, from education and career choices to financial decisions and family planning. It introduces kids to budgeting, managing expenses, and adapting to unexpected financial challenges. The Game promotes strategic thinking, planning for the future, and understanding the consequences of different choices.

Financial Football: Financial Football is an online game developed by Visa and the National Football League (NFL) to teach kids about money management in the context of football. Players answer financial questions and make choices to move their football team down the field. The Game covers saving, budgeting, banking, and credit. It combines the excitement of football with financial literacy, making it engaging and educational for young players.

Lemonade Stand: Lemonade Stand is a computer game that puts kids in charge of running their virtual lemonade stand. Players make decisions about pricing, purchasing ingredients, and managing expenses to maximize profits. The Game introduces basic business concepts, such as supply and demand, profit margins, and decision-making under uncertain conditions. Kids learn about the importance of budgeting, marketing, and adapting their strategies to succeed in a competitive market.

Stock Market Game: The Stock Market Game is an online simulation that allows kids to experience the world of investing in stocks. Players manage a virtual portfolio and make buying and selling decisions based on real-time stock market data. The Game teaches kids about investing, analysing stock performance, and the risks and rewards associated with the stock market. It promotes economic research, critical thinking, and understanding of market trends.

Payday: Payday is a board game that simulates a month-to-month financial journey, where players receive income, pay bills, and make financial decisions. It teaches kids about budgeting, managing expenses, and handling unexpected financial challenges. Players learn the importance of saving, making strategic choices, and balancing their income and expenses.

Money Bags: Money Bags is a board game that helps kids

learn about counting money and making changes. Players collect and exchange coins as they move around the board, practicing their math skills and understanding the value of different coins. The Game reinforces money recognition, basic arithmetic, and the concept of financial transactions.

Thrifty Kids: Thrifty Kids is an interactive board game that encourages kids to make wise money choices. Players learn about earning, saving, and spending wisely through various financial scenarios. The Game promotes critical thinking, problem-solving, and responsible money management skills.

Save! The Game: Save! The Game is a cooperative card game that teaches kids about saving money and achieving financial goals. Players work together to save money for a desired item or experience while overcoming unexpected expenses and temptations. The Game emphasizes teamwork, decision-making, and delayed gratification.

Finance-related games provide a playful and interactive way for kids to develop essential money management skills and financial literacy. By engaging in these games, children learn about budgeting, investing, decision-making, and the consequences of their actions. These games foster financial responsibility, strategic thinking, and the ability to make informed financial choices. By playing their way to financial literacy, kids gain valuable skills that will benefit them throughout their lives, setting them on a path to financial success and independence.

MONOPOLY: A GAME OF WEALTH AND STRATEGY

Monopoly is a classic board game that generations of players have enjoyed. It is a game of strategy, negotiation, and financial management. In Monopoly, players embark on a journey to build a real estate empire, making wise investments, collecting rent, and outsmarting opponents. This iconic Game offers a fun and immersive experience while imparting valuable lessons about money, entrepreneurship, and decision-making. Let's dive into the details of Monopoly and explore why it remains a timeless favourite.

Game Objective: The objective of Monopoly is to become the wealthiest player by acquiring properties, charging rent, and bankrupting opponents. Players move around the board, buying properties, constructing houses and hotels, and collecting rent from other players who land on their properties. The Game continues until all players, except one, are bankrupted.

Real Estate Investment: Monopoly revolves around the concept of real estate investment. Players can purchase properties, from streets to entire neighbourhoods, and become landlords. Each property has a purchase price and rental value. Wise property acquisitions can lead to a steady income stream, while poor choices may result in financial struggles. The Game teaches players to assess the value of properties, negotiate deals, and strategize to maximize their profits.

Financial Management: Monopoly requires players to manage their finances wisely. They must balance their income, consisting of rent and various card effects, with expenses such as property purchases, rent payments to other players, and potential fines. Players need to budget their money, plan for future investments, and make calculated financial decisions. The Game emphasizes the importance of budgeting, prioritizing expenses, and understanding the consequences of financial choices.

Negotiation and Strategy: Monopoly is not just about luck; it also requires negotiation and strategic thinking. Players can negotiate property trades, make deals, and form alliances to their advantage. The Game encourages players to analyse the board, anticipate opponents' moves, and strategically position themselves to gain the upper hand. Negotiation skills, strategic planning, and adaptability are crucial to success in Monopoly.

Risk and Rewards: Monopoly introduces players to the concept of risk and reward. Property developments, such as adding houses and hotels, increase rental income and incur higher expenses. Players must assess the risks associated with each investment and determine whether the potential rewards outweigh the costs. The Game teaches players to evaluate risk, make calculated decisions, and weigh the potential benefits against setbacks.

Financial Lessons: Monopoly provides players with valuable financial lessons. It introduces them to property ownership, rental income, mortgage, negotiation, taxation, and financial planning concepts. Through gameplay, players learn about the importance of diversifying investments, managing cash flow, and the power of leveraging assets. The Game also highlights the significance of financial literacy and understanding basic financial concepts.

Life Skills: Beyond financial lessons, Monopoly helps develop essential life skills. Players learn patience, perseverance, critical thinking, and decision-making under uncertain circumstances. The Game fosters healthy competition, problem-solving abilities, and the ability to handle wins and losses gracefully. It also encourages social interaction, communication, and negotiation skills, as players engage with each other throughout the Game.

Monopoly is more than just a board game; it's an immersive experience that offers many financial and life lessons. By playing Monopoly, individuals of all ages can enhance their financial literacy, sharpen their strategic thinking, and develop crucial life skills. Whether learning the art of negotiation, understanding the risks and rewards of investments, or mastering financial management, Monopoly remains a timeless classic that continues to entertain and educate players for generations. So gather your family or friends, roll the dice, and embark on a journey to build your real estate empire in Monopoly.

CASHFLOW FOR KIDS: BUILDING FINANCIAL

INTELLIGENCE THROUGH GAMEPLAY

Cashflow for Kids is an educational board game designed to teach children about financial literacy and money management principles. Created by Robert Kiyosaki, author of the bestselling book series "Rich Dad Poor Dad," Cashflow for Kids provides a fun and interactive way for young players to learn essential financial skills, develop a wealth mindset, and make informed financial decisions. Let's delve into the details of Cashflow for Kids and discover why it is a valuable tool for building financial intelligence.

Game Objective: Cashflow for Kids aims to be the first player to escape the "rat race" by accumulating enough passive income to cover their monthly expenses. The Game simulates real-life financial scenarios, where players navigate through various financial choices, such as buying assets, starting businesses, and managing income and expenses. The goal is to achieve financial freedom by acquiring assets that generate income and avoiding the pitfalls of excessive debt and overspending.

Financial Decision-Making: Cashflow for Kids teaches children the importance of making sound financial decisions. Players are given various opportunities to earn income, such as working part-time, starting small businesses, or investing in stocks and real estate. They must evaluate each decision's potential risks and rewards, consider their cash flow, and make choices that align with their long-term financial goals. The Game emphasizes critical thinking, problem-solving, and evaluating the trade-offs of different financial choices.

Cash Flow Management: One of the central concepts in Cashflow for Kids is cash flow management. Players learn the difference between active income (earned through work) and passive income (generated by assets). They must carefully manage their income and expenses to ensure positive cash flow and avoid the dreaded "rat race." By budgeting their money, tracking their income and expenses, and making wise financial decisions, players develop a fundamental understanding of managing cash flow, a skill crucial for financial success.

Risk and Reward: Cashflow for Kids introduces children to the concept of risk and reward. Players must evaluate the risks associated with different investments and business ventures. They learn that higher-risk investments may yield greater rewards but also have a higher chance of failure. Through gameplay, children understand the importance of diversification, balancing risk and reward, and making informed investment decisions. They gain an appreciation for calculated risk-taking and learn to weigh the potential benefits against potential setbacks.

Financial Literacy: Cashflow for Kids promotes financial literacy by introducing children to essential financial concepts. The Game covers assets and liabilities, income and expenses, cash flow, debt management, investing, and passive income. By playing the Game, children learn the language of money and develop a solid foundation of financial literacy that will benefit them throughout their lives. They become familiar with financial terms, understand the principles of wealth creation, and gain the confidence to navigate the complexities of personal finance.

Real-World Application: Cashflow for Kids goes beyond the game board and encourages children to apply their financial knowledge to real-life situations. The skills and lessons learned from the Game can be translated into practical financial decision-making, such as saving money, setting financial goals, investing wisely, and avoiding unnecessary debt. The Game fosters a sense of financial responsibility and empowers children to take control of their financial future.

Life Skills: In addition to financial literacy, Cashflow for Kids helps develop critical life skills. The Game promotes teamwork, collaboration, and communication as players negotiate and strategize with each other. It teaches children the importance of perseverance, adaptability, and learning from mistakes while navigating financial challenges. Cashflow for Kids also instils a sense of entrepreneurial spirit, encouraging creativity and innovation as players explore different avenues to generate income.

Cashflow for Kids is a valuable educational tool that combines fun and learning to empower children with essential financial skills. Children develop a solid foundation in money management, critical thinking, risk assessment, and goal setting by immersing themselves in the Game's interactive and realistic financial scenarios. Cashflow for Kids lays the groundwork for a lifetime of financial success and helps children build a solid financial mindset early.

THE GAME OF LIFE: A JOURNEY OF LIFE AND FINANCIAL CHOICES

The Game of Life is a classic board game that takes players through life, simulating various stages and experiences. Created by Milton Bradley (now a subsidiary of Hasbro), The Game of Life has been a beloved game for generations, offering an entertaining and educational experience for players of all ages. Let's explore the details of The Game of Life and discover why it has remained a popular choice for families worldwide.

Game Objective: The objective of The Game of Life is to navigate through the ups and downs of life, making choices that shape your path and influence your financial well-being. Players start the Game by choosing a career and a salary, then embark on a journey where they encounter various life events, make financial decisions, and strive to accumulate wealth and happiness. The goal is to reach the retirement phase of the Game with the highest net worth and the most fulfilled life.

Life Choices and Financial Decisions: The Game of Life presents players with various life choices and financial decisions. Along the game board, players encounter events such as getting an education, starting a career, getting married, having children, buying a house, and pursuing various investments. Each decision has financial implications, and players must carefully consider each choice's trade-offs, risks, and potential rewards. The Game encourages strategic thinking and helps players understand the financial consequences of their decisions.

Income and Expenses: In The Game of Life, players earn income based on their chosen careers and the outcomes of various events. They receive salaries, collect bonuses, and receive payments for investments and ventures. At the same time, players face taxes, insurance, housing, and family expenses. The Game emphasizes the importance of budgeting, managing income and expenses, and making smart financial choices to maintain a positive cash flow.

Risk and Rewards: The Game of Life incorporates elements of risk and rewards, mirroring the uncertainties of real life. Players encounter unexpected events, such as car accidents, stock market investments, and career setbacks, which can impact their financial situation. They learn to navigate these challenges, manage risks, and seize opportunities for financial growth. The Game fosters an understanding of calculated risk-taking, weighing potential rewards against potential setbacks, and making informed financial choices.

Financial Planning and Retirement: As players progress through The Game of Life, they are encouraged to plan for retirement and make decisions contributing to their long-term financial well-being. They can invest in stocks and properties, save for retirement, and make other financial moves to increase their net worth. The Game promotes the importance of long-term financial planning, building wealth over time, and preparing for a comfortable retirement.

Life Lessons: Beyond financial concepts, The Game of Life imparts valuable life lessons. Players learn the importance of goal setting, adapting to unexpected circumstances, and maintaining a work-life balance. They develop decision-making skills, negotiation abilities, and the ability to cope with both success and setbacks. The Game encourages communication, cooperation, and empathy as players interact with each other and experience the joys and challenges of life together.

Family Bonding and Entertainment: The Game of Life provides a platform for family bonding and entertainment. Players engage in friendly competition, share laughter, and converse as they navigate the Game. The interactive nature of the Game promotes communication and fosters connections among players. It offers a chance for families to come together, create lasting memories, and learn valuable lessons about life and finance in a fun and engaging way.

The Game of Life offers an exciting and educational experience combining life lessons and financial decision-making. Players gain insights into personal finance, budgeting, risk management, and long-term planning by playing the Game. They develop critical thinking skills, learn to weigh options and understand the impact of their choices. The Game of Life is a source of entertainment and a valuable tool for teaching children about financial literacy, responsible decision-making, and the complexities of real-life finance.

FINANCIAL FOOTBALL: COMBINING FINANCE AND FOOTBALL FOR FINANCIAL LITERACY

Financial Football is an interactive educational game that combines the excitement of football with the world of personal finance. Developed by Visa and the National Football League (NFL), Financial Football aims to teach players of all ages about money management, budgeting, and making informed financial decisions. By integrating the popular sport of football with financial literacy, the Game provides an engaging and interactive platform for learning valuable money skills. Let's dive into the details of Financial Football and explore how it promotes financial literacy in a fun and relatable way.

Game Objective: Financial Football aims to score touchdowns by answering financial questions correctly and strategically advancing the football down the field. Players form teams and compete against each other, utilizing their personal finance knowledge to make the right choices and earn points. The Game encourages players to understand financial concepts, apply critical thinking skills, and make informed decisions to succeed financially.

Financial Concepts and Gameplay: Financial Football covers various financial topics, including budgeting, saving, investing, credit, etc. Players progress through the Game by answering financial questions of varying difficulty levels. Questions may involve budgeting for specific expenses, identifying needs and wants, understanding credit scores, evaluating investment options, or making informed purchasing decisions. By answering questions correctly, players earn yards and advance toward the end zone, aiming to score touchdowns and win the Game.

Tailored Difficulty Levels: Financial Football offers different difficulty levels to cater to players of varying ages and financial knowledge. Beginners can start with more straightforward questions that provide foundational knowledge, while more advanced players can challenge themselves with complex financial scenarios. This adaptable approach ensures players learn quickly and gradually expand their financial literacy skills.

Teamwork and Collaboration: Financial Football can be played individually or in teams, promoting teamwork, collaboration, and healthy competition. Players can form teams, select their favourite NFL teams as representations, and work together to answer questions and strategize gameplay. The collaborative aspect encourages discussions about financial concepts, sharing knowledge and insights, and learning from each other's perspectives.

Real-Life Scenarios: One of the strengths of Financial Football is its integration of real-life financial scenarios. The Game incorporates realistic situations players may encounter in their personal finance journey, such as managing student loans, making car buying decisions, or dealing with unexpected expenses. Players develop critical thinking skills by simulating these scenarios and learning to apply financial concepts to practical situations.

Financial Education Resources: Financial Football offers additional resources to enhance players' financial knowledge. These resources include educational materials, quizzes, and interactive tools that provide in-depth explanations of financial concepts covered in the Game. Players can access these resources to deepen their understanding, reinforce key learnings, and continue their financial education beyond the Game.

Engaging and Interactive Experience: Financial Football leverages the excitement and passion for football to create an engaging and interactive experience. The Game features engaging visuals, sound effects, and football-themed graphics that immerse players in the gameplay. The competitive nature of the Game, combined with the educational component, keeps players motivated and invested in learning and mastering financial skills.

Financial Football is a powerful tool for promoting financial literacy by combining the thrill of football with practical money management concepts. The Game allows players to learn and apply financial knowledge dynamically and interactively. By tackling financial challenges and making informed decisions, players develop essential skills for financial success. Financial Football is an enjoyable avenue for individuals of all ages to gain a solid foundation in personal finance while having fun and engaging in friendly competition.

LEMONADE STAND: A FUN AND EDUCATIONAL GAME FOR YOUNG ENTREPRENEURS

Lemonade Stand is a classic and popular educational game that simulates the experience of running a lemonade stand business. Developed to teach young entrepreneurs about basic business principles, financial management, and decision-making, Lemonade Stand provides an interactive and engaging platform for players to learn valuable skills while having fun. Let's explore the details of Lemonade Stand and discover how it fosters financial literacy and an entrepreneurial mindset playfully.

Game Objective: The objective of Lemonade Stand is to successfully manage and operate a virtual lemonade stand business over a set number of days. Players must make strategic pricing, inventory, recipe, and advertising decisions to attract customers and maximize profits. The Game challenges players to think critically, analyse market conditions, and make sound business choices to succeed in their lemonade venture.

Gameplay and Decision-Making: Lemonade Stand presents players with daily decisions, such as setting the price of lemonade, adjusting the recipe, purchasing ingredients, determining the amount of inventory, and allocating funds for marketing efforts. These decisions directly impact the profitability and customer satisfaction of the lemonade stand. Players must consider weather conditions, customer preferences, and costs to make informed choices and optimize business outcomes.

Financial Management Skills: Lemonade Stand teaches players essential financial management skills. Players learn to track income and expenses, calculate profits, manage inventory, and analyse financial reports. By monitoring their revenue and expenses, players gain a practical understanding of cash flow, profit margins, and the importance of budgeting in a business context. These skills lay a foundation for financial literacy and provide valuable insights into the dynamics of running a business.

Market Analysis and Strategy: To succeed in Lemonade Stand, players must analyse market conditions and adjust their strategies accordingly. They learn to observe customer behaviour, adapt their pricing and product offerings, and consider competitive factors to attract more customers. The Game introduces concepts like supply and demand, market research, and the importance of customer satisfaction. Players develop strategic thinking skills as they assess the market landscape and make decisions based on their observations.

Risk and Uncertainty: Lemonade Stand incorporates elements of risk and uncertainty, mirroring real-world business challenges. Players must contend with unpredictable weather conditions that affect customer demand and sales. This aspect teaches players the importance of risk assessment and contingency planning. They learn to make calculated decisions, adapt to changing circumstances, and navigate potential setbacks.

Entrepreneurial Mindset: Lemonade Stand encourages players to think like entrepreneurs. They learn the value of creativity, innovation, and adaptability in a competitive business environment. By taking risks, making decisions, and experiencing the consequences, players develop an entrepreneurial mindset that fosters initiative, problem-solving, and resilience. The Game instils a sense of empowerment and encourages young individuals to explore their entrepreneurial aspirations.

Educational Value: Beyond the gameplay itself, Lemonade Stand offers educational resources and learning materials to enhance the learning experience. These resources provide insights into business concepts, financial management principles, and tips for running a successful lemonade stand. Players can access additional information and guidance to deepen their understanding of business fundamentals and apply their knowledge beyond the Game.

Lemonade Stand is an engaging and educational game introducing young players to entrepreneurship and financial management. Players develop vital skills such as financial literacy, critical thinking, market analysis, and risk assessment through immersive gameplay and strategic decision-making. Lemonade Stand fosters an entrepreneurial mindset, ignites creativity, and empowers young individuals to explore their potential as future business leaders. The Game provides entertainment and valuable life skills that can be applied to real-world scenarios.

STOCK MARKET GAME: LEARN ABOUT INVESTING AND FINANCIAL MARKETS

The Stock Market Game is an interactive and educational game designed to introduce players to the world of investing and the dynamics of financial markets. It provides a virtual platform for players to simulate the experience of buying and selling stocks, making investment decisions, and navigating market fluctuations. The Game aims to cultivate financial literacy, critical thinking, and an understanding of the stock market engagingly and enjoyably. Let's explore the details of the Stock Market Game and discover how it helps players learn about investing.

Game Objective: The Stock Market Game aims to build and manage a virtual investment portfolio by buying and selling stocks. Players aim to grow their portfolio value through strategic investment decisions and capitalize on market trends. The Game encourages players to research companies, analyse market conditions, and make informed investment choices to achieve the highest returns.

Gameplay and Investment Decisions: In the Stock Market Game, players start with a virtual cash balance and can use it to purchase stocks from a range of companies listed on the virtual stock market. They have access to real-time stock prices and market information, enabling them to make investment decisions based on market trends, company performance, and financial news. Players can buy and sell stocks, track their portfolio's performance, and adjust their investment strategy over time.

Research and Analysis: The Game emphasizes the importance of research and analysis in making investment decisions. Players learn to gather company information, examine financial statements, study market trends, and assess risk factors. They develop skills in evaluating a company's fundamentals, understanding industry dynamics, and identifying potential investment opportunities. The Game encourages players to think critically and make thoughtful investment choices based on their research findings.

Risk and Reward: The Stock Market Game introduces players to risks and rewards in investing. They experience fluctuations in stock prices and learn to manage risks associated with their investment decisions. Players understand that higher returns often come with higher risk, and they need to assess their risk tolerance and diversify their portfolios to mitigate potential losses. The Game provides insights into the dynamic nature of financial markets and the importance of managing risk in investment strategies.

Market Simulation and Real-Time Updates: The Stock Market Game simulates real-world market conditions and provides players access to real-time stock prices and market updates. This feature allows players to experience the volatility and unpredictability of financial markets. They can observe how external factors like economic news, market trends, and investor sentiment impact stock prices. The Game helps players understand market dynamics and adapt their investment strategies accordingly.

Financial Literacy and Decision-Making Skills: Playing the Stock Market Game enhances players' financial literacy and decision-making skills. They learn about investment concepts such as diversification, portfolio management, risk assessment, and long-term investing. The Game fosters critical thinking, analytical skills, and the ability to make informed decisions in complex financial environments. Players gain practical investing knowledge and develop the confidence to navigate real-world financial markets.

Educational Resources and Support: The Stock Market Game often has educational resources and support materials to deepen players' understanding of investing and financial markets. These resources provide additional information on investment strategies, market analysis, and financial literacy concepts. Players can access tutorials, guides, and interactive tools to enhance their learning experience and expand their knowledge beyond the Game.

The Stock Market Game is a valuable educational tool that enables players to learn about investing and financial markets in an interactive and immersive way. Players gain practical insights into the complexities of investing, risk assessment, and portfolio management by participating in simulated investment activities. The Game enhances financial literacy, critical thinking, and decision-making skills necessary for successful investing. With its real-time market simulation and educational resources, the Stock Market Game equips players with the knowledge and confidence to navigate the world of investing and make informed financial decisions.

PAYDAY: THE CLASSIC GAME OF FINANCIAL MANAGEMENT

Payday is a classic board game that simulates the ups and downs of managing personal finances. It provides players with an engaging and educational experience, teaching them valuable lessons about budgeting, financial planning, and making financial decisions. The Game is designed to replicate real-life financial situations and challenges, allowing players to navigate through a month of expenses, savings, and unexpected events. Let's explore the details of Payday and discover how it helps players develop financial management skills.

Game Objective: The objective of Payday is to manage personal finances wisely and accumulate the most wealth by the end of the Game. Players receive a fixed monthly income and must make strategic decisions on allocating their money, paying bills, saving, and investing. The Game spans a series of payday cycles, where players encounter various financial events and make choices that impact their financial situation.

Gameplay and Financial Decision-Making: In Payday, players move around the game board, landing on different spaces representing financial events and activities. Each space corresponds to an action, such as receiving a pay check, paying bills, making purchases, or encountering unexpected expenses. Players choose how to spend or save their money based on their current financial situation and long-term goals.

Budgeting and Expense Management: A key aspect of Payday is budgeting and expense management. Players must carefully plan their spending and prioritize their expenses to cover essential needs while saving for the future. They face decisions on whether to pay bills immediately, save money, invest in opportunities, or make discretionary purchases. The Game teaches players the importance of budgeting, distinguishing between wants and needs, and making informed financial choices.

Savings and Investments: Payday encourages players to save and invest their money wisely. They can set aside a portion of their income as savings or invest in various financial opportunities that arise during the Game. Players learn about the benefits of saving for emergencies and long-term goals and the potential risks and rewards of different investment options. The Game helps players understand the importance of balancing immediate expenses with future financial security.

Financial Risk and Unexpected Events: Throughout the Game, players encounter unexpected events and financial risks that can impact their financial situation. These events may include car repairs, medical expenses, or unexpected windfalls. Players must plan and allocate their resources to manage these unpredictable situations effectively. The Game teaches players to anticipate and prepare for financial risks and highlights the importance of having contingency plans and emergency funds.

Financial Literacy and Decision-Making Skills: Playing Payday enhances players' financial literacy and decision-making skills. They learn about financial concepts such as budgeting, saving, investing, and managing debt. The Game prompts players to think critically, analyse different financial scenarios, and make strategic decisions to optimize their financial well-being. Players develop skills in evaluating trade-offs, assessing risks, and making sound financial choices.

Fun and Social Interaction: Payday is educational and provides an enjoyable and social gaming experience. Players can engage in friendly competition, negotiate deals, and share their financial strategies with others. The Game fosters collaboration and communication as players discuss financial decisions, exchange tips, and learn from each other's experiences. It creates a dynamic and interactive environment where players can have fun while learning about financial management.

Payday is a classic game that offers a hands-on and entertaining approach to financial management. Through its gameplay and financial decision-making elements, the Game teaches players valuable lessons about budgeting, expense management, saving, investing, and navigating unexpected events. It enhances financial literacy, critical thinking, and decision-making skills, providing a foundation for responsible financial management. Whether played with family or friends, Payday offers an engaging and educational experience that empowers players to take control of their finances and achieve financial success.

MONEY BAGS: THE COIN COLLECTING GAME

Money Bags is an exciting and educational board game that introduces kids to the concept of money and basic financial skills. Designed for children aged seven and above, the Game aims to teach valuable lessons about counting money, making change, and developing good money management habits.

Through engaging gameplay and interactive experiences, Money Bags offers an enjoyable way for kids to learn about the importance of money and how to handle it responsibly.

Game Objective: Money Bags aims to be the player with the most money at the end of the Game. Players take turns moving around the board, collecting coins, and learning about their value. The Game introduces basic math skills, such as addition and subtraction, as players count their money and make changes during various transactions. The goal is to accumulate the most coins while making wise financial decisions.

Gameplay and Coin Collecting: In Money Bags, players travel around the board, landing on spaces that require them to perform specific money-related tasks. This may include collecting a specific amount of coins, changing, or learning about different coin denominations. The Game provides hands-on experiences with coins, allowing players to handle and count them. Players engage in interactive play by exchanging coins with the bank and other players during transactions.

Math Skills and Money Management: Money Bags reinforces basic math skills by incorporating them into gameplay. Players practice addition and subtraction as they count their coins, make changes, and calculate the total value of their money. By participating in these activities, players develop a solid foundation in arithmetic and improve their ability to handle real-life financial transactions confidently. The Game encourages accuracy, quick thinking, and mental math skills.

Financial Decision-Making: Money Bags presents players with various financial decision-making scenarios. They must decide how to spend their money wisely, make changes accurately, and strategize to collect the most valuable coins. The Game promotes critical thinking as players evaluate different coin values and consider the best ways to maximize their earnings. It teaches kids the importance of making informed decisions and planning financial moves.

Coin Recognition and Value: One of the primary objectives of Money Bags is to familiarize children with different coin denominations and their values. Players learn to recognize coins by their appearance, size, and value. They gain an understanding of the relationships between coins, such as how many pennies make a nickel or a dime. The Game enhances coin recognition skills and helps kids become comfortable with handling and identifying different currency units.

Teamwork and Social Interaction: Money Bags can be played individually or in teams, promoting teamwork and social interaction. Players can work together to count money, make changes, and solve money-related challenges. They learn to collaborate, communicate, and share strategies with others. The Game encourages healthy competition and friendly interactions, fostering social skills and cooperative play among players.

Financial Literacy and Responsibility: Playing Money Bags, children develop a foundational understanding of money and financial responsibility. They learn about the value of money, the importance of saving, and the basics of financial transactions. The Game instils early lessons in financial literacy, teaching kids to differentiate between wants and needs and make thoughtful spending decisions. It sets the stage for future financial independence and responsible money management.

Money Bags is an engaging and educational game introducing kids to money and financial management. Through hands-on coin collecting, math activities, and decision-making challenges, children learn valuable skills in counting money, making changes, and developing responsible financial habits. The Game fosters math proficiency, critical thinking, teamwork, and social interaction. With Money Bags, kids can have fun while acquiring essential financial knowledge and skills that will benefit them in their everyday lives.

THRIFTY KIDS: THE MONEY-SAVING ADVENTURE

Thrifty Kids is an interactive and educational board game that teaches children valuable lessons about money-saving habits and smart financial choices. Designed for kids aged eight and above, the Game aims to instil a sense of financial responsibility and resourcefulness by challenging players to navigate through real-life financial scenarios. Through engaging gameplay and interactive experiences, Thrifty Kids offers an exciting and fun-filled way for kids to learn about money management and the importance of saving.

Game Objective: Thrifty Kids aims to be the player who saves the most money at the end of the Game. Players embark on a money-saving adventure by moving around the game board, making decisions, and facing various financial challenges. The Game emphasizes the value of saving, making wise spending choices, and planning for the future. The goal is to accumulate the highest savings while demonstrating intelligent financial strategies.

Gameplay and Financial Challenges: In Thrifty Kids, players navigate through financial challenges and opportunities. They encounter scenarios such as deciding between spending or saving, budgeting, and managing unexpected expenses. The Game incorporates real-life situations that kids may encounter, allowing them to practice critical thinking and decision-making skills related to money management. Players must strategize and make choices that align with their savings goals.

Money-Saving Strategies: Thrifty Kids encourages players to develop effective money-saving strategies. Throughout the Game, players learn different techniques for saving money, such as setting financial goals, budgeting, and avoiding unnecessary expenses. They are prompted to think creatively and develop innovative ways to stretch their dollars further. The Game highlights the importance of delayed gratification and conscious money-saving choices.

Budgeting and Planning: One of the critical aspects of Thrifty Kids is budgeting and planning. Players are given little virtual money and must allocate their funds wisely to cover expenses, save for goals, and prepare for unexpected events. They learn to create and manage budgets, prioritize spending, and adjust their financial plans as circumstances change. The Game reinforces the importance of planning and making informed financial decisions.

Financial Responsibility and Consequences: Thrifty Kids emphasizes financial responsibility and the consequences of financial choices. Players experience the outcomes of their positive and negative decisions as they progress through the Game. They learn the importance of making thoughtful financial choices, the impact of impulsive spending, and the rewards of saving money. The Game fosters an understanding of the long-term consequences of financial actions and encourages responsible financial behaviour.

Cooperative and Competitive Gameplay: Thrifty Kids can be played individually or in teams, allowing for cooperative and competitive gameplay. Players can collaborate and share strategies to maximize their savings collectively. They can also compete to see who can save the most money individually. The Game promotes teamwork, communication, and problem-solving skills, fostering a sense of camaraderie and healthy competition among players.

Financial Literacy and Life Skills: By playing Thrifty Kids, children develop essential financial literacy skills and life skills that will benefit them throughout their lives. They learn the fundamentals of money management, including budgeting, saving, and making intelligent financial decisions. The Game enhances critical thinking, problem-solving, and numeracy skills as players calculate expenses, evaluate options, and strategize to achieve their savings goals. Thrifty Kids equips children with practical skills and knowledge to navigate the financial challenges they may face in the real world.

Thrifty Kids is an engaging and educational board game introducing children to money management, saving, and financial responsibility. Through interactive gameplay, players learn valuable skills in budgeting, decision-making, and setting financial goals. The Game promotes critical thinking, cooperative play, and strategic planning. Thrifty Kids empowers children to develop lifelong money-saving habits, make informed financial choices, and build a strong foundation for future financial success.

SAVE! THE GAME: A FINANCIAL ADVENTURE FOR KIDS

Save! The Game is an exciting and educational board game designed to teach children the importance of saving money and making wise financial decisions. The Game aims to instil valuable money management skills for kids aged six and above while providing an enjoyable and interactive playing experience. By navigating various financial scenarios and challenges, players learn the fundamentals of saving, budgeting and setting financial goals.

Game Objective: The objective of Save! The Game allows players to accumulate the highest savings by making strategic decisions and managing their finances effectively. Players embark on a financial adventure where they face different scenarios, make choices, and learn from the consequences of their actions. The Game encourages players to develop saving habits, practice critical thinking, and understand the long-term benefits of financial responsibility.

Gameplay and Financial Challenges: In Save! In the Game, players navigate a series of financial challenges and opportunities. They encounter scenarios like earning money from allowances, making spending decisions, and dealing with unexpected expenses. Players are prompted to consider their options, weigh the benefits and consequences, and make choices that align with their savings goals. The Game introduces players to real-life financial situations and teaches them to think critically about money-related decisions.

Saving Strategies and Goal Setting: Save! The Game emphasizes the importance of saving money and setting financial goals. Players are encouraged to develop saving strategies, such as allocating a portion of their income to savings, avoiding impulse purchases, and prioritizing long-term financial objectives. The Game provides opportunities for players to set goals and track their progress, fostering a sense of achievement and motivation to save more.

Budgeting and Financial Planning: Budgeting and financial planning are critical components of Save! The Game. Players are given little virtual money and must allocate their funds wisely to cover expenses, save for goals, and navigate unexpected financial situations. They learn to create budgets, manage their income and expenses, and adjust as needed. The Game introduces players to planning and making thoughtful financial decisions.

Financial Responsibility and Consequences: Save! The Game teaches children about financial responsibility and the consequences of their choices. Players experience the outcomes of their financial decisions as they progress through the Game. They learn the impact of impulsive spending, the benefits of saving for the future, and the importance of making informed financial choices. The Game encourages players to consider the long-term consequences of their actions and develop responsible financial habits.

Cooperative and Competitive Gameplay: Save! The Game offers both cooperative and competitive gameplay options. Players can choose to work together, sharing strategies and collaborating to achieve savings goals collectively. They can also compete to see who can accumulate the highest savings individually. The Game promotes teamwork, communication, and problem-solving skills while fostering healthy competition among players.

Financial Literacy and Life Skills: By playing Save! In the Game, children develop essential financial literacy skills and life skills that will serve them well in the future. They learn the basics of money management, including budgeting, saving, and making informed financial decisions. The Game enhances critical thinking, numeracy skills, and decision-making abilities as players evaluate options, calculate expenses, and strategize to achieve their savings goals. Save! The Game equips children with practical skills and knowledge to navigate real-world financial challenges.

Save! The Game is an engaging and educational board game introducing children to saving money, budgeting, and financial responsibility. Through interactive gameplay, players learn valuable skills in money management, goal setting, and decision-making. The Game promotes critical thinking, cooperation, and strategic planning while instilling lifelong saving habits. Save! The Game empowers children to become financially responsible individuals and lays a strong foundation for their financial well-being.

UNLOCKING THE LANGUAGE OF FINANCE

A Comprehensive Dictionary of Financial Terms

Knowledge is power. Information is liberating. Education is the premise of progress, in every society, in every family.

Kofi Annan

Financial Dictionary is an invaluable resource for anyone looking to gain a better understanding of the complex and ever-changing world of finance. With many terms and concepts finance can feel like a foreign language, but a dictionary can provide clarity and context for the most commonly used terms.

A financial dictionary provides definitions, examples, and practical applications of key terms, from basic financial concepts like savings and investments to more advanced topics like derivatives and futures. Whether a seasoned finance professional or a novice investor, a comprehensive financial word dictionary can help you navigate finance confidently and clearly.

This financial dictionary is a reference tool that provides definitions and explanations of terms and concepts related to finance. It is a comprehensive collection of financial terms commonly used in the industry, including basic terms such as assets, liabilities, and revenue and more complex topics such as options, futures, and derivatives.

This financial word dictionary is designed to help people understand the language and terminology used in finance and to provide clarity and context for these terms. It is a valuable resource for professionals in the finance industry, as well as for individuals who want to gain a better understanding of financial concepts for personal or business purposes.

Knowledge of financial terms is essential for anyone who wants to be financially literate and successful today. Here are some reasons:

Make informed decisions: Understanding financial terms can help you make informed decisions about your finances. For example, if you understand the difference between stocks and bonds, you can make better investment choices.

Communicate effectively: Knowledge of financial terms allows you to communicate more effectively with financial professionals, such as bankers, financial advisors, or accountants. This can help you understand their advice and make better financial decisions.

Avoid financial mistakes: Lack of knowledge of financial terms can lead to costly mistakes, such as taking out a loan with unfavourable terms or investing in a high-risk asset without fully understanding the risks involved.

Plan for the future: Financial planning involves setting goals and creating plans to achieve them. Knowing financial terms can help you create a more effective plan that considers your current financial situation and future financial goals.

Navigate the job market: Knowledge of financial terms is increasingly important in today's job market, particularly for positions in finance, accounting, or business. Employers expect candidates to understand financial terms and concepts, even if the position is not directly related to finance.

Knowing financial terms is crucial for personal and professional success today. It can help you make better financial decisions, communicate effectively with financial professionals, and plan for a secure financial future.

Aa

assets Things of value that an individual or organization owns, such as cash, investments, property, or equipment.

accounting is keeping financial records and preparing financial statements, such as balance sheets and income statements.

amortization is the process of spreading out the cost of an asset over its useful life, such as a loan or a piece of equipment.

APR Annual Percentage Rate, which is the interest rate

charged on a loan or credit card on an annual basis.

allocation is dividing assets among different investment options or categories, such as stocks, bonds, or mutual funds.

appreciation an increase in the value of an asset over time, such as an increase in the value of a stock or a piece of property.

annuity A financial product that pays out a fixed stream of income over a specified period, such as a retirement annuity.

accrual is the recognition of revenue or expenses before payment is received or made, such as the accrual of interest on a loan.

arbitrage is buying and selling assets in different markets to take advantage of price differences and make a profit.

audit an independent examination of financial records to ensure they are accurate
and comply with accounting standards and regulations.

ask price is the lowest price at which a seller is willing to sell a security.

Bb

bank is a financial institution that provides various financial services, such as deposit accounts, loans, and investments, to individuals and businesses.

budget A financial plan that outlines expected income and expenses over a specific period.

bankruptcy is the legal process by which an individual or company declares themselves unable to pay their debts.

broker A professional who buys and sells securities on behalf of investors.

bond A type of investment that represents a loan made by an investor to a borrower, typically a corporation or government.

bear market A market in which prices are falling, and investors are pessimistic about the future.

bull market A market in which prices rise, and investors are optimistic about the future.

balance sheet A financial statement that shows a company's assets, liabilities, and equity at a specific time.

blue chip A term used to describe a financially stable, well-established company with a long history of consistent earnings and dividends.

buy and hold is an investment strategy that involves buying securities and holding them for an extended period, regardless of short-term market fluctuations.

brokerage account is an account that allows investors to buy and sell securities through a broker.

Cc

capital refers to the money or assets that a company has available for investment or operation. It can be in the form of cash, machinery, buildings, or other assets.

credit is the ability to borrow money or receive goods or services with the promise of paying for them later. A credit score is a numerical rating representing an individual's creditworthiness to repay debts.

collateral is an asset or property pledged as security for a loan. If the borrower cannot repay the loan, the lender can seize the collateral to recover their losses.

capital gains are the profits made from selling an asset that has been appreciated. This can include stocks, real estate, and other investments.

cash flow refers to the movement of money in and out of business. Positive cash flow means that a business brings in more money than it is spending, while negative cash flow means the opposite.

cost of goods sold (COGS) refers to the direct costs associated with producing or manufacturing a product. This includes the cost of materials, labour, and overhead expenses.

currency refers to the money used in a particular country or region. It can be in the form of paper notes or coins.

consumer price index (CPI) measures the average price change over time for a basket of goods and services that households consume. It is often used to track inflation and the cost of living.

commodities are raw materials or primary agricultural products that can be bought and sold, such as oil, gold, and wheat.

commercial paper is a short-term debt instrument companies use to raise funds quickly. It is typically used to finance short-term liabilities or to cover temporary cash shortages.

compound interest earned on the household goods and services interest.

credit limit the maximum amount of credit that a lender will extend to a borrower.

certified financial planner (CFP) A professional designation for individuals who have completed a rigorous certification process in financial planning.

capital markets the financial markets where long-term debt and equity securities are bought and sold.

corporate bonds Debt securities issued by corporations to raise capital, usually with a fixed interest rate and a maturity date.

Dd

debt Money that is owed by one party to another party. In finance, debt typically refers to loans, bonds, or other forms of borrowing.

derivatives the financial instruments that derive their value from an underlying asset, such as stocks, bonds, or commodities. Examples of derivatives include options, futures, and swaps.

dividend A portion of a company's earnings that is distributed to shareholders as a reward for their investment. Dividends are usually paid out in the form of cash or additional shares of stock.

due diligence the process of conducting a thorough

investigation of a company or investment opportunity before making a decision to invest. Due diligence may involve examining financial statements, conducting market research, and assessing the management team.

depreciation the gradual decrease in the value of an asset over time. In accounting, depreciation is used to reflect the wear and tear on assets such as buildings, equipment, and vehicles.

discount rate the interest rate used to calculate the present value of future cash flows. The discount rate takes into account the risk associated with the investment and is typically higher for riskier investments.

diversification the practice of spreading investments across different asset classes, industries, and geographic regions in order to reduce risk. Diversification can help to mitigate the impact of market volatility on investment portfolios.

dollar-cost averaging an investment strategy in which an investor buys a fixed dollar amount of a particular asset on a regular basis, regardless of the asset's price. This strategy can help to smooth out fluctuations in the market and reduce the impact of market volatility on investment returns.

derivative A financial instrument whose value is based on an underlying asset, such as a stock or commodity.

dow jones industrial average (DJIA) A stock market index that tracks the performance of 30 large, publicly traded companies in the United States.

debt-to-equity ratio A financial ratio that measures the amount of debt a company has relative to its equity.

direct deposit A payment method in which funds are deposited directly into a bank account, without the need for a physical check.

de facto A legal obligation or agreement, such as making payments on a loan.

deposit A sum of money placed into a bank account or other financial institution for safekeeping or to earn interest.

due diligence the investigation or research of a potential investment or acquisition to verify all facts, risks, and potential outcomes.

Ee

equity the value of an asset after deducting any liabilities, such as mortgages or loans.

exchange rate the value of one currency in relation to another currency.

expenses the costs incurred in the course of business or personal activities.

entrepreneur A person who starts and operates a business, often taking on financial risk in the process.

earnest money A deposit made by a buyer to show that they are serious about purchasing a property.

estate the net worth of an individual, including their property, investments, and other assets, at the time of their death.

ETF (Exchange-Traded Fund) A type of investment fund that trades on a stock exchange, tracking the performance of an index, commodity, or other asset.

endowment A fund established by a donor to provide ongoing support for a particular cause, such as education or research.

escrow the holding of funds or documents by a neutral third party until certain conditions are met, such as the completion of a real estate transaction.

expense ratio the percentage of assets that is used to pay for the management and operating expenses of a mutual fund or ETF.

Ff

financial statement A record of a company's financial performance, including its income statement, balance sheet, and cash flow statement.

fixed income an investment that provides a regular stream of income, such as bonds or preferred stocks.

futures contract A financial contract that obligates the buyer or seller to buy or sell an underlying asset at a predetermined price and date in the future.

fiscal year A period of 12 months used for accounting purposes, which may or may not coincide with the calendar year.

federal Reserve The central bank of the United States, responsible for monetary policy, regulating banks, and maintaining the stability of the financial system.

foreign exchange market the market where currencies are bought and sold, often used by investors and traders to make profits from fluctuations in exchange rates.

fundamental analysis an investment analysis approach that focuses on analysing a company's financial statements, industry trends, and economic conditions to determine its intrinsic value.

financial planner A professional who helps individuals and businesses create and implement financial plans to achieve their goals.

financial leverage the use of borrowed funds to invest in assets or operations, with the goal of increasing returns.

foreclosure the legal process by which a lender seizes and sells a property when the borrower fails to make mortgage payments.

finance the study of money management, including investing, borrowing, and budgeting.

Financial Related to finance or the management of money.

forecast A prediction of future trends or conditions, such as a financial forecast that predicts future revenues and expenses.

fraud A deliberate deception or misrepresentation intended to gain an unfair advantage or cause financial harm.

fiduciary A person or organization that is legally bound to act in the best interests of their clients or beneficiaries, such as a financial advisor or trustee.

fluctuation the rise and fall of prices or values over time, such as the fluctuation of stock prices in the stock market.

fundamentals the underlying economic, financial, and business factors that affect the value of an investment or asset.

fiscal Relating to government revenue and spending, such as fiscal policy or the fiscal year.

fixed cost A cost that does not vary with changes in production or sales levels, such as rent or salaries.

Gg

gross income the total amount of income earned before any deductions or taxes are taken out.

GDP (Gross Domestic Product) The value of all goods and services produced within a country's **borders**, used as a measure of the country's economic performance.

growth stock A stock of a company that is expected to grow at a higher rate than the market or industry average, often characterized by higher valuations and lower dividends.

government bond A bond issued by a government entity, considered to be a low-risk investment due to the government's ability to repay the debt.

grant A financial award provided by a government or private organization for a specific purpose, often related to research or social programs.

guaranteed investment certificate (GIC) A type of investment that guarantees a fixed rate of return over a specific period of time, often offered by banks or other financial institutions.

goodwill the intangible value of a company's brand, reputation, and relationships, often considered in the valuation of a business.

gold standard A monetary system in which the value of a currency is directly linked to the value of gold.

general ledger A record of all financial transactions made by a company, organized by account and used for accounting and financial reporting purposes.

going public the process of a private company becoming a publicly traded company by offering its shares to the public through an initial public offering (IPO).

Hh

hedging A financial strategy used to reduce or offset risk by making investments that will counterbalance potential losses in other investments.

hedge fund an investment fund that pools capital from accredited investors and uses complex investment strategies, such as short selling, to generate high returns.

holding period the length of time an asset is held by an investor, often used to determine capital gains taxes.

high-yield bond A bond issued by a company with a lower credit rating, often associated with higher risk but also higher potential returns.

home equity the value of a homeowner's interest in their home, calculated as the market value of the home minus any outstanding mortgage debt.

human capital the knowledge, skills, and abilities of an individual or workforce, often considered a valuable asset for businesses.

health savings account (HSA) A tax-advantaged savings account used to pay for qualified medical expenses, often offered in conjunction with high-deductible health insurance plans.

hard money loan A type of loan in which the borrower uses real estate as collateral, often used by investors or individuals who cannot qualify for traditional financing.

historical cost the original cost of an asset, used for accounting and financial reporting purposes.

homeowners association (HOA) A governing body that manages and enforces rules for a community of homeowners, often associated with fees and assessments.

hourly wage the rate of pay for an employee based on the number of hours worked, often used for hourly or part-time positions.

Ii

inflation A sustained increase in the general price level of goods and services in an economy, resulting in a decrease in the purchasing power of money.

interest rate the amount charged by a lender to a borrower for the use of money, usually expressed as a percentage of the principal loan amount.

investment the purchase of an asset with the expectation of generating income or appreciation in value over time.

Initial Public Offering (IPO) The first time a company's shares are offered to the public for purchase, often used as a way for companies to raise capital.

income statement A financial statement that shows a company's revenue, expenses, and net income over a specific period of time.

intrinsic value the true or inherent value of an asset, based on its fundamental characteristics and not influenced by market conditions.

index fund A type of mutual fund or exchange-traded fund (ETF) that tracks the performance of a specific market index, such as the S&P 500.

indemnity A type of insurance contract in which the insurer agrees to compensate the insured for losses incurred, subject to the terms and limits of the policy.

invoice A document that details the goods or services provided, the amount owed, and the payment terms for a transaction between a buyer and seller.

IRS (Internal Revenue Service) The federal agency responsible for collecting taxes and enforcing tax laws in the United States.

Jj

junk bond A high-yield, high-risk bond issued by a company with a low credit rating, typically offering a higher yield to compensate for the increased risk.

joint account A bank or investment account that is owned and operated by two or more people.

jumbo mortgage A mortgage loan that exceeds the maximum loan amount set by Fannie Mae and Freddie Mac, often used for high-priced homes.

journal entry A record of a financial transaction, typically entered into a company's accounting system as part of the bookkeeping process.

jobless claims the number of individuals who file for unemployment benefits in a given period of time, often used as an economic indicator.

joint venture A business arrangement in which two or more parties agree to pool resources and expertise to achieve a common goal, typically with shared profits and risks.

Kk

KPI (Key Performance Indicator) stands for Key Performance Indicator, which is a metric used to measure the success or performance of a particular activity or business process. Examples of KPIs include revenue growth, customer retention rate, and return on investment (ROI). Thank you for pointing this out.

keogh plan A type of retirement savings plan for self-employed individuals and small business owners, allowing for tax-deferred contributions and investments.

key rate the benchmark interest rate set by a central bank, used to influence borrowing and lending rates in an economy.

knock-in option an option contract that only becomes active if the underlying asset price reaches a specified level, also known as a barrier option.

Know Your Customer (KYC) The process of verifying the identity of a customer, often used by financial institutions to comply with anti-money laundering regulations.

Ll

liability an obligation or debt owed by an individual or organization, such as a loan or unpaid bill.

liquidity the degree to which an asset or security can be bought or sold in the market without affecting its price.

leverage the use of borrowed funds to increase the potential return on investment, often associated with higher risk.

limit order an order to buy or sell a security at a specific price or better, used to control the price at which a transaction takes place.

long position the ownership of a security or asset with the expectation that its value will increase over time.

Mm

mutual fund A type of investment fund that pools money from multiple investors to purchase a diversified portfolio of securities.

market capitalization the total value of a company's outstanding shares of stock, calculated by multiplying the current stock price by the number of outstanding shares.

margin the amount of money or collateral required to be deposited by an investor in order to enter into a leveraged investment position.

maturity the date on which a financial instrument or investment reaches its final payment or expiration.

money market A market in which short-term financial instruments such as Treasury bills and commercial paper are traded, often used by investors seeking low-risk, low-return investments.

Nn

net income Net income is a company's total revenue minus its expenses, and it is often referred to as the bottom line or earnings. It is a key metric used to evaluate a company's profitability and financial performance.

Net Asset Value (NAV) Net asset value (NAV) is the total value of a mutual fund's or investment company's assets, less its liabilities. It is calculated on a per-share basis and represents the fund's intrinsic value. Investors often use NAV as a measure of a fund's performance or as a basis for buying or selling shares.

Net Present Value (NPV) Net Present Value (NPV) is a calculation used in capital budgeting to determine the value of an investment by comparing the present value of its expected cash inflows to the present value of its expected cash outflows. If the NPV is positive, it indicates that the investment is expected to generate more cash than it costs and is therefore considered a good investment. If the NPV is negative, it indicates that the investment is not expected to generate enough cash to cover its costs and is therefore considered a poor investment.

NASDAQ The world's second-largest stock exchange by market capitalization, known for listing technology and growth-oriented companies.

net worth the difference between an individual's total assets and liabilities, used to measure their financial health and ability to meet obligations.

nominal interest rates The stated rate of interest on a financial instrument or loan, not adjusted for inflation.

nonperforming loan A loan that is in default or has not been paid for a specified period of time, often considered a risk to the lender.

nostro account an account held by a bank in a foreign country, used to facilitate international transactions and settlements.

Oo

options A type of financial derivative that gives the holder the right, but not the obligation, to buy or sell an underlying asset at a specific price, on or before a certain date.

overdraft A banking service that allows a customer to withdraw more money from their account than they currently have available, up to a certain limit, usually for a fee.

operating expenses the costs incurred by a business or organization to operate on a day-to-day basis, including rent, utilities, salaries, and other expenses.

open market operations the buying and selling of government securities by a central bank in order to influence the money supply and interest rates.

out-of-the-money A term used to describe an option that has no intrinsic value, meaning the option's strike price is not favourable compared to the current market price of the underlying asset.

Pp

portfolio A collection of financial assets such as stocks, bonds, and cash equivalents held by an individual or institution.

principal the amount of money borrowed in a loan or the amount invested in an asset, excluding any interest or other earnings.

profit the amount of money earned after deducting expenses from revenue.

Price-to-earnings ratio (P/E ratio) A valuation ratio that compares a company's current stock price to its earnings per share (EPS).

pension A retirement plan in which an employee makes contributions during their working years and receives regular payments from the plan after they retire.

Qq

quantitative easing A monetary policy used by central banks to increase the money supply and stimulate economic growth. It involves the purchase of government securities by the central bank, which injects money into the economy.

quotation the price at which a financial asset is currently trading in the market. It is often used interchangeably with the term "price" in financial contexts.

quantitative analysis the use of mathematical and statistical models to analyze and measure financial and economic data. It involves the use of numerical data and objective methods to analyze financial instruments such as stocks, bonds, and derivatives. This analysis can be used to make investment decisions, risk management, and other financial strategies.

Rr

revenue the total income generated by a business before any expenses are deducted.

return the amount of money earned on an investment, usually expressed as a percentage of the initial investment.

risk the probability that an investment will lose value or fail to achieve its expected return.

ratio A mathematical comparison between two or more financial values or quantities, often used to analyse a company's financial health.

refinance The process of replacing an existing debt obligation with a new one, often with more favourable terms, such as a lower interest rate.

retirement The act of leaving the workforce and ceasing employment, often accompanied by the receipt of retirement benefits or pension payments.

royalty A payment made by one party (such as a licensee) to another (such as a licensor) in exchange for the right to use or exploit intellectual property, such as patents, trademarks, or copyrights.

Return on Investment (RoI) A measure of the profitability of an investment, calculated as the ratio of the investment's net profit to the amount of the initial investment. It is often used to evaluate the efficiency of an investment and compare different investment opportunities.

Ss

stocks Ownership shares in a publicly traded company, which represent a claim to a portion of the company's assets and earnings.

securities financial instruments such as stocks, bonds, and options that can be bought and sold on a public exchange.

savings Money set aside or saved for future use or emergencies.

solvency The ability of a business or individual to meet their financial obligations and pay off debts.

supply and demand the fundamental economic principle that describes how prices are set by the availability of a product or service (supply) and the level of consumer interest or need (demand).

spread the difference between the bid and ask price of a financial instrument, such as a stock or currency.

sales revenue the total amount of revenue generated by a company through the sale of goods or services.

stock market A public marketplace for buying and selling stocks and other securities.

securitization the process of transforming financial assets, such as loans or mortgages, into marketable securities that can be sold to investors.

settlement the process of finalizing a financial transaction, including the transfer of funds and any necessary documentation.

Tt

tax A mandatory financial charge imposed by the government on individuals or companies based on income or transactions.
treasury the department of a government responsible for managing financial resources, such as tax revenue, and overseeing monetary policy.
trade the exchange of goods or services between individuals or companies.
trading the buying and selling of financial instruments, such as stocks, bonds, and commodities, in order to generate profits.
transaction an exchange of goods, services, or financial instruments, such as buying or selling stocks or transferring funds between accounts.
trust A financial arrangement in which one party holds assets for the benefit of another party.
term the length of time for which a loan, investment, or other financial instrument is valid or in effect.
time value of money the concept that money available today is worth more than the same amount of money in the future, due to the potential for investment returns and inflation.
total return the total amount of profit or loss generated by an investment, including both capital gains and income.
turnover the rate at which a company buys and sells assets, or the frequency with which an investment portfolio is bought and sold.

Uu

underwriter an individual or institution that assumes financial responsibility for another entity's securities offering.
unit trust A type of investment fund where investors pool their money together to invest in a diversified portfolio of assets.
unsecured debt A debt that is not backed by collateral, such as

a mortgage or car loan.

uptick A small increase in the price of a security compared to the previous trade.

usury the illegal action or practice of lending money at a high interest rate.

unclaimed property such as bank accounts or securities, that has been abandoned by its rightful owner and turned over to the government.

Uniform Gift to Minors Act (UGMA) A law that allows minors to receive gifts or transfers of money or property without requiring a guardian or trust.

underlying asset an asset, such as a stock, bond, or commodity, that is used to determine the value of a derivative or other financial instrument.

Vv

valuation the process of determining the worth or value of an asset, investment, or company.

venture capital Private equity investment made in a start-up or small business with high growth potential.

volatility A measure of the amount and frequency of price fluctuations of a security or market.

value investing an investment strategy that involves buying stocks that are undervalued by the market, with the expectation of long-term gains.

variable annuity A type of annuity contract where the payout amount varies based on the performance of the underlying investments.

variable rate an interest rate that changes over time based on an underlying benchmark or index.

voluntary liquidation the process by which a company chooses to end its business operations voluntarily, sell its assets, and distribute the proceeds to its creditors and shareholders.

VIX The CBOE Volatility Index, which measures the market's expectations of volatility over the next 30 days, based on the prices of S&P 500 options.

value the worth of an asset, investment, or company based on its perceived usefulness, desirability, or usefulness to a buyer or seller.

Ww

wealth the accumulated value of assets owned by an individual, company, or society.

working capital, The amount of money available to a business to fund its daily operations and short-term liabilities.

wire transfer the electronic transfer of funds between banks or financial institutions.

warrant A financial instrument that gives the holder the right, but not the obligation, to buy or sell an underlying asset at a certain price and time.

Weighted Average Cost of Capital (WACC) A calculation used to determine the average cost of a company's capital based on the relative weight of each type of capital.

write-off A reduction in the value of an asset or account balance to zero, usually due to it being deemed uncollectible or worthless.

withholding tax, A tax deducted from income or payments made to non-residents, which is withheld by the payer and remitted to the government.

Wall Street A metonym for the financial markets of the United States, particularly the stock market and major financial institutions located in New York City.

wholesale banking services offered to large corporations, financial institutions, and government agencies, as opposed to retail banking services offered to individuals and small businesses.

Xx Yy Zz

xenocurrency A currency that is not widely used or accepted outside of its country of origin.

X-efficiency A concept in economics that refers to the degree to which a firm or organization is able to minimize costs and maximize output or productivity.

xetra an electronic trading platform used for the trading of securities and other financial instruments in Europe.

xirr the extended internal rate of return, a method of calculating the rate of return on an investment based on irregular cash flows and varying dates of cash inflows and outflows.

X-inefficiency A situation in which a firm or organization is operating below its optimal level of efficiency, resulting in higher costs and lower output or productivity.

yield the income generated by an investment, usually expressed as a percentage of the investment amount.

yield curve A graph that shows the relationship between the yield on bonds of the same credit quality but different maturities.

yen the currency of Japan.

yield to maturity The total return anticipated on a bond if the bond is held until it matures.

Year Over Year (YOY) A financial comparison that measures the change in a financial metric from one year to the next.

zero-coupon bond A bond that does not pay periodic interest payments, but instead is sold at a discount and pays the face value at maturity.

Z-score A statistical measure that quantifies the distance (in standard deviations) a data point is from the mean of a data set.

zero-sum game A situation in which one person's gain is exactly offset by another person's loss, resulting in a net gain of zero.

zigzag theory A theory that states that stock prices move in a zigzag pattern, with each zig or zag representing a change in the direction of the stock price trend.

Zacks Investment Research (ZIR) A firm that provides investment research, analysis, and recommendations to investors.

RECOMMENDED ACTIONS

Embrace the Wealthy Kids' Guide and
Transform Your Family's Financial Future

This book is a powerful resource designed to enable parents like you to teach your children about the world of finance and money. As you embark on this enlightening journey, we encourage you to take action and apply the learnings from this book in your day-to-day life. This section aims to inspire and motivate parents by emphasizing the importance of implementing the knowledge gained from this book and provides an overview of the expected results.

TAKING ACTION

1. Cultivate Financial Conversations: Initiate open and regular conversations about money with your children. Share your financial experiences and teach them about essential concepts such as budgeting, saving, and investing. Engage in age-appropriate discussions that help them understand the value of money and foster responsible financial habits.

2. Lead by Example: Remember that children learn best by observing their parents' behaviour. Model healthy

financial practices by diligently demonstrating responsible spending, saving, and making informed financial decisions. Your actions will be a powerful lesson and inspire your children to adopt similar behaviours.

3. Encourage Entrepreneurial Spirit: Nurture your children's entrepreneurial spirit by providing opportunities to explore their interests and develop their business skills. Encourage creativity, problem-solving, and the value of hard work. Help them discover the joy of turning their passions into profitable ventures.

4. Set Realistic Financial Goals: Guide your children in setting realistic and achievable financial goals. Whether saving for a special purchase or starting an investment portfolio, teach them the importance of setting goals and developing a plan to reach them. This process will instil discipline, patience, and a sense of accomplishment.

5. Emphasize Giving Back: Teach your children the value of philanthropy and giving back to their communities. Encourage them to participate in charitable activities and help them understand the positive impact their contributions can make in the lives of others.

EXPECTED RESULTS

1. Financial Confidence: By applying the learnings from this book, you will witness your children developing a strong sense of financial confidence. They will gain knowledge and skills that empower them to make informed financial decisions, paving the way for a lifetime of financial success.

2. Responsible Money Management: Implementing the teachings of this book will help your children develop responsible money management skills. They will learn the importance of budgeting, saving, and

spending wisely, contributing to their financial well-being and future success.

3. Wealth-Building Mindset: By instilling the concepts of investing, entrepreneurship, and goal-setting, you will foster a wealth-building mindset in your children. They will understand the power of long-term financial planning and develop habits supporting their financial independence journey.

4. Strong Family Bonds: Implementing the lessons from this book will create opportunities for meaningful family discussions and shared experiences. It will strengthen the bond between you and your children as you navigate the world of finance together.

"The Wealthy Kids' Guide" is more than just a book; it is a roadmap for empowering parents like you to teach your children about the finance and money world. By taking action and applying the learnings from this book in your day-to-day life, you are equipping your children with invaluable skills for lifelong financial success. Embrace the teachings, led by example, and watch your family's financial future transform. The journey may have its challenges, but the rewards of raising financially savvy and responsible children are immeasurable. Together, let's shape a future generation that is empowered, financially literate, and ready to conquer the world of finance.

Soumya Alexander
Jaison Mathew

RECOMMENDED READING

To complement "The Wealthy Kids' Guide: Equipping Children for Lifelong Financial Success"

1. "Rich Dad, Poor Dad for Teens" by Robert T. Kiyosaki: This book offers valuable lessons on financial literacy and provides practical advice for young readers to develop a mindset focused on wealth creation.
2. "The MoneySmart Family System" by Steve and Annette Economides: This book provides a comprehensive guide on raising money-smart kids by teaching them the principles of budgeting, saving, and wise spending from an early age.
3. "Smart Money Smart Kids" by Dave Ramsey and Rachel Cruze: Written by renowned personal finance experts, this book offers practical strategies for parents to teach their children about money, including saving, giving, and making wise financial decisions.
4. "The Opposite of Spoiled: Raising Kids Who Are Grounded, Generous, and Smart About Money" by Ron Lieber: This book focuses on raising children with a healthy attitude towards money, teaching them about values, gratitude, and responsible money management.

5. "The First National Bank of Dad: The Best Way to Teach Kids About Money" by David Owen: In this book, the author shares his experiences and insights on how to teach children about money management, including topics such as earning, saving, and investing.

6. "Make Your Kid a Money Genius (Even If You're Not): A Parents' Guide for Kids 3 to 23" by Beth Kobliner: This comprehensive guide covers age-specific advice on teaching kids about money, including allowances, budgeting, credit cards, and student loans.

7. "Raising Financially Fit Kids" by Joline Godfrey: This book provides a holistic approach to teaching kids about money, focusing not only on financial literacy but also on developing essential life skills, such as goal-setting, decision-making, and entrepreneurship.

8. "The Everything Kids' Money Book" by Brette McWhorter Sember: This interactive book offers fun activities, quizzes, and practical advice to help kids understand money concepts, budgeting, and saving.

9. "Growing Money: A Complete Investing Guide for Kids" by Gail Karlitz and Debbie Honig: This book introduces kids to the world of investing, teaching them the basics of stocks, bonds, and mutual funds in an engaging and accessible manner.

10. "A Smart Girl's Guide: Money" by Nancy Holyoke: Specifically targeted toward young girls, this book provides valuable lessons on money management, saving, and setting financial goals.

These books complement "The Wealthy Kids' Guide" by providing additional insights, perspectives, and strategies to help parents teach their children about financial literacy and lifelong financial success.

DISCLAIMER

"The Wealthy Kids' Guide: Equipping Children for Lifelong Financial Success" is intended to provide guidance and resources to parents and caregivers interested in teaching children financial literacy. It is important to note that the information presented in this book is for educational purposes only and should not be considered financial advice or professional guidance.

While the content of this book is based on extensive research and aims to provide accurate and up-to-date information, parents need to exercise their judgment and discretion when applying the concepts and strategies discussed. Each child's financial situation and needs may vary, and it is recommended to consult with a qualified financial professional or advisor for personalized advice tailored to your specific circumstances.

The author and publisher of this book do not guarantee the accuracy, completeness, or effectiveness of the information provided. They shall not be held responsible for any actions taken or decisions made based on the content of this book. Readers are encouraged to conduct further research, seek professional advice, and use their judgment in managing their financial matters.

By reading and utilizing the information in this book, parents and caregivers acknowledge that they are assuming full responsibility for the implementation of any financial strategies or teachings discussed, and the author and publisher shall not be held liable for any direct or indirect consequences or losses arising from the use of this book.

Reviewing and complying with applicable laws, regulations, or guidelines regarding financial education for children in your specific jurisdiction is strongly recommended.

Remember, teaching children about money is a continuous journey, and it is crucial to adapt the information and strategies to fit your family's unique needs and circumstances.

EPILOGUE

As we reach the end of this book, a journey of financial empowerment and enlightenment, we reflect on the transformation that has taken place within our children. We have witnessed their growth, newfound understanding of money, and blossoming confidence in managing their finances.

Throughout these pages, we have explored the principles of financial literacy, guiding our children on a path toward lifelong financial success. We have equipped them with the knowledge to make informed decisions, the skills to navigate financial challenges, and the mindset to embrace opportunities.

"The Wealthy Kids' Guide" has encouraged our children to dream big, set goals, and take steps towards their financial aspirations. They have learned the value of delayed gratification, the rewards of discipline, and the joy of saving. They have discovered the power of investing, the importance of giving back, and the potential of entrepreneurship.

But this journey does not end here. The lessons learned within these pages are seeds that will continue to grow and flourish in our children's lives. As parents, caregivers, and educators, we must continue nurturing their financial knowledge and skills. We must reinforce the principles of responsible money management, encourage ongoing learning, and provide guidance as they encounter new financial challenges.

By empowering our children with financial literacy, we have given them a precious gift. This gift will enable them to shape their destinies, pursue their passions, and positively impact the world. We have set them on a path toward financial security, independence, and the freedom to live on their terms. "The Wealthy Kids' Guide" serves as a reminder that financial success is not limited to a select few. Every child is within reach, regardless of background or circumstances. We are breaking down barriers and levelling the playing field by equipping our children with the tools they need to navigate the financial landscape.

As we close this chapter, let us celebrate our children's progress, the lessons they have internalized, and the future they are now poised to create. Together, we have laid a foundation for a generation of financially empowered individuals who will shape a world driven by financial wisdom, responsible choices, and shared prosperity.

Thank you for joining us on this transformative journey. May "The Wealthy Kids' Guide" continue to inspire, educate, and empower families worldwide, fostering a future where financial literacy is accessible.

Remember, our children have the power to shape a brighter financial future. Let us nurture their potential and celebrate their achievements. The legacy of financial empowerment starts with them.

With heartfelt gratitude and a commitment to lasting financial success,

Soumya Alexander

Jaison Mathew

ABOUT THE AUTHOR

Soumya Alexander

Soumya Alexander is an author and advocate for financial literacy for children. Hailing from Kerala, India, she holds an MBA in finance marketing from MG University. Soumya is a devoted wife and mother of two daughters. Her journey in finance inspired her to write  "The Wealthy Kids' Guide: Equipping Children for Lifelong Financial Success."

As an average individual, Soumya initially made some missteps in her own financial decisions. Recognizing the gaps in her financial education, she embarked on a quest for knowledge and understanding. Determined to ensure her children would not repeat the same mistakes, she delved into extensive research and developed effective strategies to teach kids about money management.

Motivated by her own experiences and the desire to empower parents, Soumya wrote "The Wealthy Kids' Guide" as a comprehensive resource to equip parents with the tools and knowledge needed to educate their children about finance. Drawing from her life lessons and successful methods she implemented with her own kids, Soumya offers practical insights and strategies to overcome financial challenges.

With a passion for helping parents become experts in training their children in financial matters, Soumya blends her research findings with her personal experiences. She aims to break through the barriers that hinder financial education and guide parents in raising financially literate and responsible individuals.

Through "The Wealthy Kids' Guide," Soumya Alexander provides a roadmap for parents to navigate the complex world of personal finance and impart essential money management skills to their children. With her expertise and relatable approach, Soumya empowers parents to shape their children's financial future and instil lifelong habits of financial success.

ABOUT THE AUTHOR

Jaison Mathew

Jaison Mathew is a Solution Architect in the networking field, currently employed at Cisco Systems Pvt Ltd. With a solid technical background and expertise in designing network solutions, Jaison brings a wealth of knowledge and experience to the field.

Driven by his passion for technology and networking, Jaison has established himself as a skilled professional in his industry. With a focus on delivering practical and innovative solutions, he has successfully contributed to numerous projects and played a vital role in the growth and success of his organization.

Outside of his professional endeavours, Jaison is a loving husband and supportive partner to his wife, Soumya Alexander, the author of "The Wealthy Kids' Guide: Equipping Children for Lifelong Financial Success." Together, they share a common goal of empowering parents to teach their children about finance and money management.

While Jaison's expertise lies in the technical realm, his support and collaboration with Soumya have been instrumental in bringing her vision to life. With his valuable insights and encouragement, Jaison has contributed to creating a comprehensive and impactful resource that helps parents navigate the world of personal finance and educate their children.

Jaison's role as a Solution Architect at Cisco Systems Pvt Ltd showcases his ability to analyse complex problems, develop effective strategies, and provide valuable solutions. His technical expertise and dedication to his work serve as a testament to his commitment to excellence.

With his professional achievements and unwavering support, Jaison Mathew is integral to the success of "The Wealthy Kids' Guide." His collaboration with Soumya Alexander reflects their commitment to empowering parents and equipping children with the tools necessary for lifelong financial success.

ABOUT THE AUTHOR

Jaison Mathew

Jaison Mathew is a Solution Architect in the networking field, currently employed at Cisco Systems Pvt Ltd. With a solid technical background and expertise in designing network solutions, Jaison brings a wealth of knowledge and experience to the field.

Driven by his passion for technology and networking, Jaison has established himself as a skilled professional in his industry. With a focus on delivering practical and innovative solutions, he has successfully contributed to numerous projects and played a vital role in the growth and success of his organization.

Outside of his professional endeavours, Jaison is a loving husband and supportive partner to his wife, Soumya Alexander, the author of "The Wealthy Kids' Guide: Equipping Children for Lifelong Financial Success." Together, they share a common goal of empowering parents to teach their children about finance and money management.

While Jaison's expertise lies in the technical realm, his support and collaboration with Soumya have been instrumental in bringing her vision to life. With his valuable insights and encouragement, Jaison has contributed to creating a comprehensive and impactful resource that helps parents navigate the world of personal finance and educate their children.

Jaison's role as a Solution Architect at Cisco Systems Pvt Ltd showcases his ability to analyse complex problems, develop effective strategies, and provide valuable solutions. His technical expertise and dedication to his work serve as a testament to his commitment to excellence.

With his professional achievements and unwavering support, Jaison Mathew is integral to the success of "The Wealthy Kids' Guide." His collaboration with Soumya Alexander reflects their commitment to empowering parents and equipping children with the tools necessary for lifelong financial success.

BOOKS BY THIS AUTHOR

"A To Z Financial Alphabets" Is An Educational And Engaging Book For Kids That Introduces Them To The Basics Of Financial Concepts And Terms. : Kids Financial Dictionary

"A to Z Financial Alphabets" is an educational and engaging book for kids that introduces them to the basics of financial concepts and terms. The book is designed to teach children the building blocks of finance in a fun and interactive way, using the letters of the alphabet as a framework.

Each page of the book features a letter of the alphabet, with a corresponding financial term and a colorful illustration that helps to explain the concept. From "A" for "Asset" to "Z" for "Zero", this book covers a wide range of financial terms and concepts and is suitable for children of all ages. Whether your child is just starting to learn about money or is already showing an interest in finance, "A to Z Financial Alphabets" is the perfect tool to help them gain a solid foundation in financial literacy.

Some Examples:
A for Assets, Accounting, Allocation, Annuity & Audit
P for Principal, Profit, Portfolio, Pension & Price-to-Earnings ratio (P/E ratio)
W for Wealth, Working Capital, Wire Transfer, Warrant & Write-Off

BOOKS BY THIS AUTHOR

Unlocking The Language Of Finance: A Comprehensive Dictionary Of Financial Terms

A financial dictionary is an invaluable resource for anyone looking to gain a better understanding of the complex and ever-changing world of finance. With a wide range of terms and concepts, finance can often feel like a foreign language, but a dictionary can provide clarity and context for the most commonly used terms.

From basic financial concepts like savings and investments to more advanced topics like derivatives and futures, a financial word dictionary provides definitions, examples, and practical applications of key terms. Whether you are a seasoned finance professional or a novice investor, a comprehensive financial word dictionary can help you navigate the intricate world of finance with confidence and clarity.

This financial dictionary is a reference tool that provides definitions and explanations of terms and concepts related to finance. It is a comprehensive collection of financial terms that are commonly used in the industry, including basic terms such as assets, liabilities, and revenue, as well as more complex topics such as options, futures, and derivatives.

This financial word dictionary is designed to help people

understand the language and terminology used in finance and to provide clarity and context for these terms. It is a valuable resource for professionals in the finance industry, as well as for individuals who want to gain a better understanding of financial concepts for personal or business purposes.

Having knowledge of financial terms is essential for anyone who wants to be financially literate and successful in today's world.